FIND YOUR "SUPER" IN 5 SIMPLE PHASES

THE Superpower Quest

A HERO'S GUIDE TO UNLOCKING YOUR POTENTIAL

JOHNNY LEVY

Dedication

Dedicated to those who feel the longing call of their potential like a whisper on the wind.

To those who never knew that greatness lives inside of them. And to those who have forgotten.

To seekers of hidden treasure. To adventurers bold and timid. To lonely kids on bus benches.

To any who have compared against others and found themselves lacking.

To the disillusioned. To the stressed. To those spinning their wheels.

To those broken hearted with themselves. To those who have despised their weaknesses. To those who have devalued their strengths, and sold themselves cheaply.

To those who have been reduced by the names others have called them.

To those who tried to pull themselves up by their bootstraps, and broke their arms in the process.

To those who live smaller than their frame. To the trapped. To those who would dare outgrow their boxes.

To Heroes on their journey.

Come and see something.

Something glorious. Something hidden.

You.

THE Superpower Quest

A HERO'S GUIDE TO UNLOCKING YOUR POTENTIAL

JOHNNY LEVY

The Superpower Quest: A Hero's Guide to Unlocking Your Potential

© 2024 Johnny Levy

All rights reserved. No part of this publication may be reproduced in any form without written permission from Johnny Levy

ISBN-13: 979-8-9900652-2-2

Cover design by Mark Rantal
Interior design by Beryl Glass

Printed in the United States of America

Gratitude

To Sarah, my wife, my "ride or die" forever; thank you for your many sacrifices to make this book happen. Thank you for believing in me. You are my home; you are my quiet strength. This book is yours.

To Isaiah, my stepson; you breathed new life into me as a writer. Your friendship and your constant encouragement to create have changed me. "Put the marks down." This book is yours.

To Eliya, my daughter; your gentle wisdom lives inside these pages, along with your steadfast love and support. Your discernment created the "Nurturer" Hero Type. This book is yours.

To Jadon, my son; your full-hearted enthusiasm is a treasure. You have no idea how much you have empowered this dream with your hard high-five-hugs and beaming smiles. This book is yours.

To Amara, my daughter, my loyal advocate, my sweet and spicy one. I've felt your belief in me, and in this work, and I treasure our conversations about this person's or that person's Superpower. So loyal to those you love. This book is yours.

To the many people who helped me push this boulder up the mountain: I cannot name you all. This book is the product of its own contents. I've Joined Forces with amazing people to accomplish something amazing. This would have been impossible for me to do alone. My community, this book is yours.

TABLE OF CONTENTS

SECTION 1
Discover Your Superpower

1.1	My Origin Story	13
1.2	Start with the End	23
1.3	The Quest	31
1.4	Core Types	37
1.5	Hero Types	41
1.6	Effective, Supporting, and Hindering Types	51
1.7	Power Words	57
1.8	Superpower Statement	63
1.9	Power Punches	71
1.10	The Mission	75

SECTION 2
Steward Your Weak Spot

2.1	Weak Spot Introduction	87
2.2	Hindering Drive	97
2.3	Hindering Hero Types	105
2.4	Weak Spot Words	115
2.5	Humility and Delight	125

SECTION 3
Join Forces

3.1	Join Forces	135
3.2	Ideal Alliances	145
3.3	Know Thyself	153
3.4	Pay Attention	157
3.5	Tend Your Garden	163
3.6	Make Swapsies	169
3.7	Create Dream Teams	171
3.8	Who First Problem Solving	177
3.9	Gain Wise Mentors	181
3.10	Initiate Transparent Accountability	187
3.11	Legos	193

SECTION 4
Build Your Utility Belt

4.1	Utility Belt	201
4.2	Pursue Truth	215
4.3	Push the Easy Button	221
4.4	Be Vulnerable	225
4.5	Know Thyself	229
4.6	Establish an Anchor Habit	233
4.7	Choose a Life System	237
4.8	Run if You Can!	247
4.9	Punch the Doohickey	251
4.10	Sequoias	255

SECTION 5
Face Your Supervillain

5.1	Face Your Supervillain	259
5.2	Your Supervillain is NOT Your Weak Spot!	265
5.3	Who is Your Supervillain?	269
5.4	Triggers	273
5.5	The Path to the Dark Side	277
5.6	Shadow Drives	281
5.7	Villain Words	287
5.8	Supervillain Names	291
5.9	Aftermath	295
5.10	The Sticky Wicket	301

SECTION 6
Final Words

6.1	Hugs and Homies	307

SECTION 1
Discover Your Superpower

1.1
My Origin Story

Have you ever wanted to not be you?

As a child, I yearned to be a hero like Spiderman or the Hulk. My best friend and I would read comics, draw, and try to will ourselves into a different world. We had this belief that if we put our backs against the wall of this abandoned building in our neighborhood, and yearned for long enough, with enough intensity, we would be swallowed up into a comic book world where we could become heroes. But in the end we were still there, standing on gravel and broken glass, denied escape. I remember a disappointment that I knew was silly. And we would walk away and go on about our business of paper airplanes and artwork and trying not to get beat up or killed. We longed to escape into a world where we could be significant, not realizing that we were already more significant than we could have imagined.

Just to prepare you, some people burst into song, but I burst into poetry. Poetry and spoken-word performance are a huge part of my passion and gifting. I've found that poetry has the ability to convey a feeling more viscerally than prose. There will be a handful of poetic snippets scattered throughout the book, like the one that follows.

The Superpower Quest

Soft wasn't the currency
In my neighborhood.

The popular kids
Were the kids who could
Punch faces bloody
And cuss, and tell
Filthy jokes on the bus.

The ones who were not victims.
Not scared of everything
Like me.

Park Hill favors
The strong and
Snacks on the weak.

I want you to smell it:
Gray air and cracked streets.

The liquor store sleeps
During the day.
Hunkered down,
Wrapped in the
Tart smell of urine.

I want you to taste it:
The delightful burst of
Sour Apple Laffy Taffy
In our mouths
That we bought with
Food stamps

That my homie's cousin
Would give to us

To buy candy and bring
Him the change. Why?

When you are a drug
Dealer, and clients pay
You with food stamps,
This is how you
Liquidate your
Assets.

Little did we
Really care.
Because … candy.

In Park Hill, my reflection
Was alleyways and
Liquor store and
Barber shop and
Broken fences
And bullies.

I learned myself.
Nothing and nobody.
Never gonna be
Anybody.

—Excerpt from "Park Hill Son." Johnny Levy, (2020)

Have you ever wanted to not be you? Yeah, I know what that's like.

Life is a journey, and many of us have stories of untold trauma. Different circumstances, different socioeconomics, different family dynamics, but somehow, we got the same rampant message: you aren't enough.

This book is about ordinary people—and the fact that there are no such things as ordinary people. It's a book for people who have not yet discovered the extent of their excellence. Or who think they don't have excellence. Or people who simply want to advance. This is a book for growers, seekers, longers; underdogs, misfits, and football stars who bear the scars. Spoiler Alert: your personal impact is proportionate to the degree in which you know and accept yourself as you were designed, and rare it is to find people who are truly comfortable in their own skin—appreciative of their strengths, gracious towards their flaws, and humble enough to receive help from others.

> Your personal impact is proportionate to the degree in which you know and accept yourself as you were designed, and rare it is to find people who are truly comfortable in their own skin–appreciative of their strengths, gracious towards their flaws, and humble enough to receive help from others.

In today's world, we can easily compare ourselves to perfect social media lives, neglecting introspection. With an excess of information and entertainment, we can postpone or bypass personal growth leading to frustration and exhaustion. We can end up crash landing into lives and circumstances that don't match up with our unique design, which always causes frustration, exhaustion, and a sense of striving. How many of us are nagged by the feeling that we are not quite living up to our potential?

For much of my life, I despised myself. I wanted to escape, as pictured above, because my neighborhood ran on a different currency than the currency I had in my metaphorical wallet. Park Hill favored brazenness, boldness, and coldness. You had to be hard, and I wasn't. You had to be strong, violent, and dominant. I grew up resenting my inability to be as powerful as the characters in my comic books and the bullies on my block.

I became miserable, petty, and cruel. I hardened my heart. I wanted to be a different person. Fear and insecurity gnawed at my guts constantly. There was nothing worse you could be in my neighborhood than a coward. And that's exactly what I felt I was. I was pretty smart at things like reading, writing, and drawing. But those weren't the currency. I would have traded it all to be more "manly." My escape was comic books, video games, and artistic creation.

A series of turning points began to change my perspective. These were providential encounters with people who saw something more in me than I could see in myself. These were few and far between, but deeply impactful.

One turning point was a government program for at-risk youth called Upward Bound. It was a fairly rigorous after-school and summer program. The staff there were gritty folks committed to helping hooligans go to college. Shout out to Paulette McIntosh and Chas Maldonado! The program director, Chas, would deliver fiery sermons laced with cuss words telling us we were going to have to work twice as hard to get half as far in this world. Chas was an expert at bridging the gap and speaking to us in our own language. Bryan Stevenson, author of "Just Mercy," has talked about the power of proximity: the fact that sometimes, for those who are struggling or who lack opportunities, simple, repeated exposure to benevolent people outside their situation can be life changing. I have experienced this firsthand. Broken down and distorted by trauma as we all were, we actually needed someone to point at us and say, "You there, yeah, you in the hoodie and baggy jeans. You can go to college, you know. Stop looking behind you. I'm talking to you. Come here, let me show you how. Yes, I'll walk through the steps with you. We'll do it together. *But I'm also not taking any of your crap.*"

I was smart enough to go to college. And my divorced parents definitely didn't have the money to pay for it. I got a series of scholarships, including a first-generation grant and student loans. And there I was one day, on a shuttle from Denver to Fort Collins, CO, with a black duffel bag containing everything I owned in the world, headed for college. And there at college, the currency was finally different from the neighborhood where I grew up. I began to leverage elements of my design, including my emotional intelligence and creativity to make progress in this new environment. Did I still despise myself? Yes, but not as much.

There were many more turning points. More than I can cover here. Getting radically saved in a 10X10 dorm room, and having an experience with the Divine that altered the course of my life. Getting married to my dream girl. Becoming a father, becoming a CEO, becoming a pastor, becoming an author. That "nobody" kid ended up with responsibilities, joys, and impacts that he never imagined. I sometimes wish I could go back and comfort that kid in the midst of his misery and self-loathing:

> And I want to go
> Back in time and visit
> Myself, that Park Hill boy
> In all his gangly
> Nappy-headed insecurity,
>
> That screechy voice that
> Makes me sick whenever
> I hear it on video.
>
> That skin that wasn't
> Black enough to be black.
> And definitely not white.
>
> That kid who was
> Always out of joint.
> Out of the socket. Kind of
> Hanging there, limp.
>
> I want to scoop him
> Up and tell him. And his homie
> Too.
>
> Like a big brother
> Who made it out, and comes
> Back with a sweet ride,

And big, booming stories
Of the big wide world,
And gifts, and secret
Handshakes and
Big hands cradling
Your knotty head,

And a grin that stares
Into your eyes, and
Knows you.

And somehow
Loves you.

And really does.
For some insane,
Incomprehensible
Reason.

And I want to tell them:

You guys are not worthless.
Look at me. Look at me.
There's more.

Park Hill isn't the world.
There are places out there
That don't eat you alive.
I'm serious.

You are precious. Park Hill
Doesn't know any better.
Pitbulls make for bad
Nursemaids.

The Superpower Quest

It was a setup
From the start.

—Excerpt from "Park Hill Son." Johnny Levy, (2020)

I sometimes wish I could go back. But convictions don't come easily, and I would not trade what my life has taught me. But it is now a personal passion, forged in the fires of my story, to accelerate others on their path to self-acceptance and progress.

Bonus Content: For more about my Origin Story, check out my full poem, "Park Hill Son" at superpowerquest.com/resources.

I want you to embrace your design, with its strengths and weaknesses. I want you to understand who and what you are so that you can live in harmony with the truth of who you are. I see the deep need for this message, in a world of untold traumas that we generally treat with the medicine of distraction in the form of scrolling and streaming. I see a growing distractedness where we are crowding out time for solitude, reflection, and simply listening to our own thoughts, much less knowing deeply who we are.

I had to learn these lessons the hard way—in closets, beneath the covers, through setbacks, in the deep anguish of prayer and self-exploration. Somewhere along the line, I learned to love myself. In all the chaos and beauty of life, I learned to embrace my design. I learned to appreciate and press into my strengths. I learned to accept and account for my weaknesses. And then I began to help others to do the same. The Superpower Quest is a process forged from intense experience, decades of observation, thousands of hours of deep connection with others, and an ongoing study of personality frameworks.

And here's the prize! For those willing to take the proverbial "red pill" and enter with me into this Wonderland of introspection and affirmation: Imagine if you could name your most earth-shaking ability in a single sentence, and then intentionally exercise that ability at will. Imagine if you could look at a new and enticing opportunity and have confidence about whether to accept or reject it based on its compatibility with your design. Imagine if you could go from spending 10% of your time doing the beneficial thing that lights you up to doing that 50% of the time? What might you accomplish if you doubled down on your unique gift and refined your area of genius over years and decades? How might the people around you benefit? What kind of satisfaction and impact might that mean for you?

Yes, you, reading this book! Not the person behind you. You have an excellence! A dazzling form of excellence, just waiting to be named.

1.2
Start With the End

Embrace your Design, Collaborate with your Community. That's what this book is about.

I go to a coffee shop in my town called Loyal, and it's the best. That's where my wife and I go to plan our life together almost every week. The baristas are all young people in their twenties, and I am always struck by the welcoming culture and the emphasis on excellence. I've had several conversations with one young man who works there. We go deep and talk about some of the struggles his generation is facing in the current era, this age of speed and distraction that has left so many young people feeling burnt out and lonely. He's passionate and vibrant and curious. We always have such awesome conversations!

One day, I was meeting with my wife, Sarah, and he came by the table. The three of us had a lively discussion about isolation, community, and redemption. We talked about how hard it is to grow without community, but how hard it is to find true community and mentorship. I talked about how rare it was for most of my early life for people to really see me and really invest in me. This has fanned the flames for my dogged dedication to finding my mentors at any cost, and exposing myself to excellence at every turn. The young man resonated with that.

The Superpower Quest

He said, "I need someone to see my potential and pull me in."

I wish you could have seen his eyes, deep with longing and intensity.

I felt that he had put words to what I have felt my whole life. I wonder how many people feel this and have never put it into words. I suspect that many of us, and especially the younger of us, are waiting for the "benevolent upperclassman" to notice us, grab our hand, and tell us how the world works. And maybe even tell us how *we* work. And it's rare that this ever happens because we are all so busy taking care of our own unwieldy lives. Many of us are treading water too hard to think about helping someone else stay above the surface.

His phrase of longing was striking enough for me to include it here, right at the front of the book, as a sort of rally cry for what this book is about.

This young man expressed a longing to be seen. To be noticed, to be recognized, to be called out for who he is. This only happens when others take the time from their busy lives to focus on someone else with a spirit of patience and curiosity.

He also expressed a desire to be *pulled in*. Assembled. Collected. Invited into a community; able to contribute corporately. Grafted into something greater than himself.

These two basic desires— to be known and leveraged—are rampant in the hearts of humans, young and old alike. These drives are a part of what makes us human. I also believe they are two sides of the same coin. We want to be known, and we want to be assembled. Self-knowledge is important, and community is equally important. What good is it to be known and to know yourself, if you don't have the impetus or opportunity to leverage that knowledge in the place of your invitation, among the people who have invited you into a worthy goal? We were not made for stagnation and passivity. We were made for the heroic. It calls to us. Even in an age of distraction. Perhaps, especially so.

This book is an attempt to address these two longings. It is an attempt to name them and to equip the honest seeker with tools for self-exploration and for effective collaboration. Radical self-knowledge is the goal, but this doesn't exist apart from using that knowledge to effectively benefit the people in your circles. Healthy self-interest flows outward into healthy investment in the world. We were designed for this.

> "Everybody, unashamed, lock your arms, plant your feet,
> Look around, they need you! Follow the banner!"
> —"Raise the Banner." (Propaganda, *Excellent* Album, 2012)

My design? I'm a Connector. I love being with people, understanding people deeply, encouraging, and connecting with people. I love watching people thrive in their gifts and reach their potential. I love making introductions between people that can mix together to make an explosive combination. I'm kind of a mad scientist that way.

My wife, Sarah, sometimes sends me to the store for milk and eggs, and I'll come back an hour later with just milk (forgot the eggs) and a story of how I spent thirty minutes talking to my barista from Starbucks who happened to be shopping with his wife. On a first meeting, some people will tell me things that they don't tell anyone. This is my Superpower of Connection at work.

I was sitting at the auto repair shop next to a rumpled man with gray hair and dirt beneath his fingernails. Neither of us really wanted to talk. And suddenly I thought, "Let's see if the magic works every time." I began asking him questions out of the blue. I uncovered vulnerability, passion, and a story inside this man, waiting to be told. This man who almost tricked me into thinking he was commonplace.

This book is the output of that love for humanity and the power of connection that gets me into so much adventure and trouble, and that fills my life with the faces and gifts and sufferings of so many fellow humans.

The great writer and philosopher C.S. Lewis said, in his essay, *Weight of Glory*, "There are no ordinary people. You have never talked to a mere mortal."[1] I agree wholeheartedly. We are tragically glorious. We are angels in gutters, royals in restaurants, Michelangelo's on bus benches. We are common, we are extraordinary.

There are no ordinary people. You are no ordinary person. And this book is no ordinary book.

I'm starting with the end in mind. I'm picturing you at the end of this book. I'm picturing you closing the back cover, or shutting your Kindle, and taking a moment to close your eyes and reflect on the experience. I'm picturing the feeling you may have, and I hope it is excitement; a sense of accomplishment. A calm clarity and a sense of confidence. A readiness. And most of all, a sense of your significance and value, with a gentle acceptance of your flaws, and an eagerness to give your gifts to the world.

You will have invested many hours into figuring out how you specifically work with your strengths and weaknesses. You will have a language for articulating your unique Superpower, and you'll be able to accurately describe the weaknesses that hinder you from effectiveness (Weak Spot). Armed with this knowledge, you will be more open than ever to join forces with others for mutual benefit, giving your strengths to their weaknesses, and their strengths to your weaknesses.

But I don't want to stop there.

As a Connector, I want this book to be the beginning of an ongoing relationship. My ultimate goal is not to sell books. It's to create a vibrant community of people with radical self-knowledge and a common language, and to experiment with what's possible if we collaborate. I've created an online portal to facilitate this community.

As you go through the process outlined in this book, you will learn things about yourself that will surprise and delight. You can enter your findings into the different printables that you can access throughout the book, or you can go to superpowerquest.com/myprofile (see the QR code at the end of chapter) to input your findings into your Hero Profile. Each chapter will have a call to action for you to input your Superpower Quest findings into your personal Hero Profile.

This is my goal for you with this book: Embrace your Design; Collaborate with your Community.

You will hear this call repeated throughout this book. When all is said and done:

SECTION 1 | Discover Your Superpower

- I want you to know yourself better and feel more confident about your unique gifts.
- I want to equip and challenge you to put those gifts into practice for your joy and for the benefit of the communities in which you participate.
- I want you to be excited to lock arms with others in your areas of weakness.
- Finally, I want to connect with you and partner with you on that journey, far beyond this book.

Superpower Design Map

The following is a map for your journey through this first section of the book. Once completed, you will be able to see the full map of your Superpower design. You can access a printable version at superpowerquest.com/resources.

Superpower Quest Resources Page

As noted above, you can also register for the online version at superpowerquest.com/myprofile.

Superpower Quest Hero Profile

The Superpower Quest

CORE DRIVES	
Harmony, Order, Progress	
Effective Core Drive	
Supporting Core Drive	

HERO TYPES		
Connector, Nurturer, Leader, Organizer, Dreamer, Achiever		
Effective Hero Types		
Supporting Hero Types		

POWER WORDS	
Positive traits and tendencies	
1.	4.
2.	5.
3.	6.

SUPERPOWER STATEMENT
Focused description of your special ability

SECTION 1 | Discover Your Superpower

	POWER PUNCHES
	Specific schedulable actions within your areas of Superpower

1.3
The Quest

Simply put, this book is about leveraging your unique design for greater joy and effectiveness in life. The goal is radical self-understanding for a radical focus on the activities that best suit your design, with the secondary goal of helping you collaborate with others for greater impact.

The statement above implies a series of assumptions.

Every human has an unchosen, rational design. You were born with certain tendencies, both strengths and weaknesses. You have many choices in life, but you didn't get to choose your original design. Each person has a purpose, or reason, for existing.

This book takes for granted that part of the reason you exist is to benefit the people around you. Embedded in your design are certain special abilities for benefiting others. There are also flaws that will require you to access the strengths of others. This is in line with the comic book trope that heroes use their powers to serve and protect the community, while villains use their powers to destroy and exploit the community. We are all designed to be, and have the potential to be, heroes.

Many of us resist or fight our design, often because of stories we've told ourselves, or stories that others have told us. Many of us have internalized the idea that we are faulty, broken, or inferior to others. Many of us wish to be something other than what we are, rather than embracing and leveraging what we are.

You were designed with strengths and weaknesses so that you can interlock with a community. Self-sufficiency is a myth. The need for community is in your design.

You may agree or disagree with some or all of these assumptions. Regardless, if you are seeking greater joy and impact, this book can move you towards your goal. I invite you to eat the meat and spit out the bones.

Now, why use the *superhero trope* for a personality framework? First of all, I am Alfred Levy's son, and Alfred Levy has a room in his apartment that has nothing but comic books in it. I've maybe been in there once in my life—other than that, I've only seen him disappear into that room to bring out treasures from time to time. My dad was always passionate about comic books from as early as I can remember. Some of my fondest memories are around going to the comic book store with my dad and brothers, or tenderly taking one of my dad's precious comics out of the plastic and turning pages with careful, reverent fingers; or going to the movie theater, sneaking in our own candy and snacks, and watching superhero movies. Superheroes are in my blood. That's one reason I've chosen this theme.

The other reason is that the *Superhero Trope*, like nothing else, speaks to the deep desires of human beings to strive and grow and prevail in life. We are empowered vicariously through the heroes we watch. We become them—or at least, we long to become them in some way. And I believe this is far more ancient than the modern iteration of comic books.

The superhero story is the modern rendition of the Hero's Journey archetype. Joseph Campbell's influential book, *The Hero with a Thousand Faces*,[2] illustrates the common heroic themes that are found in myths and legends across cultures, across history. Every culture has its own heroic legends and lore, and there are strong common themes in even the most divergent cultures of what it means to be a hero. The hero's journey is the ideal life, intended to spur people and even civilizations towards virtues and accomplishments. By using hero language, I am tapping into age-old, cross-cultural principles of what it means to be heroic, and what we're striving for across the centuries.

In this framework, on a primal level, Superheroes save the world. Supervillains destroy and oppress it. Heroes love and serve the community. Villains exploit, enslave, and harm the community. Heroes are ultimately sacrificial. Villains are ultimately selfish. Heroes are ultimately driven by love. Villains are ultimately driven by power.

This recurring theme is the scaffolding upon which many of the principles of this book are built.

You're on a journey to discover your Superpower so that you can serve your community, fight your Supervillain, join with other heroes, and live for a higher cause, as heroes have done since time immemorial. This book is here to help you along the way.

What is the meaning of a Quest? The quest is a long or arduous search for something, generally precious. The quest is an adventure in which the hero will encounter adversity and allies along the way. A quest requires fortitude and a firm resolve. The hero is aiming for a lofty goal that is not guaranteed to the faint of heart. Growth is a requirement. The hero, if successful, will be changed along the way. This means that humility is required, because humility is a prerequisite for change. The *Superpower Quest* is just such a journey, requiring action, fortitude, and humility. You came to this book because you are looking for something. If you walk this path, you will encounter a treasure the likes of which you might never have imagined. You'll discover yourself in a new way.

The *Superpower Quest* is a five-phase process. Each phase is a funnel to clarity. Each section will start at the broad top of the funnel, and guide you downward into narrower, sharper, actionable understanding so that you can live out your design with focused intent. It's like angling the sun through a magnifying glass. It takes a while, but once you narrow that beam, it starts to burn through stuff. I want to help you focus down to the ways you can make the most impact.

The Superpower Quest

Here are the five phases of the *Superpower Quest:*

Phase #1: Leverage Your Superpower
Part of your design is your unique *Superpower,* which is your area of unique gifting that, when exercised, brings you a sense of joy and effectiveness. We will help you narrow your strength-set down to your top super strength that can knock down walls and barriers. The process starts with helping you identify your Core Drive, and then moves into defining your Hero Types and selecting your Power Words. The output at the end of this chapter unveils your unique Superpower Statement, which is a single, razor-clear sentence that sums up your area of greatest effectiveness and joy, with strategies for how to press into this area for exponential progress. This will be a GAME CHANGER.

Phase #2. Steward Your Weak Spot
Another part of your design is your Weak Spot, which represents your areas of weakness that can lead you into ineffectiveness and frustration. This book will help you leverage your Weak Spot for maximum growth. Yes, you heard me correctly. Your weaknesses can be leveraged as well as your strengths. At the end of this chapter, you will be able to articulate your lifelong areas of weakness in three to five words—and you'll walk away with strategies for how to manage your weakness so well that it can actually become strength.

Phase #3. Join Forces
A third part of your design is your ability to Join Forces wisely. You were designed for community. You were designed to collaborate. Loners and mavericks set a cap on their impact, due to their very decision to remain loners and mavericks. Understanding the best ways to interlock your strengths with the strengths of others leads to exponential progress. The final output of this chapter will be your "Ally Profile," which will be a clear description of the type of person who fills in your gaps, so you can team up like a boss for huge wins.

SECTION 1 | Discover Your Superpower

Phase #4. Build Your Utility Belt
This section contains tools, habits, and systems to manage your Weak Spot and enhance your Superpower. This chapter will help you build your "tool box" for navigating life more effectively.

Phase #5. Face Your Supervillain
Your Supervillain is your dark side; your worst self. We will explore the difference between faults (Weak Spot) and vices (Supervillain). Sometimes we make bad decisions and there are patterns to the ways we arrive at our worst selves. Your Supervillain represents the ways you destroy yourself and others when triggered. Once you have completed your Supervillain journey, you will be able to identify your three to five Supervillain Profiles, so that you can guard yourself and others from the havoc they can tend to wreak in your life.

When all is said and done, this is a book about human flourishing. If you can understand your design, then you can cooperate with your design. And if you cooperate with your design, you will experience greater flourishing.

Picture a tree that is so heavy with fruit that its branches are literally bending downward to accommodate the weight. We were designed for this kind of fruitfulness. And it's also remarkably rare to find someone who is flourishing in this way. The goal of this book is to help you embrace your design and collaborate with your community for amazing progress.

It's time to cross the threshold of this journey, as heroes have done from time immemorial. Sail away from the world you thought you knew, and take the road to adventure. The first foundational step of your Superpower Quest is identifying your Core Drives.

1.4
Core Drives

As noted before, the Superpower Quest is a funnel drawing you down into a tighter and tighter stream of focus. In phase one of your Superpower journey, finding your Core Drive is the top of the funnel. This is where your journey begins.

There are three Core Drives that represent the broad categories of our priorities in the world and how we serve others. The three Drives are Progress, Harmony, and Order. People will tend to have an Effective Core Drive, a Supporting Core Drive, and a Hindering Core Drive. Which of the following rises to the top for you?

Progress

If Progress is at the top of your pyramid, you will be a person who craves forward motion. You are not comfortable staying where you are. You want things to be dynamic, not static. You want to grow and prevail. Maybe you are more abstract, and dream of new ideas, new possibilities, or big creative endeavors. Or maybe you are more concrete, and you just have the determination to get things done and make things happen. Either way, you are looking forward with an eye for *more, bigger, better,* and a deep desire for a sense of accomplishment.

Harmony

If Harmony is your Core Drive, you care much more about people and relationships than you do about getting things done. You care about people, and you want your people to get along. You want peace and intimacy. You hate relational discord and conflict, unless you see it as a means to create deeper intimacy. Maybe you're the life of the party, and everyone is your friend. Or maybe you focus your energy on a small circle of "ride-or-die" friends and family. Either way, you long for thriving human relationships, and thriving humans.

Order

What do Order people hate most? Chaos. Aimlessness. Inefficiency. Wastefulness. They prefer routine, stability, and excellence. Order people believe there is a right way to do things, and they want things done the right way. They cringe at a lack of structure. If your Core Drive is Order, you long to bring things into a state of proper fine-tuned perfection. You want to bring all people and processes into the state of optimal operation.

Which of these Drives most resonates with you; Progress, Harmony or Order? It might be very, very close between two, or even all three. But which one is even a millimeter ahead of the rest?

It might help to invert this. When you are most upset, is it because of chaos, lack of authority structure, or inefficiency? Then Order might be your Core Drive.

Are you most triggered by relational tension or betrayal? Then Harmony is probably your thing.

Are you disproportionately frustrated when you feel stuck, boxed in, or stymied? Then Progress could be your jam.

Take a moment to reflect and rank your Drives. First will be your Effective Core Drive, followed by your Supporting Core Drive, and finally, your Hindering Core Drive.

Don't overthink this; you can change your answer later. Make a note of the order of your drives, or you can go to superpowerquest.com/myprofile to input your Core Drives into your online Hero Profile.

SECTION 1 | Discover Your Superpower

Superpower Quest Hero Profile

Effective Core Drive
Your Effective Core Drive is the place where you feel most comfortable and confident. It comes to you as naturally as breathing. Pay attention to this because you want to be spending most of your time and energy letting your Effective Core Drive guide you towards fruitful activities.

Supporting Core Drive
Your Supporting Core Drive may be nearly as strong, or just as strong, as your Effective Core Drive. Or it could be just a place of competency where you are functional, but not excellent. At this stage, it may be hard to tell, but the next chapter will give you a lot more insight as we work our way down the funnel.

Hindering Core Drive
Everyone has strengths and weaknesses. Generally, your Hindering Core Drive is the area where you most struggle. Activities in this area are going to be draining. The things you dread doing in a given day are generally going to reside in this area.

Results
Understanding your deepest motive will help you recognize why you are drawn to certain activities and away from others. For example, you might wonder why you have always struggled with organization. Surprise! Your Hindering Core Drive is Order. Why do you have trouble making friends and investing in relationships? Maybe because your Hindering Core Drive is Harmony.

This does not mean you are automatically relegated to a life of disorder or loneliness. This book will give you some great tools for leveraging weakness. The fact that these things are difficult does not mean that there's something wrong with you. What's *wrong with you* is that you are human, and no human is good at everything.

Your Core Drive discoveries will provide you with clues for the next phase of your quest, which is identifying your Hero Types. Let's go!

1.5
Hero Types

"With great power, comes great responsibility." For my comic book fans out there, this is one of the most iconic statements in the Marvel universe, and it's a part of Spiderman's origin story. Although attributed to Peter Parker's Uncle Ben in the comic books, other real-life figures, such as Winston Churchill, have made nearly identical statements. This is a prevailing theme in comic books, and it is a foundational understanding for this book.

Heroes Serve the Community
Villains consistently seek to destroy and exploit the community. Heroes consistently serve and protect the community. The fundamental difference between heroes and villains is that villains are selfish, and heroes seek the good of others. This comic book theme is just one of a billion reflections of a fundamental truth. We were designed to serve the world around us, and at our best, we reflect this design.

Every one of us can and will choose the way of the Hero, or the way of the Villain. However, our design points us towards the heroic. It is the fitting reflection of our design. Villainy is a distortion of that image.

You were designed to serve the world in ways that fit with your unique passions and giftings. No one else was ever designed to do exactly what you can do. I find this to be breathtakingly amazing. Many of us cannot, or will not, slow down long enough to take stock of ourselves and press into our Superpowers.

When I say *you were designed to serve others*, I know that it may conjure up images of being a doormat or a martyr, which is not what I mean.

It might also give you mental images of giving Christmas gifts to orphans, or activists rallying for justice, or a fireman rescuing a cat out of a tree. "Those are the people who are really serving," you might say. And that kind of service is necessary, true, and beautiful.

But I am referring to service in a wider sense. We serve the world when we press into our giftings in ways that benefit the world, even if it doesn't always look or feel like *service* in the traditional sense.

Serving Examples

I am serving the world by writing this book. Writing this book also happens to bring me great joy, because it is a project that is 100% within the wheelhouse of my design. Writing this book does not feel like work to me. It falls squarely within my Hero Type of being a Connector/Dreamer. Much of this writing process does not drain energy from me. In fact, it gives me energy.

I have a co-worker named Caleb who is a systems and process genius. His sister, Lydia, also works with us, and she is similarly gifted, but even more tactical. I recently promoted him to be the operations director, and promoted her to project manager. I began to pass them all my duties that fit more in the Organizer/Achiever camp than the Connector/Dreamer camp. These were the tasks that required high conscientiousness and directional practicality. I gave them oversight of the detailed minutiae that I hated. I felt bad passing off all these tasks to them. It sometimes felt unfair or lazy of me. But the truth is, those were the tasks where I was doing a mediocre job, and I was often causing problems for the organization in those areas. Caleb and Lydia rose to the challenge and began to optimize everything, creating structures and systems and documentation for all the chaos.

One day, in our weekly meeting, Caleb told me that he was almost feeling bad because his new role "didn't feel like work" to him. Can you imagine my surprise!? In doing what he was built to do, which felt energizing and not draining, he was giving the best possible service to both me and the organization. But it felt so effortless that he actually felt bad!

We have somehow gotten the idea that *real* serving means drudgery, sacrifice, and the sense of striving. It is true that this is sometimes the case, and should be, as we sacrificially put other people's interests above our own, when this is actually needed. But we can definitely sacrifice unnecessarily because of a misguided conception that work must feel sacrificial in order to be valid. Greg McKeown debunks this idea beautifully in his book *Effortless: Make It Easier to Do What Matters Most*. The truth is, you can live a life in which you are working extremely hard within the boundaries of your design, where the majority of what you do doesn't even feel like work at all. And the end result can be exponentially better for the people around you.

> We have somehow gotten the idea that *real* serving means drudgery, sacrifice, and the sense of striving.

We were not only made to serve others, we were made to serve others in accordance with the way that we were designed. This is why it is vitally important to understand your Hero Type, which helps you identify your sweet spot for effective and joyful service. This will also bring us a step closer to discovering your unique Superpower, which is even more specific to you.

The Six Hero Types

Hero Types are the categories that describe the different ways humans serve the world. There are six Hero Types that align in pairs with the three Core Drives we discussed in the previous chapter. The six Hero Types are Connector, Nurturer, Leader, Organizer, Dreamer, and Achiever.

If your Primary Drive is Harmony, then one of your Primary Hero Types has a strong possibility of being *Connector* or *Nurturer.* If your Primary Drive is Order, then one of your Primary Hero Types is likely *Leader* or *Organizer*. If your Primary Drive is Progress, then one of your

Primary Hero Types has a good chance of being *Dreamer* or *Achiever*.

This is not always true. As I have said before, people cannot be stuffed into spreadsheets. People are unique, beautiful, complex creations. But patterns and trends do exist, and those patterns and trends can help us accelerate the journey.

All people possess elements of all the Hero Types. The goal here is not to say that a Dreamer can never be organized, or that a Connector can never be driven to achieve. But everyone has areas of relative strength and relative weakness.

To be most effective in life, you'll have to carry out activities on a daily basis that pull from all the different Hero Types.

We're not all accountants, but most of us have to do taxes at some point. We're not all handy, but we all have to fix stuff from time to time. We're not all social butterflies, but we all have to engage with groups sometimes.

Knowing your strengths and weaknesses enables you to intentionally press into your areas of strength for exponential results, while strategically supplementing your weaknesses in order to create a well-rounded outcome. This is leveraging your design.

The following are descriptions of all of the different Hero Types. Pay attention to which ones most resonate with you. Which are the ways that most align with how you joyfully serve the people around you?

The Connector

Community: Connectors are the peacemakers within a community. Unity is their passion. They serve their communities by connecting with others, and by connecting others in the community with one another. They generally have a high capacity for many relationships. They tend to be more concerned with forging new relationships than with maintaining existing ones. They are often extroverted and charismatic, but not necessarily so. Great at networking, they can be the life of the party or the common denominator beneath a community. They are good at lassoing people in from the fringes, and making sure everyone is included. They can rally people around themselves, because people tend to see them as winsome and benevolent.

Adjectives: Charismatic, Gregarious, Open, Inviting, Accepting, Engaging, Tactful.

Contrast: Leaders also interface with groups, but for the purpose of order rather than connection. Leaders want to assemble people towards orderly action, and they can be more concerned with outcomes than people's feelings. This can be appalling to Connectors, who care much more about peace and harmony than about orderly outcomes.

Struggles: Connectors can also become insecure and people-pleasing. They hate conflict; it makes them feel uncomfortable and threatened. Because of this, they are more likely than other types to sacrifice truth and accountability for the sake of keeping the peace. They care a lot about what people think about them, and this can be their downfall.

The Nurturer

Community: Ever had a friend who stood by you, no matter what? Someone you could always rely on; someone who you knew, in your soul, was in your corner? Nurturers are the caretakers within a community. They make sure that individual needs are being met. Nurturer's prize loyalty above all. When a nurturer is your friend, he or she will bleed for you. Nurturers invest in their stable of relationships, using attentiveness and concern to make sure their people are well taken care of. They are diligent caretakers, supporters, encouragers, consistently showing up for their people no matter what.

Adjectives: Loyal, Dedicated, Helpful, Empathetic, Sincere, Faithful, Committed, Compassionate.

Contrast: Where the Connector has a high capacity for a lot of relationships, the Nurturer has a capacity to go deeper with a smaller number of people. Nurturers show up for their close relations, and can seem like Achievers in this way. The difference is that Achievers are motivated by the tasks themselves, and bringing tasks to completion. Nurturers are motivated by people's needs and welfare.

Struggle: Nurturers can be loyal to a fault. With a focus on others, they can forget to tend to themselves. Thus, they can overextend themselves and become unhealthy and resentful. They can also become resentful when others don't reciprocate to their standard. They can have a hard time forgiving others because of the high premium they place on loyalty. However, on the flip side, they can use their empathy to rationalize and make excuses for others who mistreat them, thereby becoming doormats.

The Leader

Community: Picture a drill sergeant who whips a bunch of ragtag cadets into an effective unit. He's firm, unyielding, and blunt. He has no issue with conflict. In fact, he almost seems to enjoy it. The cadets hate him at first, but they learn to respect and value his ability to challenge and mold them into their potential as a team. Leaders assemble communities and provide them with direction. They serve the community by being decisive and practical, and they often value their opinions as facts. They have the ability to lead others because they have the conviction that they know better than others. They hate aimlessness and insubordination. They hate haphazardness and sentimentality. They hate fuzzy authority structures and a lack of accountability. They love delegating tasks. They do this to bring groups up into their well-oiled potential, where everyone is doing what they are supposed to be doing, and being held accountable to do it well.

Adjectives: Decisive, Authoritative, Blunt, Intentional, Bold, Confident, Assertive, Determined.

Contrast: Where Organizers are concerned with optimizing processes for efficiency, Leaders are concerned with optimizing groups of people for maximum productivity and effectiveness. Dreamers inspire, but tend to lack the decisiveness to mobilize people into specific roles and tasks.

Struggles: They have a low tolerance for laziness or excuses and are compelled to hold people accountable to their commitments. In doing so, they can ruffle feathers. They can be seen as harsh, insensitive, and tyrannical. They can over-control people, leaving resentment in their wake. They can often see feedback as a challenge to their authority, which can make them unapproachable by people with good ideas and good intentions. It's very hard to change their minds, which can be both good and bad. Motivated by self-determination, they are assertive. They prize their autonomy and ability to choose their own destiny. In Supervillain mode, they can become tyrannical dominators who oppress and invalidate the people they're supposed to be serving.

The Organizer
Community: The Organizer serves the community by bringing reform in the direction of efficiency. Organizers have a gift for solving complex problems and breaking them down strategically. They tend to be more introverted than leaders, and prefer organizing processes over managing people. They have a knack for carving big vision down into actionable steps. They are concrete thinkers, map makers, legislators, architects, handbook authors, standardizers. They create and hold to routines.

Adjectives: Conscientious, Systematic, Efficient, Ritualistic, Disciplined, Pragmatic, Discerning, Thrifty, Aware.

Contrast: As concrete thinkers, they tend to be uncomfortable in the abstract realm of Dreamers. They do not tend to produce big ideas or dream of new possibilities. However, they are essential instruments for translating dreams and goals into achievable steps, and equipping teams with streamlined processes and clarified procedures.

Struggles: Their compulsion to follow routines and maintain rituals can set them up for difficulty coping with change. When plans change, or the unexpected happens, they can become flustered, frustrated, and even angry. They can get hung up on details that others are able to set aside. They can become perfectionistic and controlling, frustrating others with their highly specific expectations. They prize control and consistency as an antidote for being overwhelmed.

The Dreamer

Community: Dreamers are high level, creative, abstract thinkers who serve the community by bringing vision and creativity. The Dreamer sees things from afar and often struggles with the details. Dreamers are imaginative, innovative, original, and conceptual. They can be deeply inspiring because they see possibilities that others can't see, often leading to new horizons and unexpected outcomes. They are artists, idealists, visionaries, nonconformists. They have active and vibrant imaginations that enable them to foster unique perspectives.

Adjectives: Inspirational, Big-Picture, Creative, Abstract, Visionary, Entrepreneurial, Innovative.

Contrast: Where the Achiever can be nearsighted and driven by the practicality of what needs to be done now, Dreamers are far-sighted and long to make big, lofty, creative possibilities into realities. Where the Achiever gets dopamine from checking tasks off of the list, Dreamers are content to conceive of, describe, and discuss exciting possibilities or things they are discovering. They get dopamine from building invisible frameworks—castles in the sky.

Struggles: They deeply desire to bring their ideas into fruition, but they often struggle to formulate plans and execute, which can be deeply unsettling and disappointing for them (and people around them). In addition, they can be unfocused and distractible by "shiny things." They can flit from idea to idea like butterflies going from flower to flower, never sticking with any single one long enough to make it a reality. They can also have tunnel vision for their own ideas, unable to make room for the ideas of others. When triggered, they can escape into their own minds, becoming narcissistically obsessed with their own creative ideas, and neglecting the community around them. This tendency can be seen in the personal lives of many great artists who married their craft and abandoned or mistreated loved ones in the process.

The Achiever

Community: The Achiever is like an engine that just won't stop. Achievers are big-time doers and heavy lifters who drive progress step by thundering step. They have huge (metaphorical) shoulders and can bear massive physical, mental, and emotional weight. They are often described as driven, motivated, and prolific. They have strong willpower. Achievers measure their days by how many things they got checked off their lists. They don't have much use for talking about things in high and lofty terms. They're all about execution and tangible results.

Adjectives: Driven, Unstoppable, Productive, Intense, Practical, Determined, Steadfast, Tireless.

Contrast: Where an Organizer would rather spend ten hours on a system that shaves ten minutes off of a repetitive task, the Achiever would rather plow through without stopping, not wanting to overthink things and waste time.

Struggles: Achievers have the will to prevail, get the job done, and cross the finish line. As a result, they can struggle with creating intentional inactivity and getting the proper rest. They have a hard time defining a point at which they have achieved enough for the day, which means they can carry a deadly sense that they have never done enough. When triggered, they can become workaholics who neglect their families and friends by escaping into their work. They can bulldoze right over people in their eagerness to take action.

Selecting Your Types

Now that you have reviewed all of the Hero Types, it's time to rank your Hero Types. This will help you begin to discern your areas of strength, your supporting areas, and your areas of weakness. Everyone has capabilities in all of the different Hero Type categories. However, a few will rise to the top. Some will settle toward the middle, and some will sink to the bottom. Take a moment to rank them one to six, with one being your strongest area and six being your weakest.

Make a note of the order and rank of your Hero Types, or you can go to superpowerquest.com/myprofile to input your Hero Types into your Hero Profile.

HERO TYPES		
Connector, Nurturer, Leader, Organizer, Dreamer, Achiever		
Effective Hero Types		
Supporting Hero Types		

When asked, "What is your Hero Type?" use the shorthand of putting your top two Hero Types together with a slash. For example, I am a "Connector/Dreamer." My wife is a "Leader/Organizer." I recently met someone who is a "Dreamer/Connector" which has a different emphasis than my type (shout out to Jason Campbell!) Everyone is unique, even people with the exact same Hero Types. You'll see this as we work our way down to your unique Superpower Statement. Still, people with similar Hero Types will find it much easier to understand each other, because the ways they see and serve the world will have some substantial similarities.

Now you know how your Hero Types stack up against each other! This is a foundational building block for discovering and refining your Superpower. In the next section, we will identify which Hero Types are your Effective Types, your Supporting Types, and your Hindering Types.

1.6
Effective, Supporting, and Hindering Types

This chapter will help you interpret your Hero Type results. Your strongest Hero Types are your Effective Types. Your middle Hero Types are your Supporting Types. Your last place Hero Types are your Hindering Types.

For most people, you will have two Effective types, two Supporting Types, and two Hindering types. Some people will have slightly different combinations, which will affect the balance of the remaining distribution. No worries if this is the case, but you should definitely have Hero Types landing in all three categories.

You'll have to make some decisions here, but don't push to the point of frustration. This is a guideline, not a law. You are a unique and complex person, not a math problem. You can change things later.

The following descriptions will help you classify your Hero Types, and form a tiebreaker if you're having trouble.

Effective Types
Your Effective Types are like your native language, or like riding a bike. They come so easily to you that you barely notice you're using them. Working in these areas often doesn't feel like work at all.

My wife is like this with organizational problem solving. I present a complex workplace situation to her, usually from a place of agonizing over a decision. She listens carefully, gets a look in her eye, and then gives me roughly five sentences about what needs to be done. "You're a genius," I say. She looks at me, puzzled, and says, "It's just common sense." It's common sense to her because of her Effective Types of Leadership and Organization. It's so effortless to her that it just feels like common sense. Which Hero Types are like that for you?

Supporting Types
Supporting Types represent things you can do with moderate effort. Working in these areas can be rewarding, but also mildly draining. Supporting Types are often activated in tandem with an Effective Type, serving the purposes and goals of that type. You might refer to yourself as "adequate" or "intermediate" in your Supporting Type areas. Maybe even "expert" or "skilled." But they don't quite have the effortless magic of your Effective Types. For example, no one would call me an Organizer. I can be forgetful, tunnel vision-y, and inefficient. But…I can sometimes create amazing organizational systems for topics and projects that I am passionate about. I have The Organizer as a supporting type, and it comes alive (when needed) in tandem with my Effective Type of The Dreamer. This Superpower Quest framework that you are reading is an example of my Dreamer type thriving with the support of my Organizer type.

Which Hero Types feel like this to you? You're good at them, but maybe not great. Or maybe you are great, but only under very special circumstances, or because of extensive practice.

Hindering Types
The number one clue that you are operating in a Hindering Type is that the activity is draining. I once knew a lady that had a job where she had to use ten key to key in numbers on a repetitive basis. And she told me she loved it. I remember thinking this was the most preposterous thing I'd ever heard. Who could enjoy sitting at a keypad pecking in numbers for hours at a time?

When I have to perform rote, repetitive tasks like that, it's extremely draining for me. I end up feeling like my guts are going to bubble up out of my mouth in protest and my brain is going to pop. I have very little willpower for the grind. I need variety and fun to stay engaged. It's not that I can" do these things. But it makes me very cranky if I have to do too much of it. And it's exponentially exhausting.

Hindering Types can represent the areas that make you feel the most insecure and inadequate. Areas that might make you feel like an imposter. Your stress level goes up. You might notice that it requires twice as long or twice as much effort to get the same results as others. You wish someone else could do it. Maybe you procrastinate. There's no joy in it for you. No payoff.

Which Hero Types feel like this to you? Your hindering types may not feel this dramatic—but as a rule of thumb, just look for the types that most drain you, compared to other types.

Allocating Your Types

Make a note and allocate your Hero Types into their proper category of Effective Types, Supporting Types, and Hindering Types. You can also go to superpowerquest.com/myprofile to allocate your Hero Types within your Hero Profile.

Effective Types.
These are your primary ways of impacting the people and the world around you. These are the areas where you have your biggest wins and experience the most joy. Growth in these areas can be exponential.

Supporting Types.
These are your secondary areas of strength. They support your primary strengths and make you more versatile. Though you may sometimes be highly effective in these areas, they come harder to you, and do not provide as much satisfaction. Growth in these areas can be moderate-to-high.

The Superpower Quest

Hindering Types.
These are your areas of least effectiveness. You may experience frustration and insecurity when you are forced into—or you force yourself into—performing in these areas. Growth in these areas, though sometimes necessary, can be hard-fought, slow, and proportionately small.

What Now?

Remember, this book is about leveraging your design for greater effectiveness and joy in life. The idea is to know yourself so well that you can go with the grain of your design instead of against it. Our endeavors are more effective when we cooperate with our design. We know this, instinctively. If you are 6'9", agile, and great at jumping, are you more likely to get excited about basketball or horse jockeying? It feels like common sense. Your Superpower is harder to see and put into words, but it follows the same principle. You will be more successful if you play the game that is rigged in your favor. Yes, there are edge cases. Humans are complex. Exceptions exist. There will always be the Spud Webbs who defy the odds to carve out an unlikely place for themselves in history. But even these edge cases leverage some aspect of their design to make up for whatever they seem to lack in their design.

> You will be more successful if you play the game that is rigged in your favor.

Effective Types: Press In

Pay attention to the areas of performance where you feel the effortless magic of your Effective Types at work. Then, find ways to do more activities in the realm of your Effective Types, and less of everything else. This simple and profound mental shift can have an immediate impact on your sense of joy and effectiveness. There's not much more to it. I almost feel silly saying something so obvious in writing; but this simple principle is profound and wonderful. Now that you know your Effective Types, do yourself the favor of doubling down on them and serving the world in those ways.

If you are a Leader, look for opportunities to mobilize people towards a goal. A Dreamer? Then dream big and cast wonderful visions. A Nurturer? Find your people and dig in hard for their healing and nourishing. Insofar as you are able, bend your life around your design instead of vice versa.

Supporting Types: Use With Care

Use supporting types to supplement your Effective Types. Supporting Types are not your star players—they are your bench. Supporting types are not an end to themselves, but they can be powerful contributors. Don't get tricked. You might be really, really good at actions that fall within a Supporting Type. So good that you might get offered a job or promotion that primarily leverages that type. In general, don't accept such offers, except as a bridge to where you really want to be, which is operating in your Effective Types. Like I said before, I have a powerful Organizer gift that activates in service of my creativity. But if someone offered me a job to create and manage systems all day, I would run the other way. I've learned that I need to stay in the big picture. I need the freedom to dream and create and invest deeply in people in their progress. Systems, for me, are the means to the end of creatively helping people unlock their potential.

Supporting types are gold. I love my supporting types. Your supporting type abilities will help you serve the world more robustly. The thing to watch out for is mistaking your supporting types for your effective types, and leaning into the good instead of the best. Lean hardest into your Effective Types. That's where exponential joy and impact are going to be most possible for you.

Hindering Types: Avoid If Possible

Hindering Types are part of your Weak Spot, which we will discuss in later chapters. Hindering Types are the areas where you most often fail, experience frustration, and get drained of enthusiasm and joy. When you have let yourself down, or feel disappointed about an outcome, it's often because you were operating in a Hindering Type.

What is the danger? Your Hindering Types represent your weaknesses. They can be very bothersome. They can represent the areas where you wish you were better. They can cause you immeasurable inconvenience, pain, and even tragedy. What you don't want to do is brute force your weaknesses and try to eliminate them by sheer willpower. That's a really draining way to spend your energy, and it will lead to exhaustion and mediocre results. It's fighting against your design.

So what do you do? A better way to look at your weaknesses is that they are the areas where you need the most help. A low-hanging fruit strategy is to avoid situations that force you to act heavily in the areas of your Hindering Types; and this is a good partial strategy. But there are many areas in your life where this is simply not possible. There are times when every human must perform actions that are associated with all six Hero Types in order to be functional in society. I hate doing my taxes, but my taxes have to get done. The rest of the equation of managing your Hindering Types is that you will need to leverage systems (Build Your Utility Belt) and the talents of other superheroes (Join Forces). All of this will be discussed in later chapters with more detail.

Congratulations!
Now that you know your Hero Types, and the nuances behind your Effective, Supporting, and Hindering Types, you are ready to move on to the next step of the Superpower discovery process: selecting your Power Words. Power Words will help you get even more specific about calling out your unique characteristics. These words will ultimately help you write your hyper-specific and unique Superpower Statement.

1.7
Power Words

Down the funnel we go, seeking a razor thin stream of clarity. We're going from abstract principles to concrete application, because everyone needs both in order to take the right actions.

The Power of Power Words
Now you will select your Power Words, which are core values that describe and fine tune your Hero Type discoveries. Your power words are the adjectives that best describe how you relate with the world at your best. They describe your optimal state of being.

If you're a Leader, your Power Words will answer the following: What kind of leader are you? What do you value in your leadership?

Are you a Nurturer? Power Words will answer these questions: How do you nurture? What ways of nurturing are important to you?

Power words are a sharp-pointed instrument that will help you color in the gaps in a complete design description.

Your Power Words are instinctively important to you. Maybe they always have been. Or maybe they result from powerful lessons learned through experience. Life may have reinforced them or, on the other hand, stolen them from you. But we are here to claim and reclaim them.

Your Superpower is what you do, automagically, when you are truly in step with your design. It's what you do more of when you are at your best, and happiest, and healthiest, and most confident. Power Words will guide you closer to this internal treasure trove.

The following table lists power words that are commonly associated with the different Hero Types. Circle ten to fifteen words that best describe you and how you benefit the world around you. Start with your Effective Types, but you may circle words in any Hero Type. As stated before, we are not trying to box you in. Your Power Words will tend to align with your stronger Hero Types, but that's not a hard and fast rule.

Sample Power Words by Hero Type

Leader		
Bold	Delegating	Just
Confident	Intense	Self-Controlled
Decisive	Blunt	Truthful
Assertive	Passionate	Determined
Persuasive	Strong-Willed	Disagreeable
Authoritative	Driven	Competent
Poised	Responsible	Forceful
Commanding	Steadfast	Fiery
Organizer		
Discerning	Conscientious	Self-Controlled
Planning	Responsible	Objective
Efficient	Structured	Punctual
Reforming	Rational	Thorough
Perfectionistic	Logical	Thrifty
Systematic	Consistent	Attentive
Automating	Disciplined	Cautious
Connector		
Peacemaking	Forgiving	Gregarious
Non-Judgmental	Rescuing	Witty
Tolerant	Humorous	Talkative
Enthusiastic	Curious	Hospitable
Connecting	Teachable	Liberating
Networking	Personable	Accepting

SECTION 1 | Discover Your Superpower

Nurturer		
Hospitable	Welcoming	Meek
Affirming	Embracing	Agreeable
Authentic	Caretaking	Committed
Sensitive	Comforting	Empathetic
Sincere	Concerned	Protective
Gentle	Compassionate	Supportive
Loyal	Benevolent	Available
Achiever		
Productive	Conqueror	Initiating
Driven	Persevering	Obedient
Perfectionistic	Nonstop	Dependable
Impressive	Overachieving	Determined
Unstoppable	Workhorse	Enduring
Impatient	Overcoming	Diligent
Tireless	Reliable	
Dreamer		
Visionary	Faith-Filled	Daydreaming
Inspiring	Resourceful	Inventive
Prophetic	Wise	Imaginative
Creative	Flexibility	Idealistic
Far-Seeing	Optimistic	Romantic
Futuristic	Philosophical	Quixotic
Abstract	Profound	Hopeful

Start a List

On a blank piece of paper, write down the words that you selected above. This will be your Master List. You will use this list to add some additional words (see instructions below), and then narrow down from there. As a second step, after you have added your words from above, then add any more words that come to your mind that resonate with how you serve the world at your best.

Phone a Friend

Next, ask one or two friends or family members who know you very well to help you. The "ask" will sound something like this:

> *"I am going through an awesome process to learn my Superpower. I am trying to get a deeper understanding of the ways that I most joyfully and effectively benefit the people around me, and I need an outside perspective. Can you list four to five adjectives that best describe me when I am operating at my best?"*

Once you have collected words from your family and/or friends, add them to your Master List. Pay special attention to words that come up more than once.

Narrowing Down

Okay! At this stage you will probably have ten to twenty Power Word candidates. This is your reserve. You'll use the following process to narrow down your reserve to the four to six words with the most relevance and impact. Follow the steps below.

- Keep this in mind: **The four to six words that you end up with should be distinct from one another.** For example, "authenticity" and "honesty" are not the same thing, but they are too close to both make the cut. Same with "innovative" and "creative." Same with "courageous," "bold," and "confident." You get the idea.
- Give priority consideration to the words that came up more than once.
- Group similar words into pairs or sets. In that set, identify the word that feels the strongest and resonates the most. Cross out the others in that set.
- Write the winning words in order of how much they resonate with you. See what rises to the top. Cross out whatever falls to the bottom.
- Pay attention to yourself. If you're having a really difficult time crossing out a word, don't be too fast to cut it. Come back to it later.

Enter your final four to six words into the table below, or you can go to superpowerquest.com/myprofile to input your Power Words into your Hero Profile.

SECTION 1 | Discover Your Superpower

POWER WORDS	
Positive traits and tendencies	
1.	4.
2.	5.
3.	6.

Thundercats, HOOOOOOOOO! These are your words that give important insight into your core values and how you carry out your stated Core Drive and Hero Types.

You're making progress! Now you know your Core Drives, Your Hero Types, and your Power Words. This is more self-understanding and clarity than many people achieve in a lifetime. I hope you are already beginning to see your life through the lens of your design, and gaining clarity about where to pull back and where to double down.

Your Power Words are like a cheat sheet that helps you remember your best and most effective ways of being. Memorize them. Bring them to mind daily. Let them help guide you toward your best opportunities, and away from bad, mediocre, and merely "good" opportunities.

Once I realized that my Power Words are Authentic, Creative, Humble, and Enthusiastic, I made an acronym to help me remember: "A.C.H.E." My friend David gets extra credit, because his words formed the acronym "D.A.V.I.D." (Determined, Adventurous, Versatile, Imaginative, and Diligent.)

Once I understood my Power Words, I began to press into these characteristics unapologetically. At my best, I get *crazy* hyped for other people's accomplishments and passions (Enthusiastic). I'm always coming up with wild new ideas (Creative). I'm willing to sacrifice my own opinions and agenda to invite others to offer their ideas and opinions for honest consideration (Humble). I reveal more personal information about myself than most people ever would, in order to invite others to share authentically, and to feel safe doing it (Authentic). This is me. I got over my fear of being "too extra" and stopped dialing down these characteristics for public consumption. My job isn't to make myself palatable for every other person on earth. My job is to live out my unique design, not someone else's opinion of the way I should be.

This is true for you as well! Power Words will help you understand and press into your unique design for more effectiveness in your community. For those of you who deal with Imposter Syndrome, I hope your Power Words will help you stop trying to be something you're not, so you can enjoy the beauty and rarity of what you actually are.

The next chapter will take all of these wonderful pieces of self-discovery—your Core Drive, your Hero Types, and your Power Words—and help you distill them down into a single Superpower Statement that illustrates the one thing you do that most benefits the world and brings you the most satisfaction. This will be the tip of the spear as you learn to redirect your energy towards your most special ability.

I want to help you focus the beam of your design-energy so tightly that it burns through barriers and opens doorways to places you never imagined.

1.8
Superpower Statement

Welcome to the key step of the "Superpower" phase of the SPQ process. The goal of the whole process has been to funnel you down into actionable clarity. This is that moment. This is the treasure chest at the bottom of the hole we've been digging together. Once you know your Superpower Statement, you can use it to change the direction of your life.

I'm not talking about quick fix shortcuts. I'm not talking about immediate results, although these are possible. I'm talking about the kind of fundamental clarity that can help you fine-tune your trajectory. I'm talking about the magic that comes from knowing the ordained output of your complex and beautiful design. I'm talking about radical achievements that you can't even imagine in areas that you're passionate about, given a sufficient amount of practice and experience.

> Your Superpower Statement is a core ability
> where you can keep getting better over a lifetime,
> and where there is no ceiling on your progress.

In the book *Unique Ability* by Catherine Nomura, Julia Waller, Shannon Waller, and Dan Sullivan, the authors describe a concept called *Unique Ability,* which is similar to this concept of your Superpower.

The Superpower Quest

One characteristic of *Unique Ability* is that "... there's a sense of never-ending improvement...you keep getting better and better, and never run out of possibilities for growth." [3] Investing time and energy into your Superpower is like investing in a low-risk investment with high returns, instead of a high-risk investment with low returns.

I don't personally know Lin-Manuel Miranda, the creative genius behind the Broadway hit "Hamilton" and other productions. I also have the benefit of saying that I have not, at this point, researched his creative process. What I know of him, I know mostly through the experiences that he's given me through his creative works. I'm curious how he came to the level of clarity that he seems to exhibit in his productions. Regardless of how he got there, he has reached a level of excellence and clarity about *who he is creatively* that is rarely seen in a generation.

He creates delight by reconciling the best of wildly disconnected genres. He raises the bar by embedding excellence in the small details that others would overlook. I suspect his Power Words include excellent, unstoppable, creative, and non-conforming. This leads me to believe he's very high on the Dreamer and Achiever Hero Types.

If l were to surmise, I would guess that his Superpower Statement is something like: "Making unexpected connections for the sake of excellence."

I would imagine that he exercises his Superpower in nearly all aspects of his life, not just the finished products that we get to see and enjoy. I bet he does this in his emails. I bet he does this in his conversations. I bet he did this when he participated in freestyle rap battles. I bet he writes his inspirations on toilet paper squares if he has to. I'll bet he quickly and decisively says "No!" to opportunities that are outside of his Superpower.

And now, here's the big reveal for why I included that extended treatise on the popular playwright.

What if we are all Lin-Manuel Miranda, but we just haven't all clarified our Superpower to the point of investing in it for decades? No, I do not mean we're all intended to be playwrights and artists. Your Superpower might be a galaxy apart from his. But you might be the Lin-Manuel Miranda of small business accounting. You might be the Lin-Manuel Miranda of being a stay-at-home mom or dad. You might be the Lin-Manuel Miranda of barbering for inmates. You might be the Lin-Manuel Miranda of office management for B2B software sales. You might be the Lin-Manuel Miranda of enjoying nature and inviting others into that enjoyment.

We're all bad at many things. Mediocre at many things. Good at many things. But we usually only have one thing that we are straight-up geniuses at. And you probably don't even know it, because it feels effortless. Or because you don't think it's marketable. Or because you think other people's Superpowers are cooler. Or because it's not what you would have picked for yourself. Or because someone told you that you were supposed to be something other than what you are.

> We're all bad at many things. Mediocre at many things. Good at many things. But we usually only have one thing that we are straight-up geniuses at. And you probably don't even know it, because it feels effortless.

That one "thing" lives inside of your Core Drive. It lives inside of your Effective Hero Types. It lives inside of your Power Words.

Review the notes you've taken up until now. You can also go to your Hero Profile and download or print out your conclusions. Reviewing your characteristics all in one place will be the basis for the next step.

Now, you are going to look at all your conclusions from the previous chapters as the raw materials to make something beautiful. This part of the process is kind of like those old "Magic Eye" puzzles from the nineties. At first glance, it looks like a page covered with colors and dots. Keep staring. Nothing happens. Keep staring. Still nothing. All of a sudden your eyes do this weird unfocusing-flip, and you see this awesome three-dimensional shape hovering before your eyes. Maybe it's an eagle. Maybe it's pyramids. It's magic!

I want you to put on your magic eyes and gaze at your materials; the list of all of your superhero descriptions above. Your Superpower Statement will be a single sentence that harnesses the power of these words in a single direction. This is art, not science. It will require some abstract thinking. If you're a more concrete person, don't worry. I will provide some templates below that will help you. But I'd suggest trying without them first.

Your Superpower Statement probably won't contain all of the words that you listed above. It might not use any of the words you listed above. But it will somehow harness the essence.

Gaze at the words. Think about what they are saying to you and about you. Reflect or pray. Think about your design. Think about the things you do that bring you the most satisfaction. Think about the things you do that most impact the people around you. Think about the last time you felt effective and confident, like a fish in water. Write down a few potential phrases, no matter how strange they sound, just to get the blood pumping. Expect it to take you twenty tries before you find something that really resonates. That way, if you do it in five or nineteen, it will feel like a win.

Remember, you can always phone a friend. Because your Superpower is the way that you serve your community, it's a great idea to enlist your community to confirm or add color to your conclusions. They're the ones that have experienced your Superpower for themselves. They know the good it can do.

Enter your Superpower Statement into your notes; or you can go to superpowerquest.com/myprofile to input your Superpower Statement into your Hero Profile. You can also go to **superpowerquest.com/resources** for printable versions.

SUPERPOWER STATEMENT
Focused description of your special ability

If you are having trouble with this step, you're not alone. I don't want you to push to the point of frustration. A shortcut is to look at all your words, including Effective and Supporting Core Drives, Effective Hero Types, and Power Words, and circle the handful that seem to most deeply resonant for you.

Then, take try to insert them into a format like this:

[ADJECTIVE] [NOUN] for [ADJECTIVE] [NOUN]

For example, my Superpower Statement is "Authentic Connection for Mutual Progress." That fits the format above. You may need to convert some of your adjectives to nouns, or vice versa. Try a few combinations, and see which one feels the most true.

The first adjective-noun combo is WHAT you do, and the second is the ultimate GOAL of what you do. For example, my first adjective-noun is Authentic Connection. I connect with people constantly, authentically, deeply. But I am always doing this *for the sake of* moving people forward, or moving myself forward in learning and growth, so the second adjective-noun is Mutual Progress.

Where you land may not feel like a 100% fit at first—but if you can find a statement that feels like a 70% solution, go with it for now. You will most likely tweak it a few times as you begin taking it out for a spin.

Again, once you are done, you can input your statement at **superpowerquest.com/myprofile**.

Superpower Quest Hero Profile

Congratulations!
You have discovered your Superpower Statement. This phrase is unique to you. It gives words to the passion and skill that live in your heart. This is a major part of leveraging your design.

Next Steps
Here are some concrete strategies for using your Superpower Statement:

- Memorize it. These words are precious, and you've worked hard to get to this point. Now is the time to imprint this sentence on your mind and heart, so you can have access to it at all times.
- Look for more opportunities to exercise your Superpower. Because it's an area that brings both joy and effectiveness, you'll find it easy to invest time and energy, and you will grow exponentially over time.
- Factor in your Superpower when it comes to big decisions. When considering job opportunities, volunteer roles, or day-to-day tasks that you can say yes or no to, ask the question: how well does this fit with my Superpower? This isn't the only factor for your decisions, but it should be a factor.
- More and more people are investing in a side hustle. A side hustle is a great opportunity to begin experimenting with your Superpower.
- Tell people your Superpower, and encourage your community to help you find more opportunities to exercise it. As you activate your Superpower inside your community, you will have more and more value to offer people outside of your community for expanded reach.

In my experience, your Superpower represents an area of limitless growth opportunity. Lifelong dedication to using and enhancing your Superpower will keep you from becoming a "has-been" who plateaus later in life.

We are getting down to the pointy end of the funnel. Now we're going to dive even deeper into specific applications of your Superpower by generating your "Power Punches."

1.9
Power Punches

Down the funnel we go! Power Punches are where the rubber meets the road…or rather, where the fist meets the wall. Power Punches break through walls of mediocrity. They open doorways to new opportunities. They are the heartbeat of progress. If you are executing some or all of your Power Punches every day, you are swinging for the fences every day. It's like getting your engine fully in gear.

You know your Superpower Statement, which is a sentence encapsulating your unique way of effectively and joyfully impacting your community. Now we're going to translate this down into a handful of repeatable activities. These are the activities that you do, or can do, on a regular basis, that highly reflect your Superpower. These are the high-leverage outputs of your design.

Power Punches are the four to eight consistent applications of your Superpower Statement. They can be scheduled into your life. The goal is to build a cadence in your life where you are using your Power Punches consistently. Your Power Punches are going to break through barriers and create opportunities, especially if you double down and intentionally work them into your life.

My Superpower Statement is "Authentic Connection for Mutual Progress." This powerful way of being extends down into the following activities. I double down on these activities, and they provide me with exponential results.

As an illustration, my Power Punches are the following:

- **Intimate Quiet Time with God.** For me, authentic connection with others starts with authentically connecting with God. Any progress I might possibly bring to others comes from my intimate connection with God. This connection enables me to be my best for others.
- **Effective Meetings.** Meetings are where the magic happens. Meetings are where I listen deeply and help people clarify and accomplish their dreams. Planned or unplanned, I define a meeting as any opportunity for authentic connection. This can be a scheduled Zoom meeting, a spontaneous conversation with a stranger, or anything in between.
- **Creative Works.** I use my creativity to connect with people and move them forward through written works such as poetry, stories, and personal development books. My enthusiasm about these creative works is contagious, and it's one of the ways I draw people into connection.
- **Targeted Learning.** I am constantly learning new things (within areas of my key interests) that I can use to move my connections forward. Books, seminars, coaching appointments, and other development opportunities stoke my enthusiasm and fill me up with more ideas to benefit others.
- **Consistent LinkedIn Engagement.** I have used the LinkedIn platform for many years as a way to connect and inform people in my community. The platform is a great vehicle for my Superpower, because it creates conversations.
- **Focused Acts of Service.** I come up with creative ways to benefit others through giving gifts and acts of service. These actions create deeper connections. They also convey my authentic care.
- **Passionate Public Speaking.** I have a passion for addressing whole communities with messages of hope, reconciliation, encouragement, and empowerment. I connect with communities to move them forward through these creative messages.

SECTION 1 | Discover Your Superpower

- **Strategic Connections.** I am constantly meeting with people, listening deeply, and understanding their stories and Superpowers. I use this knowledge to create mutually beneficial strategic connections.

How can you figure out your Power Punches? Follow these simple instructions to unlock this amazing technique.

- Reflect. Start by thinking about your Superpower Statement and the actions you already perform on a regular basis that bring joy to you and effective service to others. Pray or reflect, and write down what you come up with.
- Be Specific. Your Superpower is an ability, and your Power Punches are specific applications of that ability. For some Power Punches, you might use an adjective/descriptor that ties it back to your Superpower Statement or Power Words. For example, Fixing Things could be Enthusiastically Fixing Things or Efficiently Fixing Things. Instead of Making Meals, you could say Making Meals that Delight. Regardless, the goal is to get as specific as possible.
- (Achiever Extra Credit) Add Color. For each Power Punch, give a small two to four sentence description that ties it back to your Superpower. Pack this sentence full of all your superhero words and phrases from this entire section.

What are your Power Punches? Make a note for later, or you can input them into your Hero Profile at **superpowerquest.com/myprofile**.

Now that you've identified your Power Punches, you can immediately aim to start redirecting energy from other roles, tasks, and responsibilities into these higher-leverage activities. Do what you need to do to start doing more of these things. Your community needs your unique contribution, reflected in these clarified manifestations of your Superpower.

In the next chapter we will wrap up the "Leverage Your Superpower" section, and begin our preparations for the next phase of the journey: "Stewarding Your Weak Spot."

1.10
The Mission

You have identified your Effective and Supporting Core Drives, your Effective and Supporting Hero Types, your Power Words, your Superpower Statement, and your Power Punches. I get excited thinking about the potential this has to change your life, like it has changed mine.

The logical question now is, what do you do with all this information? How do you best use these powers? How do you increase your margin for Superhero activities, when life is so packed with the things that drain you? How does a kid with spider strength become a masked webslinger for justice and still get his homework done on time?

The answer is the statement that I first heard from coach and author Alan Briggs, a friend and mentor of mine: "Progress over perfect." With this book, I hope to do more than offer quick results. I hope to help you change your trajectory. I hope to help you make a long-term shift towards more joy and more excellence, and away from being drained and overwhelmed and mediocre.

As we begin to close this section, we will proceed with practical steps to begin leveraging your unique design for satisfaction and success. Then we will zoom out to make sure we are keeping the big picture in view.

Here are eleven pieces of advice to help you gain momentum on your quest, with an eye towards long term results. Here is your Superpower Mission, should you choose to accept it!

#1. Take One Small Step

Take one small step, and don't plan the next step until you have taken that step. This one small step can include any of the actions below, or something else of your own design. Just make sure it's something that could be done in less than fifteen minutes. Take that action, and then take another small step.

In the book *Atomic Habits: An Easy & Proven Way to Build Good Habits & Break Bad Ones,* author James Clear notes that "Small changes often appear to make no difference until you cross a critical threshold. The most powerful outcomes of any compounding process are delayed. You need to be patient." [4]

This is why so many people don't succeed in getting traction for change. The currency of change is consistency, and consistency is extremely hard for most of us to come by. If you are going to have long term success, you will need to gain momentum and learn to trust yourself by achieving small victories, compounded over time.

Your next small steps could be as simple as telling your friends your Superpower Statement, or asking them for ideas about how you can apply your Superpower in your life. This will open up new opportunities you never thought of. We were designed to serve our community, but we need our community to serve us as well, in order to become all that we were meant to be.

#2. Schedule It

There's incredible power in going from abstract to concrete through the simple act of scheduling. Take one of the steps in this list, or some other step that gets you closer to your goal, and put it on your calendar or task list. Make this real to yourself. Release what you've learned out into the wild of your actual life. Write it down. Mark it. Schedule it.

#3. **Share**

As noted above, sharing your Superpower goals with others can be a catalyst for momentum. Be specific and tell them about your different elements. Tell them your Superpower Statement. Tell them about your Power Punches. Ask them if the conclusions you've come to seem to accord with their experience of you. This can feel very vulnerable, so make sure to share with people you trust. Saying things out loud has a way of making them feel more real. Bringing others into the equation compounds the "realness" factor even more.

Here's the actual notice I posted on LinkedIn in December 2022. As of the time I'm writing this, it was the most viewed of all my LinkedIn posts for the whole year.

> *OK, I am posting here as a flag in the ground for accountability. I have begun actively working on a book called "The Superpower Quest" that will help people radically understand, and press into, their unique design. I will be finished with the first manuscript by June 30, 2023.*
>
> *For some background, I have greatly benefited from frameworks like #enneagram and #myersbriggs and #ikigai. My experiences in pastoral ministry, building a business, and raising and equipping my children, have fueled a fiery passion for developing and releasing people into exponential effectiveness by leveraging their unique design.*
>
> *My goal is not to replace the frameworks mentioned above, but to stand on the shoulders of giants and create a unique funnel to help people develop a razor-sharp clarity for how they were uniquely designed to impact the world.*
>
> *Writing this book is actually an intentional manifestation of my superpower, revealed through this process, which is "authentic connection for mutual progress."*
>
> *You can see some of my rough work at superpowerquest.com.*
>
> *Please do take this post as an invitation to check in on me from time to*

time, ask questions, and help push me towards my Big Hairy Audacious Goal. *Deep breath.

My wife cringed when I showed her that post, after I had just hit the button to make it live. It was like signing my name in blood. Scary!

But this simple act created incredible momentum for me. I put my big dream out into the open. People began asking me how the book was coming along. I felt like I had raised the stakes on myself significantly, and it was scary and exhilarating, all of which translated into a greater drive to finish. Like many Dreamers, I have no problem starting things. It's finishing things that gets very tricky and inconsistent for me.

I think that was the moment this book was born. That was the beginning act of dragging it out of the realm of possibility and across the finish line into reality. All from an act of sharing. Share what you've learned! Share what you intend to *do* with what you've learned!

#4. Memorize and Reinforce

Create strategies to keep the elements of your design in a mental space where you can freely call them to mind. Commit all the elements to memory, from your Core Drive, to your Hero Types, all the way down to your Power Punches. This may sound like a heavy lift. But if you believe in the process, and you believe your conclusions to be true, then committing them to memory will be a worthy investment. It will help you disqualify activities outside your Superpower that you shouldn't be doing, except for a very good reason.

A parallel step to memorization is reinforcement. You can have something memorized, and never give it a second thought, like your times tables, or your states and capitals, etc. You can set a time, such as the early morning, or in tandem with some other daily or weekly ritual, to check back in with your Superpower Design Map. Press it into your mind until it makes a dent.

#5. Help Others

Sharing things you are excited about with your friends and family (#2) can lead others to engage. They might even want to join you in your exciting endeavor. Consider the joy of spreading what you've learned to others, and helping them begin to leverage their unique design in ways they never imagined!

#6. Say "Yes"

Start saying "yes" to invitations and opportunities that are in the realm of your Superpower. It feels good to identify opportunities where you have the highest percentage chance to be effective and successful. Look for moments to contribute your special gift to the world around you. You may be surprised how much "that effortless thing you do" creates exponential benefit for the people in your life. I am crying out for you to GET YOUR REPS IN. Give your value to the world. Give generously, find opportunities, and don't worry about compensation at this point. Bob Burg and John David Mann say in their bestselling book, "The Go Giver," that "Your true [professional] worth is determined by how much MORE you give in value than how much you take in compensation." Go, be the gift you are, and lavish your Superpower upon the people around you. And watch what comes back to you.

My brother, Bobby, creates custom art pieces upon request. When he has a new commission, he will do a short interview to learn about the subject, and then he will dedicate time and space to fill his mind with that person, and with love. Then he will create a painting from that mental and emotional space that is unique to that person. What an amazing gift! When he's doing this, he is saying "yes" to his Superpower. I want you to say "yes" to your Superpower, more and more.

#7. Say "No"

In his book, *Essentialism: The Disciplined Pursuit of Less*, Greg McKeown gives the following instructions for setting prioritization in your life: "If it isn't a clear yes, then it's a clear no." [5] He also writes, "Non-essentialists say 'yes' to everyone, and essentialists say 'no' to almost everyone." [6] The idea, here, is that we need to learn to say "no" to tasks and obligations that are not in our wheelhouse, because those tasks and obligations are often hindering us from doing the really important things that most contribute to our greatest goals. I am putting the spin on this that the realm of your Superpower is a great clue to determining the activities that you should and shouldn't be doing, so that you can learn to say "no" to the wrong opportunities.

This must be taken within reason. I know that we all have roles and responsibilities that we cannot simply abandon just because they are outside of our best use. Sometimes we are called to sacrifice for others; and this is true, good and right. But what if there are many, many roles and responsibilities in your life that can, and should be, abandoned, for your own good, and for the good of your community? The idea of abandoning duties for the benefit of your community may feel counterintuitive. But the reality is, every second you spend doing something outside of your Superpower is a second that could have been spent acting within, and investing in, your Superpower. And your Superpower represents the most effective ways that you can serve your community.

Of course, this principle can be transcended, and only applies as an indicator and not a law. It would be sad and misguided, for example, to forego helping someone in need because empathy and mercy are not your *Superpower*. I hope that no one will apply these ideas counter to virtue, but rather in the service of virtue and love. We are aspiring heroes, not villains. We don't excuse ourselves from responsibility to serve the world; but we must be selective about how we serve.

#8. Build Your Systems

The greatest challenge for any significant change is consistency. You need habits and systems in your life to help you make progress in the areas where you are weak. These can also enhance your strengths. We will cover this more in-depth in the upcoming section, Build Your Utility Belt.

#9. Join Forces

One way to multiply your effectiveness is by joining forces with people who have complimentary Superpowers. This is how we facilitate the give-and-take, necessary in a community, that enables us to rise together.

This means you will not only need to understand your own design, but you will need to be able to recognize clues to identify the designs of others. As a Dreamer, I don't work well with Leaders who are too overbearing. They can make me feel constricted and stunt my creativity. Alternately, I can make life really difficult for Organizers, who crave concrete details, if I stay in the abstract clouds and refuse to come down a few paces. But I deeply need Organizers for that very reason. So I've learned, through mighty struggle, to come down from the clouds and meet them halfway.

We can be intentional to look for ways to interlock our design with the complimentary designs of others. We will discuss this in more detail in the Join Forces section of the book.

#10. Join the Superpower Community

Go to **superpowerquest.com/myprofile** to input the information from your Design Map. This will automatically register you as part of the Superhero Community Newsletter and will unlock a whole new world for you, as you will get to join a movement of heroes who have been through the SPQ process, and who are looking to grow their Superpowers and Join Forces with other heroes. You can also go straight to the newsletter at **superpowerquest.com/community**.

Superpower Community Newsletter

In the Superpower Community, you will get the opportunity to:

- Receive articles and content about how to maximize your Superpower.

- Participate in forums to discuss the application of your Superpower in various aspects of life, such as job search, side hustles, creative collaboration, and more.

#11. Swing for the Fences

I love the business author Jim Collins's term "Big Hairy Audacious Goals." I use it all the time to encourage people to think bigger. Some of us have stopped dreaming. The monotonous thrum of life has broken us in some way. Have you forgotten the childlike awe of discovery? I want you to dream again. What is swelling inside you, so big that you can't necessarily put it into words? What accomplishments do you want carved into your gravestone, when you're finished with this short, wild, unpredictable life?

Let's start thinking in terms of years, decades, and lifetimes. What do you want in the long-term?

Great Power and Responsibility

In the original Spider-Man comic book series, Peter Parker's Uncle Ben was shot and killed by a burglar whom Peter had allowed to escape earlier. The incident took place after Uncle Ben and Peter had an argument about responsibility and the importance of using one's power wisely.

Uncle Ben's last words to Peter Parker were, "With great power comes great responsibility." This quote has come to define Spider-Man as a character.

As in comic books, you, the protagonist, have now discovered that you have a special ability. And now you are faced with the daunting task of discovering why it was given to you, and what to do with it. What kind of difference can you make in this overwhelming world? What kind of difference do you want to make? What are the fundamental governing principles of your life? How will you shepherd the design you were given?

These are big questions. Some of you have wrestled them already. Maybe you are still wrestling. Maybe you haven't engaged with them, and don't intend to. The scope of this section was to lead you to this

SECTION 1 | Discover Your Superpower

place, and no further. I wanted to show you the beauty and power of your design, and then help you embrace it. I wanted to send you forward with a clarified understanding of the way you work, so you can reduce friction in your existence. I wanted to help you go "all-in" on your glorious design, and stand in awe of your miraculous potential.

Ultimately, I want to help you see what I could not see for many, many years. I could not see that I was beautiful. Yes; ugly, flawed, traumatized, broken. But above all, beautiful. Now, I commit you to the implications of your excellence.

Should you choose to accept it, your mission from here is bi-directional. It is both micro and macro. It is both the telescope and the microscope.

On the "micro" side, your mission is to test drive your Superpower in new ways, taking practical steps to make more and more room for your unique design to sparkle and sing. Schedule your Power Punches. Use your Hero Types as filters to accept and reject opportunities. Tell people your Superpower Statement.

On the "macro" side, your mission is to make some space for the big questions, in light of Uncle Ben's wisdom about the implications of your wonderful design.

Think about your great power and your great responsibility. What does that responsibility look like for you? How will you leave the world a better place than you found it?

You've now graduated from my primary school for the gifted. Time to get out there and get your reps in, saving the world!

Now that you know your Superpower, the next phase of your education has everything to do with how to embrace and leverage your Weak Spot.

SECTION 2
Steward Your Weak Spot

2.1
Weak Spot Introduction

I used to work as a head counselor at a sleepaway camp for at-risk kids in New York. The director of the camp at that time was an author/educator named Ousmane, and he was one of my first wise mentors. One year, I did a stint helping with hiring interviews. Ous taught me to ask a key question: "What's your greatest strength and greatest weakness?"

Weakness as something you would freely admit during a job interview was foreign to me. Weren't you supposed to hide weakness, or excuse it away? But in Ous's worldview, weakness was something to be aware of, to own, and to freely discuss. This was a revolution.

I remember interviewing a guy, and when I asked him about his greatest weakness, he said it was "that he cared too much about the kids." In other words, his greatest weakness was actually a strength. His application quickly went into the rejection pile. We were looking for people with self-awareness and a desire to grow. Ous taught me that the willingness to acknowledge weakness was a sign of emotional maturity.

Abraham Lincoln is quoted to have said, "It has been my experience that people who have no vices have very few virtues." To be human is to be flawed, and to be authentic is to be willing to admit those flaws.

Everyone has weaknesses. Real, debilitating weaknesses. These are characteristics that do not flatter us when revealed. And the mature response to weakness is to understand it, own it, and not be ashamed of it. Not to hide it, or dismiss it, or gloss over it. The clear-eyed owning and acceptance of the fact of weakness is a hallmark of both wisdom and humility.

If you are to thrive, you have to understand and name your Weak Spot. By Weak Spot, I mean your weaknesses. I mean your flaws and deficiencies. No one has strengths without weaknesses. No one has Superpowers without Weak Spots.

Every hero on the Hero's Quest must, at some point, come to terms with his or her limitations and fatal flaws. It is only through a process of identifying, confronting, and ultimately embracing those limitations that the hero becomes mature and resilient, finding the inner peace to complete the mission.

> We wrestle, he and I.
> My Weakness is strong. And it's
> Ugly fighting, the gritty, grunting
> Kind that happens
> In back alleys where no one
> Is looking. No crowds leering,
> No one to break it up. Just
> Awkward punch and kick
> And bite if you can, blood
> And bruise and exertion
> Until you are both swinging
> In drunken slow motion, falling on
> Each other, breathing hard.
> Tasting blood.
>
> There comes a point
> When you realize
> There is no winning.
> He is my equal in every
> Way. The counterpoint
> To every point. The Weakness
> To all my strength.

And I know, with my face
Rubbed raw against the concrete,
I know, with the salted copper
taste of blood, I know,
Laying down, looking
Up at him, that I am not
God. And I will never win.

And this is beautiful.
This is beautiful.
My heart begins to understand.

—Excerpt from "The Beautiful Distance." Johnny Levy (2015)

Superpower, Weak Spot, Supervillain.
I will reiterate here the distinction between Superpower, Weak Spot, and Supervillain. These are distinct ideas that must be separated.

Superpower. Your Superpower represents your greatest design strengths. These are the areas where you experience the most effectiveness with the least effort and most satisfaction. The clarion call of the previous section was to identify and press into these areas.

Weak Spot. Your Weak Spot represents your design liabilities. These are the places where your imperfection is most apparent to you. Weak Spots are on the inside of you—in the realm of your tendencies and your proclivities.

Some of us are high achievers, and some of us lean towards laziness. Some of us are gregarious, and some of us lean towards isolation. Some of us are secure and confident, and some of us lean towards insecurity. Some of us are conscientious, and some of us struggle to manage the details. None of this makes you a good or bad person. Your strengths and weaknesses all contribute to who you are as a person.

I have a dear friend who has a tendency towards indecision, especially when the decision confronting him is high stakes or weighty. We

The Superpower Quest

know each other's strengths and weaknesses, we trust each other, and we've given each other carte blanche to really name it when we see the other person's Weak Spots manifesting themselves. I remember, we were talking about a situation where he had gone back and forth on a decision, and it was creating a crisis in his business and causing people to lose confidence in him. I was able to tell him, "Hey, that's that indecisiveness that you deal with sometimes. And that's OK, you just need to be aware of it, so that you can manage it." You should have seen the relief on his face! And I know this might seem counterintuitive! The relief comes from having permission to be human, and to have flaws, and not to be judged or criticized for them. We all have Weak Spots, just as surely as we have Superpowers. It's nothing to be ashamed of! He was able to acknowledge, "Yes, that is what's going on!" and we were able to talk about the best course of action, so he could be empowered to make a decision and stick with it. This is the power of naming your Weak Spots.

> To be human is to be flawed, and to be authentic is to be willing to admit those flaws.

Insecurity is my greatest Weak Spot. It comes up a lot; and in the past, I really hated this about myself. It made me feel so weak and worthless. I could find myself crippled with worry about what other people thought about me. But I have done a lot of work to accept and embrace both my strengths and my weaknesses. The other day, I found negative feelings rising up in me, based on some interpersonal interaction (I don't remember what.) I began to worry what the other person would think of me, and my heart dropped. My heartbeat quickened. I was going down. Those wretched, acidic sensations began to rise in my stomach. Then, I had a cool moment where I said in my mind, "Wait a minute, I see you, insecurity! You're just my Weak Spot!" Immediately, my feelings changed, and a smile came to my face. I recognized that this reaction was just a part of how I sometimes respond, but that I also had the option to name this and choose whether or not to let it own me. This doesn't always happen this way, like some sort of magic wand, but it's a possibility that comes available when we have a language for naming our weakness. We can experience freedom to decide on our course of action, instead of being dragged along with the powerful current of our Weak Spot.

Supervillain. The Supervillain is what occurs when a hero voluntarily deviates from the healthy path of benefiting the community and/or self, and into the unhealthy path of exploiting and destroying the community and/or self. Where Weak Spot is weakness, the Supervillain is malevolence. Where Weak Spot is *tendency,* Supervillain is *motive.* The line can be thin between the two, but there is a line. It has to do with the role of our volition in any behavior that destroys ourselves and others. It has to do with intention.

We'd generally agree that I have moral culpability for stealing, or murdering, or lying, or cheating, or tearing someone down verbally.

But I think we'd also agree that I have no moral culpability for being bad at math, or having a tendency towards laziness or insecurity, or struggling with anxiety, or even having a tendency towards anger. I don't get to control my factory settings. There are things about me that I didn't, and wouldn't, choose; but they exist nonetheless. So…what are the different categories?

We all have these "factory settings." I have three children under age twelve. When triggered, one resorts to sadness, one resorts to defensiveness, and one resorts to anger. These aren't primarily learned behaviors— these tendencies surfaced for each child early in their lives; some, even before they were verbal. These are proclivities –design imprints. My daughter who defaults to anger has anger as a part of her Weak Spot, but she has many strengths that make this weakness inevitable. She is bold, assertive, and passionate. As parents, my wife and I have to teach her to name her anger, and manage it, and we also need to affirm the strengths that are on the flip side of the coin. But when she hits her brother, or calls her sister a mean name, it's no longer Weak Spot. Now we're dealing with the Supervillain. You might think of Weak Spot as potential energy and Supervillain as kinetic energy. The key factors for the Supervillain are willful action; volition and choice. The key factors for Weak Spot are tendency, limitation, and proclivity. The two are related, but they are not the same.

And just to be clear, just because I have a proclivity towards anger, I don't get to absolve myself of responsibility when I unleash that anger into destructive actions or words. That's the Supervillain, and we don't overcome the Supervillains by making excuses.

Just because I have insecurity as my Weak Spot, doesn't mean I am not responsible for my actions when I deceive others to try to make them think better of me. That's my Supervillain.

Here are some comparisons to help get to the heart of the distinction. Weakness is the opposite of strength, where malevolence is the opposite of virtue. Strength is not virtue. Strength can be used for malevolence or virtue. Weakness is not malevolence. Weakness can be handled with either virtue or malevolence. We often conflate strength with virtue and weakness with malevolence, but in order to have a healthy knowledge of self, you need to be able to separate the two paradigms. Your weakness is not inherently evil. Your strength is not inherently good. Mind blown yet?

A Note About Design
You may notice me repeating the following idea many more times along the way: Like any tool, your design can be used for glorious benefit or unspeakable harm. Every one of us has acted the hero and the villain in our lives, just like every comic book superhero has fallen into the dark side at some point in the journey.

But just like the countless heroes in our lore, I trust that you will ultimately harness your design for the good of the world. And part of that process is humbly investigating your Weak Spot.

Why is a Weak Spot Discovery Process Needed?
We have been taught in our culture to see weakness as negative and shameful. I spent many years of my life crushed by this shame over the weaknesses of my design. In the U.S., this has roots in our entrenched philosophy of rugged individualism and meritocracy. These ideas certainly have their benefits when it comes to survival and work ethic.

However, their dark side is their tendency to leave many people feeling inadequate and to perceive themselves as shameful disappointments if they lack in the abilities that are deemed most desirable. In a lifetime of reading and learning, I have found very few frameworks that advocate a healthy relationship with weakness. No, the answer is not to pull ourselves up by our bootstraps, gut it out, and prevail in all circumstances. The real answer is more nuanced. Weaknesses don't make us failures—they make us human. We need a framework for facing our weaknesses unemotionally, and embracing them as a part of our design, and then acting in harmony with them wherever possible.

What are the Elements of Weak Spot?
In the SPQ framework, *Weak Spot* is an umbrella term that contains the following components:

- Hindering Drive
- Hindering Hero Types
- Weak Spot Words
- Triggers

As we did in the previous Superpower section, we will now funnel downward towards a distilled and actionable understanding of your areas of weakness and struggle.

In comic books, the Hulk is a big green rage monster who appears whenever his alter ego, the scientist Bruce Banner, becomes scared or angry. The Hulk represents Bruce Banner's psychological response to childhood trauma. The Hulk has the mental capacity of a five-year-old, the destructive power of an earthquake, and a primal desire to destroy evil (or anyone who attacks him.) In the comic books, there's a moment in time when the Hulk/Bruce Banner enter therapy. This was a crazy abstract comic book episode, because they are the same person! They have a shrink, Doc Sampson, who is basically doing guided meditation that allows both personas to manifest.

The Hulk sees his *Weak Spot* as his frail alter ego, Bruce Banner. Bruce Banner sees his *Weak Spot* as the destructive and irrational Hulk persona. At some point, they come to terms with each other, and with the traumatic childhood that they share. This reconciliation leads to a new entity being formed, a new Hulk with the strength of the green monster and the intelligence of the scientist. By reconciling with his weaknesses, the Hulk makes peace with himself and becomes a more balanced and effective individual. And he starts wearing custom tailored clothes, instead of shredded purple pants. And I think he gets a girlfriend. It's pretty amazing.

That's my ultimate goal for this section: to help you understand and embrace your weakness in a way that makes you stronger. At some point the Hulk's got to stop bashing things apart long enough to do a little deep soul work. You feel me? The strongest people are those who have deeply wrestled to embrace the fact of their weakness with clear eyes.

If you haven't already, remember that you can add your Weak Spot findings to your Hero Profile by registering online at superpowerquest.com/myprofile. You can also use the printables provided.

Going back to the original vision of this book, remember that my goal can be summed up as: "Embrace your Design, Collaborate with your Community." Understanding your Weak Spot will be a huge and necessary part of embracing your design.

Weak Spot Design Map
The following is a map for your journey through the second section of this book. Once completed, you will be able to see the full map of your Weak Spot. You can access a printable version at **superpowerquest.com/resources**!

Superpower Quest Resources Page

As noted above, you can also register for the online version at **superpowerquest.com/myprofile**.

Superpower Quest Hero Profile

HINDERING CORE DRIVE
Harmony, Order, Progress

HINDERING HERO TYPES		
Connector, Nurturer, Leader, Organizer, Dreamer, Achiever		
Hindering Hero Types		

WEAK SPOT WORDS	
Adjectives that describe challenging tendencies and areas of weakness	
1.	4.
2.	5.
3.	6.

TRIGGERS
Life events that cause you to experience disproportionately strong negative emotions, and even act in ways that are destructive to yourself and others.

Bonus content: Check out the full poem, "The Beautiful Distance" at **superpowerquest.com/resources**

Superpower Quest Resources Page

2.2
Hindering Drive

Between Order, Progress, and Harmony, what was your Effective Core Drive from the first section? What was your Supporting Core Drive? You discovered your Hindering Drive at that time, but we didn't spend much time talking about the ramifications of your Hindering Drive.

You may be super strong in one, or even two of the Core Drives. But there's always going to be one that lags behind. This is your Hindering Drive

We see this reality played out in front of us all the time. Maybe you know a groundbreaking innovator who's late to every meeting and can't balance a checkbook. Or an accountant who can work wonders in excel, but she can barely look you in the eye. Or the coffee shop squatter who has intense, meaningful conversations across a dozen people, but you can't for the life of you discern what he does for a living because you never see him do any actual work.

We all struggle with something. We all have our Weak Spot. Understanding and addressing that Weak Spot starts with naming the broad category of your Hindering Drive.

Harmony Hindering Drive
If Harmony is your Hindering Drive, you may have a hard time connecting with people. Whether it's groups, or an individual, you feel a

disproportionate angst when it comes to truly knowing people, and truly being known by others. Maybe you feel misunderstood or lonely. Maybe you have a deep longing to find your people. Maybe you feel like a poor communicator, especially when it comes to sharing your feelings. And honestly, maybe you aren't really interested in sharing your feelings. Maybe emotional connection feels like too much work, and you can take it or leave it. Or maybe you just roll over people, and you've come to terms with the fact that most people just don't like you. But I suspect that even if you're a pretty clinical, objective person, there's still a wound and a longing. If asked what area of life you'd like to improve, I suspect you would say something like "improving my ability to build or maintain healthy relationships."

Order Hindering Drive
If Order is your Hindering Drive, you may simply struggle with the concrete details of life. You may struggle with punctuality, because your awareness is lacking. You may struggle with disorganization or haphazardness. Maybe your mind wanders. You're not huge on planning or thinking ahead—you prefer to wing it. You might forget important details and events. Disorder can bite you a thousand different ways, and sometimes it bites hard. You let people down. You're inconsistent. You don't have good systems in place. You feel like you're constantly reacting to your environment. You're unprepared. It's hard to get ahead and be a responsible citizen when Order is your Hindering Type. You miss deadlines and opportunities with no one to blame but yourself. Or maybe you're just sloppy, because you care more about getting things done than getting them done right.

Progress Hindering Drive
Without Progress in our lives, we languish. We're uninspired, lazy, unmotivated. We're prone to paralysis. If Progress is your Hindering Type, you dig deep for the will to prevail and overcome, and find the reserve empty. Maybe you sleep a lot. Maybe you use substances, or entertainment, or social media to zone out. You're not really competitive, you're not really ambitious. You're not really out to challenge the

status quo. You might have settled for B's and C's in school because you didn't quite see the point of doing all the extra work to get the A+ grade like the teacher's pets. You don't have the same longing for big outcomes, or strong work ethic as some of your peers. Sometimes you wish you had bigger dreams, or maybe just some more drive. You end up feeling stuck sometimes, just spinning your wheels. You endure certain circumstances longer than you should because you don't have the energy to make a change. You can be sluggish, lethargic, paralyzed.

Which of these is your Hindering Drive? Where do you run into the most trouble and friction in life? Think about the times your Hindering Drive has let you down. Think about the times when you feel like you should have been better. Think about the times when you cursed yourself silently under your breath, wishing you were a different person.

> I'm proposing that we don't have to look at our areas of weakness as negative. We don't have to look at our failures as shameful. There's another way.

Now consider that everyone has an area like this. Whether we acknowledge it, or not, everyone has areas of performance that feel this way. I'm proposing that we don't have to look at our areas of weakness as negative. We don't have to look at our failures as shameful. There's another way.

We often measure ourselves against an impossible ideal. It's human nature. In the book *The Gap and The Gain: The High Achievers' Guide to Happiness, Confidence, and Success,* Dan Sullivan and Benjamin Hardy describe how they have observed this trend of thinking in even the most successful and wealthy people. It's easy to get caught up obsessing about our deficits. Our failures often carry more weight with us than our successes. This is called living in *the Gap*, and it's where most of our unhappiness and stress lives. Dan Sullivan and Benjamin Hardy write: "When you're in the Gap, you focus is on your shortcomings and limitations, which gives you a negative perspective on your abilities and opportunities."[1]

The Superpower Quest

You have a design with inherent strengths and weaknesses. A baseball bat is great for hitting baseballs and terrible for hammering nails. A baseball bat shouldn't aspire to be a hammer, or vice versa. If you chart yourself against some ideal person, who has only strengths and no weaknesses, you are setting yourself up for a life of frustration and angst. That would be living in *the Gap* in regard to your design.

Living in *the Gain* in regard to your design, would be accepting your Weak Spot as an important fact of life, and relishing the reality of your design, with all of its pluses and minuses. What if you could truly, radically accept your shortcomings, not as something to be fixed, but as something to be managed?

What if the hammer says, "How awesome it is to be a hammer, and not a baseball bat!"

What if the baseball bat says, "I'm not great at hammering nails. And that's okay! I think I'll go swing at more baseballs."

I know this analogy falls short, and that we have to mitigate our Hindering Drive to some degree. Here, I'm simply advocating a different mindset in regard to your Hindering Drive.

Maybe you'll make more progress if you have compassion for your weakest Drive, instead of disdain. Maybe you'll find a path to becoming more well-balanced if you embrace your Hindering Drive instead of fighting it. Self-loathing, self-flagellation, and resentment against your unique shape and form are the wrong tools for overcoming your personal challenges. How do I know?

I've used those harmful tools many times in my life, and they never really improved my station. Self-loathing has a cannibalizing effect. You might get short-term results, but ultimately you will fail to meet the expectations of that cruel taskmaster, and you'll end up worse off than before.

A greater tool is curiosity. This entire book is advocating a spirit of curiosity rather than condemnation. Be curious about yourself. Withhold judgment on your failures. I know this is hard, but seek to look at them objectively.

I have a daughter, Eliya, who is a Nurturer/Organizer, with Order as her Core Drive. I have a son, Jadon, who is a Nurturer/Connector, with Order as his Hindering Drive. Jadon's Superpower Statement is "jumping in enthusiastically with others for their benefit." I have a lot of parenting failures under my belt, but here's a parenting win. I've helped my kids understand their Core Drives, Hero Types, and Superpowers. This has become a regular dialogue in our household.

One day, I asked Eliya and Jadon to go outside and put the cushions on our lawn furniture so we could all sit out in the sunshine.

Eliya began to put the cushions on the furniture in a very methodical way. Jadon began to throw them all over willy-nilly. This caused incredible frustration for his sister, which she expressed to Jadon in an outburst. Jadon received her feedback as an act of bossing him around and criticizing him. They began to fight.

Once I got everybody quiet, I asked Jadon, "What is your sister?" He answered, "An Organizer." Then I asked him, "Is organizing a strength for you?" He shook his head and answered, "No." Then I asked, "Can you let her take the lead on this, and then jump in enthusiastically for her benefit?" It was like the lights went on behind his eyes. He did exactly that; their complementary strengths were aligned, and they finished the task with joy. No, this does not always work. But it worked that time!

I was able to help my kids step back and look at the situation and their design unemotionally. I tried to help them replace contempt with curiosity.

I have a great family friend who is one of the most gentle, caring, loving people you can imagine. He grew up in a household where Order was the highest value. But, uh-oh, Order is his Hindering Drive. So he grew up feeling like something was wrong with him. He has despised this deficit in himself for his whole life, never quite able to overcome it. In a casual conversation, I drew this out of him, inducing tears of pain and frustration. I was able to tell him the truth, which was to the effect that, "There was never anything wrong with you. The game you were forced to play was just stacked against you. To this day, you judge yourself by a false standard that you never should have been judged by in the first place." He acknowledged that this could be true, but was honest about how difficult it was to shift a lifelong perspective on his Hindering Drive, to see it not as something to be despised, but something to be embraced and managed.

I'm convinced that many of us, maybe the majority of us, carry some sort of trauma due to some variation of this dynamic in our family of origin. The family ran on a different currency than we had in our pocket, and we felt all the uselessness, self-loathing, self-disappointment, and longing to be a different person that came with that dynamic.

If this rings true for you, and you have pain associated with being forced to play in a rigged game, I want to tell you what I tell my friends and family: You are "fearfully and wonderfully made." You are not accidental. You were never supposed to be perfect. You were never supposed to be exempt from weaknesses. Your Hindering Drive is okay; your Hindering Drive is a fact of life. Sure, it's inconvenient. But it's also part of what makes you human. How you manage your Hindering Drive can be a thing of beauty that inspires others to be gentler and accepting of themselves, rather than being a source of self-loathing.

Hindering Drives, and Weak Spot overall, can be managed, but not eliminated. We'll talk about this more, later in the chapter.

For now, remember! Weakness is not malevolence, and strength is not virtue. It's what you do with both of these things, strength and weakness alike, that counts. Sometimes we make horrible choices and do horrible things. Sometimes we respond to our Triggers by unlocking our Supervillain, and we destroy ourselves and the people around us. The Supervillain, your dark side, is to be earnestly withstood, with a grave awareness of the damage he can do, and an earnest desire to be free of his control.

But not your Weak Spot, such as your Hindering Drive. Have compassion for your Hindering Drive. Have understanding. Have tolerance for your imperfections. Have curiosity. Seek to understand before you judge. Learn to love and appreciate your design, including the limitations of your design. More than anything else, this will help you to love and appreciate the designs of others, for greater impact in the world than you could ever imagine.

Now that we have explored the ramifications of your Hindering Drive, and we've discussed replacing condemnation with curiosity, let's zoom in a little bit and discuss the applications of these findings in regard to your Hindering Hero Types.

2.3
Hindering Hero Types

For review, the Hero Types are Leader, Organizer, Dreamer, Achiever, Connector, and Nurturer. In general, for most people, two of these are your Effective Types. Two of these are your Supporting Types, and two of these are your Hindering Types, which you have identified in the previous section.

Your Hindering Types are classified as a part of your overall Weak Spot. What follows are the types of effects that you might experience in your life for each of the possible Hindering Types.

Hindering Type: Leader
If Leader is your Hindering Type, you're simply not built to delegate, direct, or command. You probably lack assertiveness and decisiveness. Managing others makes you feel uncomfortable or gives you a feeling of imposter syndrome. You really don't want to be concerned with holding other people accountable, or for rallying teams towards specific goals. This is how it bites you—when there is a leadership void, you have to endure the chaos and indecision until someone takes the wheel. When you do take charge, it feels stressful and ineffective.

Hindering Type: Organizer
If Organizer is your Hindering Type, then you probably lack a systematic and methodical approach. You're not always as efficient as you

could be. You may lack time-awareness. You may have a tendency towards haphazardness, and a lack of quality control. This is how it bites you—you find yourself spinning your wheels, or painting yourself into corners because you didn't accurately discern the "how" of what needed to be done. You end up wasting time.

Hindering Type: Dreamer
If Dreamer is your Hindering Type, you can't see the forest—you can only see the trees. You have a hard time seeing the big picture, preferring to stay locked into the concrete details. This can lead to shortsightedness. You have a really hard time coming up with new ideas. You struggle with abstract thinking. You can be fearful and risk averse. You may lack inspiration. This is how it bites you—you end up doing a lot of activities without a higher sense of purpose, which can be depressing, confusing, and demotivating. You can feel stuck in the box.

Hindering Type: Achiever
If Achiever is your Hindering Type, you struggle with being motivated to get things done. You hate the feeling of slogging through just to get something checked off your list. You leave things unfinished. You are more passive than driven. Maybe you procrastinate. You lack ambition. You sometimes feel overwhelmed with the weight of things that need to be done, or consequences of things that are left undone. Here's how it bites you—you avoid or forget potentially important things. You let people down. You feel ineffective and inconsistent.

Hindering Type: Nurturer
If Nurturer is your Hindering Drive, then you may be lacking in empathy. You may have a hard time reading emotional cues. Showing up for your tribe is not top of mind. Feels inconvenient when people ask you for things, especially emotional support. You may feel bad about this, but it doesn't change it. You either lack the desire, or the ability to express yourself to the people in your circle. Deep, active listening is a problem for you. This is how it bites you—you feel misunderstood.

Relationships can be confusing and frustrating for you. You escape into other things, but have a nagging feeling that you're failing the people closest to you.

Hindering Type: Connector

If Connector is your Hindering Type, you struggle with groups. You definitely don't have bandwidth for lots of relationships. You come across as shy, introverted, or standoffish. Social situations take a huge toll on you. You have real difficulty making friends, and sometimes you feel lonely. Maybe you feel unworthy. You feel like you're a burden because you struggle to find words to break the silence. It's not that you're not curious about other people. Maybe you're not. But, whatever muscle enables you to reach out and take risks, and somehow transverse the distance between you and another human, that muscle is weak. This is how it bites you—you can end up feeling lonely for long periods of time. You miss out on opportunities to advance or have fun because you're nervous about seizing new social opportunities.

Do you see yourself in any of the descriptions above? Consider these examples to be guidelines, not rules. One of these might apply only 50% to you, and still be your Hindering Type. The combination of your other Hero Types can affect the intensity of your experience of any given Hindering Type.

To reiterate from the previous chapter, I'm encouraging you into a space of curiosity over condemnation. Your hindering types may have caused you great harm in life. You may have let people down in ways that you can't seem to forget. Others may have condemned you for your shortcomings. They may have looked down on you for your inability to be good at things that come easily to them. You may have concluded that you're simply damaged.

But maybe your factory settings are just different than what was expected of you. Maybe your settings are different than you wanted them to be. You came off the manufacturing line as a minivan instead of a sports car. Well, people need minivans, too. There's a lot that you control. There's a lot that you can change in your constitution. There's a lot of room to grow and branch and stretch. But there is a limit to this. There's a sacred design that exempts itself from such factors, because it resists the idea that it contains any mistakes that need to be corrected.

I find this beautiful. I find this breathtaking. That's why I can look at my kids, with all their faults, and say "Child, I would never change a thing about you, even if I could." Sure, we have behaviors that need to be improved. But we don't need to be improved upon. We don't look at an adult as an improved baby. We never get more or less precious than when we were born. If this is not true, then we have to contend with the idea that some humans can be more valuable than other humans based on their characteristics. I don't believe that. Your design is an extension of your untouchable essence. Beware that you do not dishonor this essence by seeking to become other than what you are.

And look, I'm not saying you don't have issues. We've all got issues, we've all got shortcomings. And we're ultimately responsible for our destructive and malevolent choices.

But I must continue to reef on the fact that weakness is not equivalent to evil or moral failure. Weakness is a category all its own. Superman doesn't get jacked by Kryptonite because he's a bad person. It's a fundamental weakness of his constitution. Hating himself for it doesn't help. There are certainly measures that he can and should take. But self-loathing isn't one of them.

There's possibly some part of yourself that you hate and resent that doesn't deserve hatred and resentment. It's a part of you that's just…you.

You're a hammer, not a baseball bat. You are whatever you are. Truly unique and special and handcrafted. Fundamentally incomparable to any other human being, at least at your core.

Let us learn to be gentle and curious.

I have a very good friend whose life is an open book to me, and mine to him. We worked together closely for many years, so I've gotten to log hundreds, if not thousands of hours seeing both his Superpower and Weak Spot in action. And he's seen all of mine.

This is a man that I respect and love like a brother. He's a Nurturer/Achiever. He's fundamentally driven by loyalty, and has a massive capacity for working through complex problems. He's both loving and determined. Pretty unstoppable once he sets his mind to something.

He also has a deficit in the Organizer Hero Type.

So, here's how things play out. He has an incredible, almost supernatural, drive to show up for his people. He will work long hours to make sure that he fulfills his commitments even in the face of unexpected sacrifice. But once he has delved into executing a project, he often runs into unforeseen snags. He struggles with time management and prioritization, which are both squarely in the realm of the Organizer. This means that he has a natural tendency to overcommit himself. When a series of deadlines converges, suddenly he's pulling all-nighters and stealing time from his domestic responsibilities.

One day, he and I were discussing this unfortunate pattern on a plane. I heard him describing his inability to get himself properly organized, and the ways that it had cost him and cost people that were close to him. I heard contempt in his voice. This is a man fundamentally driven by loyalty, speaking about the part of himself that lets people down. Of course this was emotional. Of course, this pattern made him angry.

This was in my early-middle stage of building the Superpower Quest framework, so I was able to use Superpower Quest language to begin to paint the picture for him. He had been processing my SPQ ideas with me and had even been a guinea pig for some of my early worksheets, so he was familiar with the concept.

I affirmed him in his Effective Types as a Nurturer/Achiever. I tried my best to help him see how truly remarkable he was in his design, and how powerfully his particular combo impacts the world around him.

Then I named his deficiency in the Organizer Type, which he readily accepted. And I told him something like this:

"The Organizer is never going to come easy to you. Let's say you rate yourself a three out of ten right now in the Organizer. And let's say you work ridiculously hard to brute force yourself to make it better. Maybe you'll get to a four or a five, and it will be soul-sucking. Organization is never going to be an Effective Type for you. It's never going to be a design strength. And that's okay. The way God made you is amazing. There are certainly things you can do and ways you can grow, but there's nothing fundamentally wrong with you. You just have a comparative weakness, like we all do."

I got to watch my friend come to tears over this realization. I got to watch him begin to shed the burden he had been carrying towards himself. I got to see him begin to come to terms with himself. What an amazingly precious moment.

He has since made some incredible changes in his life. He'" thriving more than I've ever seen. He's taken significant and tangible steps to right-size his life and tune it towards his giftings.

There were many factors that led him this direction. That conversation was only one of many revelations that helped him to move forward with clarity. But for me, that conversation was a seminal moment in helping me grasp the power of the Superpower Quest framework in action.

It also showed me the power of naming and embracing your Weak Spot.

I have a Hindering Core Drive of Order. I'm naturally messy and spontaneous. But I do have the Organizer as a Supporting Hero Type, and I can access Order at some key moments due to that. Organization, most of the time, feels like a Hindering Type— until the right circumstances fall into place, and then I feel a momentary competency there.

Also, you'll probably notice that I'm holding some cards close to the vest for later. It may seem like I'm saying that if you have a weakness, and that weakness is making life hard for you, then there's nothing you can do about it. True, I'm not an advocate of trying to brute-force change in the area of your Hindering Types. I don't think the cure for a Leader-deficit is gritting your teeth and willing yourself to have more Leader-type characteristics. Step one of dealing with this deficit is acknowledging it, and step two is embracing it. But I don't think it ends there. There are steps you can take to mitigate your Weak Spot, and even turn a weakness into a strength. But spoiler, it's not the teeth-gritty way, or the pull yourself up by your bootstraps way, or the berate-yourself-until-you-change way. There's another way. So, we will go into that later. For now, I just want to make it plain that you will have options.

First, we must accurately identify our Weak Spot, then develop a healthy posture towards our Weak Spot. Then we can begin to master it.

Weak Spot versus Supervillain

I want to take another moment to solidify the difference between Weak Spot and Supervillain by giving a concrete illustration.

My wife and I take our parenting very seriously. It's our joy and responsibility to love, instruct, and discipline our children. Children are complex mixtures of virtue, strength, malevolence, and weakness. Each of these categories must be handled differently. If I'm constantly complimenting and praising them on a design strength, "You're so beautiful, you're so smart, you're so creative," and never teach them virtue, they can grow up incredibly gifted, and incredibly selfish. What good is a high IQ or a particular talent, if you lack humility and resilience?

In the same way, if I spend all my time criticizing a design weakness, then neglect to address malevolent actions, they may grow up apologizing for their weaknesses and totally excusing their malevolence. This leads to performance-based humans who elevate success over virtue, judging themselves and others by utility and capability over inward integrity and character.

In our parenting, our strongest discipline is reserved for malevolence, such as defiance. It's reserved for when kids hit out of anger, lie, put people down, etc. We are teaching them the sovereign responsibility of choice. When you're young, you don't feel like you have a choice. We're guiding them towards being responsible humans who take responsibility for their actions, and feel sorrow when they do harm.

We handle weakness very differently. There's a lot more leniency and mercy. We're more instructive than disciplinary. This is how you address things like sloppiness, anxiety, laziness, and tendencies toward temper, over-controlling, rambunctiousness, etc.

A child struggling with her temper is different, and requires a different response, than when a child goes a step further and exercises her temper by punching a sibling.

> Ability and virtue are fundamentally different. One is the function of power, and the other is a function of love. Still, they are sticky and intertwined.

One requires instruction. The other requires discipline and is a matter of character. In matters of ability, it's about training that helps them build habits to counteract areas of weakness. In matters of virtue, it's about the proper use of their volition, for good or evil. Our kids, like us, will need to decide if they want to become Heroes or Villains. We seek to discipline them away from the malevolent, and towards the heroic.

Admittedly, this landscape can be difficult and complex. Sometimes the line between Weak Spot, such as Hindering Hero Types, and the Supervillain is invisible, since it is a question of motivation and choice.

In a classroom setting, when required to participate in a group discussion, one person might decline to participate because she is intensely introverted. Another might decline to participate as an act of rebellion against the teacher's authority. One is a function of the Weak Spot, the other is a function of the Supervillain. This can be impossible to navigate! And yes, we must try, without simply waving away the categories.

Ability and virtue are fundamentally different. One is the function of power, and the other is a function of love. Still, they are sticky and intertwined. But this fundamental distinction is the reason we send some criminal perpetrators to prison, and we send some to mental institutions. The former has intentionally and willingly broken the law (lack of virtue). The latter has a mental deficiency that indicates that the legal transgression was more a function of sickness than of choice (lack of ability).

SECTION 2 | Steward Your Weak Spot

We need frameworks to identify and respond to both of these human realities—ability and virtue. We have many frameworks for addressing behavior and performance. Much of this book is dedicated to that endeavor. In contrast, we have fewer accepted frameworks for morality and virtue. Why? Because these concepts have generally originated from religious discourses which can be complicated in a pluralistic society.

Still, I have met no person who does not see him or herself as a moral agent, applying at least a portion of their closely held moral standards to the people around them. We do ourselves a disservice by pretending to obliterate moral absolutism from the conversation. I also recognize the Pandora's box that this idea opens up in a pluralistic society, and why this pretense has been made to try and facilitate conversation between disparate groups.

In the Supervillain section, I will try to produce a basic framework of virtue and malevolence (Hero versus Villain) in a way that is generally accessible.

For now, suffice it to say that the proper response to the Supervillain is understanding and opposition, while the proper response to your Hindering Types is curiosity, acceptance, and management.

A Note on Criticism

The criticism of a friend can be beautiful. It can be loving, and it can be true. Even the criticism of an enemy can be true, and a very humble person can even benefit from this. But in my experience and observation, much criticism given and received is selfish, prideful, and intended to manipulate its object to conform with something in the giver of the criticism. Certainly I have done this. We all have. For example, if I pride myself on productivity, I'm more likely to be harsh with people who struggle with productivity. If I pride myself on emotional intelligence, I might be overly critical of people who lack this characteristic.

Sometimes people will criticize you for your Hindering Types. Your Hindering Types can be very inconvenient to you, but also very inconvenient for others. How do you process it when someone condemns you for your weaknesses? Put another way, what do you do when someone makes you feel like your weakness is evil, or that a design flaw is a moral failure?

- **Have grace.** The differentiation between weakness and malevolence, Weak Spot and Supervillain, is not common knowledge in the world. From what I can tell, people have a hard time distinguishing between the two. Many people see their weakness as evil in itself, and have little tolerance for their limitations, or limitations of others. Have some grace and resist the urge to snap back or take it personally.
- **Don't internalize.** Another may judge you. But…you are not required to judge yourself by the same standard. It is neither desirable, nor possible, to become what someone else wants you to be, if it's different than what you are.
- **Outside perspective.** No one is an island. Our grasp or reality is hindered and tenuous at best if we do not have loving people around us to help us check our assumptions. If you are unsure about how much of a criticism is valid, and how much is not, give the healthy and wise people in your life an opportunity to weigh in.

Don't forget to register at superpowerquest.com/myprofile to add your Hindering Core Drive and Hindering Hero Types to your Hero Profile!

Superpower Quest Hero Profile

Now, let's get more specific in this Weak Spot Journey. In the next chapter you will identify your Weak Spot Words.

2.4
Weak Spot Words

This section will mirror your process of generating your Power Words in the last section. You'll end up with four to eight words that describe your specific areas of lack, frustration, and lower competency.

Consistent with the delineation between Weak Spot and Supervillain, your Weak Spot words will describe tendencies as opposed to actions. You may have irritability as your Weak Spot, where your Supervillain would be the act of lashing out. You may have insecurity as your Weak Spot, where active deception is the realm of the Supervillain.

Knowing my Weak Spot words has been very precious to me. Being able to look back at my life, and put a name to the tendencies that have most hindered me has been life-changing. It was like being introduced to myself in reverse time lapse. Why has anxiety been such a struggle for me? Why have I been so deathly afraid to let people down? Why does relational conflict and confrontation make me physically ill? The answers to these questions and many more were hidden within my Weak Spot. There were precious secrets of my design, waiting to be discovered.

So much of this book is about naming things. A name is like a handle you install on something that makes you able to grip it, move it from side to side, examine it. Naming things helps to make things less overwhelming, less scary, and more able to be confronted.

There are two types of Weak Spot words. Some proceed from your Hindering Drive, and some come out when you push your Effective or Supporting Drives to the extreme. This is called an Over Drive.

If I am a Leader, and have a tendency to push to the extreme, then assertiveness may turn into aggressiveness and domination. That's an example of an Over Drive tendency. If I'm a Nurturer, my Over Drive tendency can look like being overbearing, overprotective, and over-controlling of the people that I keep closest to me.

Let's give words to your Weak Spot. We'll start by looking at a list of common Weak Spot words, grouped by Hero Types, in both the Over Drive and Hindering Drive categories. Circle the ones that most resonate with you. Feel free to introduce your own words—these sample words are just here to accelerate the process.

LEADER

Over Drive Weak Spot Words	Hindering Drive Weak Spot Words
Overbearing	Timid
Insensitive	Indecisive
Brash	Passive
Dominant	Yielding
Pushy	Self-Deprecating
Inflexible	Fearful
Over-Controlling	Insecure
Stubborn	Aimless
Demanding	Permissive
Intolerant	Spineless

SECTION 2 | Steward Your Weak Spot

ORGANIZER

Over Drive Weak Spot Words	Hindering Drive Weak Spot Words
Anxious	Sloppy
Controlling	Inconsistent
Picky	Random
Perfectionistic	Unstructured
Tense	Disorderly
Stressed	Inattentive
Critical	Flaky
Ungracious	Careless
Inflexible	Disorganized
Neurotic	Unconscientious

DREAMER

Over Drive Weak Spot Words	Hindering Drive Weak Spot Words
Unfocused	Small-Minded
Distracted	Uninspired
Flaky	Hopeless
Impractical	Melancholy
Unrealistic	Short-Sighted
Obsessive	Detail-Obsessed
Scattered	Dispassionate
Distant	Settling
Oblivious	Insular
Addictive	Resigned
Untethered	Nitpicky

ACHIEVER

Over Drive Weak Spot Words	Over Drive Weak Spot Words
Overcommitted	Lazy
Overworked	Unmotivated
Preoccupied	Apathetic
Prideful	Tardy
Overconfident	Disengaged
Self-Determined	Uncaring
Isolated	Undisciplined
Help-Rejecting	Inconsistent
Impatient	Lethargic
Reckless	Under-achieving
Stressed Out	Passive
Hasty	Helpless

CONNECTOR

Over Drive Weak Spot Words	Hindering Drive Weak Spot Words
Insecure	Anti-social
Fearful	Awkward
Passive	Inarticulate
People-Pleasing	Stifled
Indecisive	Standoffish
Spineless	Stiff
Obsequious	Cold
Flattering	Anxious
Patronizing	Bashful
Wheedling	Disengaged
Fake	Timid
Insincere	Lonely

NURTURER

Over Drive Weak Spot Words	Hindering Drive Weak Spot Words
Stubborn	Noncommittal
Defensive	Disloyal
Oversensitive	Insensitive
Needy/Clingy	Merciless
Unforgiving	Distant
Presumptuous	Indifferent
Insecure	Callous
Entitled	Harsh
Overprotective	Unkind
Suffocating	Inconsiderate
Resentful	Ruthless
Controlling	Detached
	Uncaring

Start a List

On a blank piece of paper, write down the words that you selected above. This will be the start of your Weak Spot Master List. After you have added your words from above, then add any more words that come to your mind that describe your areas of weakness and struggle.

Phone a Friend…Again
As with the Power Words section, it's time to ask one or two friends or family members to help you. The "ask" will sound something like this:

"I am going through a process to identify my weaknesses. I am trying to name my weaknesses, so that I can accept and manage them. Can you list three to four adjectives that best describe the areas where you most notice that I struggle? I know this is a sensitive ask, but please be honest and don't worry about offending me."

Once you have collected words from your family and/or friends, add them to your Master List. Pay special attention to words that come up more than once.

Narrowing Down
Use the following process to narrow down your reserve to the four to six words with the most relevance and impact. Follow the steps below.

- Keep this in mind: **The four to six words that you end up with should be distinct from one another.**
- Give priority consideration to the words that came up more than once.
- Group similar words into pairs or sets. In that set, identify the word that feels the strongest and resonates the most. Cross out the others in that set.
- Write the remaining words in order of how much they resonate with you. See what rises to the top. Cross out whatever falls to the bottom.

Enter your final four to six words in the table below. These are your Weak Spot Words that give important insight into your core hindrances. You can also add these to your Hero Profile at **superpowerquest.com/myprofile**

The Superpower Quest

Superpower Quest Hero Profile

Weak Spot Words	
#1.	
#2.	
#3.	
#4.	
$5.	
#6.	

Congratulations for Continuing the Quest!

Pushing down to discover your Weak Spot can be uncomfortable and even painful. It's much easier and more intuitive to learn about our strengths than to confront our weaknesses. Weak Spot work is the work that many people cannot, or will not, do.

I remember having a team retreat several years ago. Using the *Good to Great* model by Jim Collins, we got very serious about diving into the company's dysfunction and mediocrity in a push towards true excellence. The company was made up of seven people and we all walked through a series of penetrating questions intended to isolate the areas where the company was failing. As the president of the company, I was totally bought into the process, and I was serious when I invited the leaders and employees to be brutally honest about their experience, and where they saw the cracks in our infrastructure.

As we walked through the questions in a team retreat, all sitting in a circle, an uncomfortable trend started to surface. I was the one who frequently over-committed the company to projects that were either a bad fit, or risky. I was the one creating haphazard and undocumented processes. I was the one who was often the bottleneck.

People began to feel uncomfortable and apologetic, but to their credit, they didn't pull punches. The book *Good to Great* had changed us. We wanted to be excellent more than we wanted to be comfortable. This enabled us to face a reality that had never been fully articulated up to that point.

The biggest problem our company faced was—*surprise*—me!

I had been working so hard, but so much of what I was doing on a day-to-day basis was in the realm of my Weak Spot, and my weaknesses in the area of *Order* were being felt throughout the enterprise. I struggle with consistency. I struggle with being detail-oriented. I struggle with being realistic. It was evident that I needed to get my hands out of the kitchen.

I kept reassuring people that it was okay and that I could handle it. I earnestly thanked them for being honest. But there was a real pain I felt, sitting in that circle with people I loved and respected and felt accountable to. I felt naked, exposed, and embarrassed. I felt like a wet blanket had been thrown over my soul.

And at the exact same time I felt relief, and a fledgling sense of hope. We had delved down deep into the caverns of my fear, and faced the Balrog in the heart of that mountain. And apart from a bit of bruised ego, I was alive and intact. My weaknesses and shortcomings were on display; but rather than disdain, I received understanding and mercy from the people around me. My team did not respect me less, but perhaps more. We were all deeply committed to getting me out of the areas of the business where my abilities were not a good fit so I could spend my time doing more of the Dreamer/Connector things that I thrived at doing. So, from the heart of the mountain, we rescued the jewel that is precious above all others: Truth.

We may not always like or enjoy the truth. The truth may be inconvenient or even shattering. But without truth there can be no clarity. And without clarity there can be no real progress.

Your Weak Spot is an inconvenient and precious truth. Cherish it. The clarity you gain has the potential to remove age-old boulders from your path and give wings to your feet.

- Memorize your Weak Spot Words!
- Begin the process of naming them when you see them operating in your life. Be curious. Do this without beating yourself up; just practice noticing.
- Talk about them with others. This is hard, but so freeing. When you give yourself permission to have weaknesses, you give others permission to have weaknesses, too.

> Your Weak Spot is an inconvenient and precious truth. Cherish it. The clarity you gain has the potential to remove age-old boulders from your path and give wings to your feet.

Cowabunga! You've done the deep work required to fully explore your Weak Spot. You've discovered all of the components of your Weak Spot, including your Hindering Drive, Hindering Types, and Weak Spot Words. I hope that you have continued to maintain a posture of gentle curiosity during this exploration, instead of harshness, self-criticism, or condemnation.

Now that you've identified your Weak Spot, you must neither hate your Weak Spot nor excuse it away. You must embrace it as a part of your design without abdicating responsibility for your actions. This is the way of proper stewardship.

Let's say inconsistency is your Weak Spot, and you miss a deadline that negatively affects other people. What will you say to them? Will you say, "Oh well, what can I say? I'm inconsistent. That's why I missed the deadline. You should never count on me!" God forbid! No one will want to work with you, if this is the way you handle your commitments.

It is right to apologize when we intentionally OR unintentionally do harm to others based on our actions or omissions. Sure, malevolent intent and accidental weakness come from utterly different places in the heart. Malevolence is the realm of the Supervillain. But, regardless of intent, they can both have inconvenient, and even disastrous, effects on ourselves and others. We must take full responsibility for the harm that we do, whether malicious or accidental. To embrace your Weak Spot is to take full responsibility for its effects, while being careful not to judge yourself too harshly for the inconvenient parts of your design.

That's a difficult balance, but it's very important. I still miss deadlines. I still forget important details. But this happens, probably, eighty to ninety percent less than it used to. I've worked very hard, and set up great systems, and leveraged alliances with others to make this level of improvement possible. But with all my structures and safeguards, my Weak Spot still comes out. And it's very inconvenient when it does. I've learned to take full responsibility, rectify the damage the best I can, and forgive myself very quickly. There's not a bunch of self-analysis to wade through. The explanation is simple. I am imperfect, and I understand my imperfection, and therefore I can have mercy for it. I'm a minivan, not a sports car. I'm a dreamer, not an organizer. I'm an artist, not a project manager. I no longer hold myself to a standard that doesn't account for my innate limitations. And that allows me to take a deep breath, pick myself up, and walk it off when I have one of life's little fender-benders. I wish only the same for you!

Now, let's spend some precious time talking about the role of your Weak Spot in your life, and what can be gained from a proper, healthy, relationship with your weakness. From there, we will formulate the actions and systems needed to bring strength to your weakness. We will discuss these strategies in the upcoming *Join Forces* section and the *Utility Belt* section.

2.5
Humility and Delight

> "You shall not pass!"
> —Gandalf, *The Fellowship of the Ring*

In the archetypal hero's journey, the hero almost always comes to a place of pressure and despair. It's a moment when the hero has endured many trials, and must now face the greatest trial of all. He spends his entire strength, he risks all that he has, only to fail at the zenith of his struggle. He must face the fact that he is not strong enough to complete his mission, and he begins to question his whole existence. This is usually part of the *Ordeal* phase of Joseph Campbell's "hero's journey." [2]

Picture the end of the movie, "Avengers: Infinity War," when the hero Thor has his one chance to defeat Thanos. Thanos, the arch-nemesis, has just taken the final Infinity Stone, placed it into his gauntlet, and is just about to use his newly acquired power to "snap" away half of the population of the universe. Thor, high in the sky, unseen by Thanos, throws his magical ax with all of his Asgardian strength and rage. The ax flies, end over end, locked onto its target. Before Thanos can snap, the ax buries itself deep in the tyrant's chest. Thanos gasps. The universe holds its breath. Thanos looks up.

He smiles. Too little, too late. He snaps his fingers. In a blinding flash, fifty percent of all lives in the universe are snuffed out, including many of Thor's beloved companions, right before his eyes.

Thor gave his all, and it wasn't enough. In the sequel, after this event, we find that Thor has fallen into total depression, frittering his life away brooding, drinking, and playing video games. Ultimately, he must pick himself up, join forces with the remainder of his team, and engage in a risky plan to go back in time and somehow rewrite events. Ultimately, they all succeed together where he failed.

Here, as in so many tales, Thor has to wrestle with his greatest enemy— his own limitations. The fact that he cannot always be the savior. The fact that, when the stakes were highest, he failed. His Weak Spot is his pride, self-reliance, and arrogance, which are only highlighted by his journey into depression and apathy, post "snap."

The real enemy, beneath all other enemies, is Thor himself. If he cannot accept his limitations, and get back on mission to be a part of the solution, then the universe will remain in its defeated, fragmented state. But to admit one's limitations, and somehow move beyond them back into a place of hope and productivity, requires a particular form of virtue that can only be wrought in us through the very weakness and failure we seek to avoid.

Our Weak Spot teaches us something. Our Weak Spot does something for us that nothing else could ever do. It has the power to teach us humility. This is what's at stake. This is what is being forged in the deep, dark caverns of our failure and frustration. Humility. Acceptance of our limitations. A healthy embrace of our incompleteness, and our need for help.

We are not gods and goddesses, but men and women. We are not infinite, but finite. An ancient Greek philosopher once said, "A man cannot surpass his strength, even though he strives." We realize that we are not striving for some external standard of perfection. We are striving to be fully ourselves, and only ourselves, nothing more or less than ourselves. Ourselves, with all of our warts and blemishes and beauties and strengths.

What is humility? Humility is the understanding and embracing of one's limits.

Humility asks for help. Humility does not see the self as the answer to every problem. Humility is an honest estimation of one's strengths and weaknesses, and an openness to the critiques and contributions of others. Humility is not defensive. It doesn't need to be. We are defensive when we are slaves to protect an image of ourselves that we cannot bear to be challenged. Prideful people fight and strive to maintain an image of rightness and perfection. Failure is horrifying to them. Weakness is detestable to them. Humble people can entertain the idea that they might be wrong without having their identity threatened, because their identity isn't anchored in the need to be perfect. They have embraced the reality of weakness as the antidote for the burden of perfection.

To be flawed, and responsible for my flaws, and still content, is humility. To fail, and not have that failure threaten my identity, is humility. Our Weak Spot has the power to teach us humility. It will not automatically teach it. There are three fundamental responses to encountering your Weak Spot. Everyone one of us must choose.

#1. Deny. If you are in denial and rebellion against your Weak Spot, you cannot accept it. You make excuses. You defend yourself. You blame other people, you blame circumstances. You complain about your rotten luck. You avoid taking responsibility.

#2. Despair. You think you are broken. You compare yourself with other people and find yourself lacking. You curse and criticize yourself. You are constantly trying to improve, but it's because of shame. When you fail, the emotional consequences of failure are multiplied.

#3. Delight. You embrace your Weak Spot, and you embrace full responsibility for your Weak Spot. You do not Deny your Weak Spot, but neither do you Despair over it. You take hope in the understanding that no one is perfect, and you accept your imperfections. You reject the idea that you could ever totally eliminate your imperfections through hard work. In Delight, embrace, and resignation, you can rest from the perpetual striving that comes from judging your human self against an inhuman standard. This idea of *delighting* in your weakness may sound hopelessly idealistic. The most concrete example I can give you is this: I delight in my children, not because they are perfect, but because they are themselves. If I can learn gentleness towards myself, then I can take a similar posture of unconditional love towards my own design. This is rooted in the idea that we do not need to be perfect to be precious. Each unique human being, including you, is invaluable simply for being. You have innate and infinite value. If you truly believe this, you can rest, finally rest, from earning your value through external workmanship, which is the root of both Denial and Despair. This is the path to humility, and humility is the path to strength.

To avoid plagiarism, I must here give credit for this idea of each person's "innate and infinite value" to the Judeo-Christian, Biblical teaching of the *imago dei,* the belief that all humans are created in the image of God, and that this fact is the fundamental and incontrovertible basis for human dignity, identity, and flourishing. I hold this idea to be essential for any conversation about a universal standard of human worth, which is necessary for a universal understanding of human progress, which is the central concern of this book.

Now, to close this section and transition us to the next, I will sum up in this way. The whole goal of this section has been to give you an opportunity to reckon with, and ultimately delight in, your Weak Spot. Your weakness is the path to humility, and humility is the path to strength.

I made a very bold promise in the beginning of this book that I would not only show you how to identify and embrace your weakness, but also how to turn weakness into strength. The conversion of weakness into strength is contingent upon humility.

By *strength,* I mean the ability to accomplish things. You can accomplish a lot with your Superpower, but there are a ton more things that your Superpower is not geared to accomplish. That's the reality of being finite and flawed. One hero has power over fire, which is awesome. But there are a million Superpowers that this hero doesn't have—magnetism, mind control, teleportation, etc.

You need something melted? Call the fire dude! But what happens when the mission is a deep sea rescue operation? For every mission matched with a particular Superhero's might, there are countless others that require nothing of the sort.

Humility is present inside the person who recognizes that she is not always the answer. She recognizes the need for help and pursues help. This is the person who candidly realizes that *Superpower* is narrow, and *Weak Spot* is broad.

> To be willing to acknowledge your weakness, and thus to be open to receiving help, is a form of great strength, and opens up the doorway to exponential accomplishment.

To be willing to acknowledge your weakness, and thus to be open to receiving help, is a form of great strength, and opens up the doorway to exponential accomplishment.

This help can come in the form of systems, hacks, mentors, and collaborators. It's the humility, the openness, that is the strength that calls forth strength. It is the posture of spirit that calls for the contributions of others. It is the precondition for the highest quantity of opportunities.

It takes weakness to truly appreciate the strength of others. It is our felt limitation that produces the force of awe. I am the most impressed and awestruck when I witness a work of art that I know I could not have created myself. It is when I feel small that my awe grows big.

I'm great at writing poetry. Not so great at music. My brother-in-law, Drew, is a gifted improv pianist. A church in town offered us a low-cost recording session, technician included. We rented out the music studio one morning, and proceeded to lay down five tracks in two hours; spoken word poetry over improv piano. Drew was effortless. He was totally unfamiliar with each poem, and generated lively music out of thin air. It was magical. He was truly operating in his Superpower, and I was operating in mine.

I'm not great at technology, and wanted each piece turned into a video. I tapped my friend Preston, who is great at that stuff. A poetry EP was born out of the contributions of many. I could not have done this without Drew, without Preston, without the tech, without the church connection. We leveraged each other's strengths and weaknesses to accomplish something special.

My stepson and BFF told me one day that I seem to him a man of extremes. Extreme gifts and extreme flaws. This was spoken and received in love, not criticism. For much of my life, I felt the weight of my flaws more than the buoyancy of my gifts. I think that's a very human tendency, even for optimists like myself.

I always felt like I was less than others. Less of a man, less of a leader, less of a "go-getter." Tragic and untrue as this was, and toxic as it was to believe, it also tenderized my pride a bit. It became the raw material for a genuine appreciation for the wisdom and skill of others, and an openness and awe towards the accomplishments of others. I would not trade this. I truly think this posture of awe and appreciation is a discipline that can be learned.

This is the greatest lesson of my life, as far as I can see. Own your weaknesses. Depend on others. Receive others. Covet mentorship.

I no longer dream as much of personal conquest as I once did. I'm not a rugged individual. I shudder at the idea of trying to execute a big dream without leveraging the Organizers in my life for discernment; the Achievers in my life for heavy lifting and determination; the Leaders in my life for mobilization and direction, and so forth.

The ancient Biblical proverb says, "Many hands make for light work." Having experienced the glory and exponential quality of light work, you couldn't drag me back to my days of rugged individualism, striving, and frustration. I like the "easy button." I like the fact that there are people out there who are ten times better at almost everything than I am. I love the fact that there are a few things that I'm so good at, I'm basically one in ten thousand.

In his book, *Mind Shift: It Doesn't Take a Genius to Think Like One*, bestselling author and pastor Erwin McManus has a chapter called, "Be Average (At Almost Everything)." This chapter puts forth the view that our culture is rigged to make us think we have to be good at everything, which really means we will be average at everything. If we narrow the investment of our energy, then we have a shot at achieving true greatness in a specific area. McManus says, "Instead of pressuring people to make straight A's, maybe we should have been helping them to find their one A in an ocean of C's. Maybe the first eighteen years of our lives would have been better spent learning to be average at almost everything –except your one thing."[1]

Isn't that a crazy thought? Embracing your "average," embracing your Weak Spot, and funneling all that energy into the area where you have the most potential to exceed and excel? This will mean there are a few areas in your life where people will come to you for help, and rightly so, because you are a BEAST in those areas. And in a hundred other areas, you can have the humility to ask for help from your bettors without resenting them for being better.

This is the gift I would give you—the ability to press into your Weak Spot, embrace humility, and come out the other side stronger than you were. And I don't mean able to bench press more weight, you Hulk-a-maniac. I mean the ability to ask for, and receive, the kind of help that dwarfs all the resources you could muster alone. I want you to be an exponential giver, but I equally want you to be an exponential receiver.

In the next several chapters, we will talk about the practical ways that you can manage your Weak Spot and turn weakness into strength; but all of the tactics I have for you will leverage this principle of humility. Once you have acknowledged your weakness, and embraced your Weak Spot as a fact of life, then you can begin to strategize around it without embarrassment or shame.

SECTION 3
Join Forces

3.1
Join Forces

"If you want to go fast, go alone. If you want to go far, go together."
—Proverb

I cringe in spite of myself when I hear people quote this proverb, which makes me a hypocrite, because here it is in my book. It's one of those sayings that gains momentum until it loses meaning, and carries a "we are the cool kids" feel to it wherever it's uttered. It didn't help when I looked it up to see if it really was an African proverb, and found that the jury is out on that. But with all my old-man crankiness about this particular quote and its usage and roots, the more important thing is that I believe it to be true, and it aptly sums up the spirit of this section.

An isolated approach is a way of playing the short game. Going it alone will carry you only to the brink of your limitations; no further. Some people have a lot of capacity before they hit their limits, and some don't. Regardless, in isolation, you become your own ceiling. The "hack" to this ceiling is collaboration. Collaboration is the long game. "If you want to go far, go together." If you want to accomplish bigger things; if you want to surpass your limits, you will need to "go together" with the right people. I'm going to teach you how to do that.

The Superpower Quest

There is personal greatness, and there is corporate greatness. Up to this section, we have been discussing the individual pursuit of self-understanding as a vehicle for achieving excellence. Now we are exploring how you can move beyond individual excellence and into the realm of corporate excellence.

In this section we will answer the following questions:

- Why is Joining Forces so important?
- Who should you Join Forces with, and how do you know?
- What are some habits and techniques for Joining Forces?
- How does Mentorship fit into this equation?

Why is Joining Forces so Important?
I wonder what it was like to be a part of some great movement in history, like the American Revolution, or the Civil Rights movement, or William Wilberforce and his crew pushing to abolish the European slave trade, or creative movements like the Modernists, Impressionists, or Surrealists. I try to imagine the energy, the unity of purpose, and the build up towards memorable greatness that endures the ages.

There are marked moments in history when the right people come together at the right time, and stunning things happen. The right people in the right place at the right time can have an insane multiplying effect, like a chain reaction producing exponential force.

Why is this? Certainly there are environmental factors—social and cultural forces at work. But there are also people. People of passion, people of excellence and will and strength, people with gifts. People with parts to play in a grand production.

Have you ever been a part of something greater than yourself? Can you think of a time when you collaborated with others to achieve results bigger than you could have achieved yourself? By definition, "greater than yourself" means that you accomplished something that you never could have accomplished alone.

For me, I have experienced this feeling in my job. As the CEO of a small company, I have gotten to hand pick my people and contribute to a vibrant culture in which each person is "unleashed" to operate in his or her gifts. We've achieved amazing things together, and this has produced confidence in our team and trust in each other. We've been through the fire together and come out the other side.

I remember a time when our company was on the verge of going out of business. At our annual team retreat, I had to break the news that our financials were suffering, and that we had a six-month shelf life if things didn't change drastically. I was a complete wreck going into that meeting. Seldom have I prayed more desperately than I did before going into that meeting. My business partner and I decided to be transparent with the team, and we didn't know what was going to happen. Were the people going to bail and look for a new job? Were they going to be shocked? Dismayed?

My team took the news with calm determination. We spent two days of our team retreat facing the difficult realities, identifying our weaknesses, and creating plans to change our future. I stood in complete awe of the wonderful, productive, heartfelt atmosphere that engulfed us. In my grateful mind and heart, this was truly a miracle. We all left that meeting with a sense of purpose and a willingness to put our hands to the plow and execute. Within three months, we had turned things completely around, and the company's financial performance was greater than anyone could have expected for the year.

How did this happen? I was keenly aware, the whole time, that something was happening that was greater than me or my ability. Our solution to the problem was complex, and it required all of us to contribute in our own way, in accordance with our own gifts. We forged together to form something greater.

It's kind of like the Dinobots in the old 1980's "Transformers" cartoon. These were four fearsome robots: Grimlock, Strafe, Slug, and Scorn. They were crazy powerful on their own. But they had the ability to fuse together into a single entity—the terrible Volcanicus— a mega-robot who could wreak havoc on a massive scale that dwarfed what any of them could do individually.

We were made with strengths and weaknesses so that the need to Join Forces with other people would remain non-optional. We were made with interlocking parts, like Transformers. This is one of the stunning things about the idea of design. There's intentionality behind both the strengths and the weaknesses, the areas of surplus and the areas of lack. Your being, with its holes and protrusions, with its hills and valleys, makes you a candidate for interlocking connection, just like everyone else in the human race. There is no "me" without "us."

This is the most important revelation of my forties, as I near the end of this decade of life. When I was a young man, I wanted to make a name for myself. I wanted to be the solution. I wanted to get out on the field and perform, score my points, win my games. As I have gotten older, this desire hasn't disappeared, but I've had less desire to be a star player, and more desire to be a coach. I'll talk more about this in the *Gain Mentors* chapter of this section.

> Everyone has a Superpower. This isn't just a maxim for me, it's a conviction. Part of living as if this were true is placing a high value on the Superpowers of others, and always looking for ways to join my powers with the powers of others.

As I came to understand and appreciate the gravity of my own weakness, I began to gain a proportionate appreciation for the people who had those strengths and characteristics that I knew I didn't have. This helped me to stop eternally striving to become all things.

From there, a fire began to blaze in my heart, and I began to stand in awe. I've never met a boring person. Neither have you. Every human being is a gift waiting to be unwrapped, for there is beauty in every human. This beauty can be distorted and twisted by evil, but rare is the case when it can be totally snuffed out. I've never met anyone who wasn't beautiful in some way.

So, I began to stand in awe, and I began to dig. I began to take every opportunity to peel back the layers and get beneath the surface with people around me. And for those who would let me in, I always found gifting and excellence and pain and longing. And this, too, was beautiful.

Everyone has a Superpower. This isn't just a maxim for me, it's a conviction. Part of living as if this were true is placing a high value on the Superpowers of others, and always looking for ways to join my powers with the powers of others. As a *Connector,* this includes assembling others together into pairings, small groups, and large groups in which everyone's powers are leveraged. When you assemble people together around a common purpose, with gifts that contribute to a high and lofty outcome, hearts can engage and amazing things can happen.

This is the power of Joining Forces. Much of life is interlocking with the right people at the right time for the right goals. In fact, this is the greatest accelerator of progress that I've ever discovered. The "why" behind collaboration is that we need each other. Full stop. We were not designed to reach our potential by ourselves, and we hinder potential when we withhold ourselves from collaboration, or when we undervalue collaboration.

My first formal exposure to this idea was in one of my most influential books, *Good to Great,* by Jim Collins. This book is a data-driven exploration of excellence using a combination of empirical research practices, including public data analysis and formal interviews of executives and employees at successful companies.

Early in the book, Collins and his team made an unexpected discovery.

"When we began the research project, we expected to find that the first step in taking a company from good to great would be to set a new direction, a new vision and strategy for the company, and then to get people committed and aligned behind that new direction. We found something quite the opposite. The executives who ignited the transformations from good to great did not first figure out where to drive the bus and then get people to take it there. No, they first got the right people on the bus (and the wrong people off the bus) and then figured out where to drive it. They said, in essence, 'Look, I don't really know where we should take this bus. But I know this much: If we get the right people on the bus, the right people in the right seats, and the wrong people off the bus, then we'll figure out how to take it someplace great.'"[2]

The Superpower Quest

The first and foundational ingredient of "greatness" as defined in *Good to Great* is the right people. This is the clear essence of what I mean when I say that success comes from Joining Forces. It's good to know your design. It's even better to know how your design interlocks with other people's designs. The best situation is locking arms with the right people to accomplish lofty goals that are a shared passion for the group.

Who should you Join Forces with, and how do you know?
The output of this chapter is your *Ideal Alliances Map*. You'll work through this step by step in the next chapter. For now, here's a snapshot of the full map:

REQUIRED PARTNERSHIP VALUES (RPVs)	
These are two non-negotiable values that I look for in a partner. They are the characteristics I most value in a relationship. (For example: Humility, Gentleness, Follow Through, Willingness to Risk, Honesty, Patience, Communication.)	
Required Partner Value #1	
Required Partner Value #2	

NON-STARTERS FOR PARTNERSHIP (NSPs)	
Two non-negotiable flaws or vices that cannot be present in someone I partner with. These probably reflect the ways I've been most damaged by others. For example: dishonesty, selfishness, pridefulness, overbearingness, etc. (It's OK if these are just the opposites of the above, or not RPVs, or not.)	
Non-Starter #1	
Non-Starter #2	

SECTION 3 | Join Forces

COUNTERPART ALLIANCE PROFILE (CHALLENGE)	
This covers the people who are most opposite to me, with the potential to provide the most value and progress to my life.	
Ideal Core Drive *This is my Hindering Core Drive, which is also my Counterpart's Ideal Effective Core Drive. (Order, Progress, Harmony).*	
Ideal Hero Types *These are my Hindering Hero Types. These are my Counterpart's two Ideal Hero Types.*	
Challenges *When I partner with someone described above, here are some problems that can happen.*	
Positive Outcome *When I partner with people like this, in a healthy way, then "x" happens.*	

COMRADE ALLIANCE PROFILE (SAFETY)	
These are the kinds of people who make me feel safe and understood.	
Ideal Core Drive *I am most comfortable with people who have the following as their Effective Core Drive. (Order, Progress, Harmony)*	
Ideal Hero Type *I am most comfortable with people who are strong in the following two Hero Types.*	
Challenges *When I partner with someone described above, here are some problems that can happen.*	
Positive Outcome *When I partner with people like this, in a healthy way, then "x" happens.*	

CUSTOM ALLIANCE PROFILE (#1)

These are the kinds of people I've worked well with, or think I would work well with.

Ideal Core Drive *(Order, Progress, Harmony)*	
Ideal Hero Types (2) *(Leader, Organizer, Dreamer, Achiever, Connector, Nurturer.)*	
Challenges *When I partner with someone described above, here are some problems that can happen.*	
Positive Outcome *When I partner with people like this, in a healthy way, then "x" happens.*	

CUSTOM ALLIANCE PROFILE (#2)

These are the kinds of people I've worked well with, or think I would work well with.

Ideal Core Drive *(Order, Progress, Harmony)*	
Ideal Hero Types (2) *(Leader, Organizer, Dreamer, Achiever, Connector, Nurturer.)*	
Challenges *When I partner with someone described above, here are some problems that can happen.*	
Positive Outcome *When I partner with people like this, in a healthy way, then "x" happens.*	

What are some habits and techniques for Joining Forces?

Once you are done filling out the Ideal Alliances Map, we will move onto habits for success. These are some ways to leverage the *Join Forces* philosophy for practical, mutual gain. We will address each of these areas in greater detail in this section:

- Know Thyself. Understanding your strengths and weaknesses is the foundational key to collaborating effectively with others.
- Pay Attention. Start intentionally noticing the strengths and weaknesses of the people in your life.
- Tend Your Garden. Rather than focusing energy on extending your network, focus on reconnecting with and serving your existing network.
- Make Swapsies. Start looking for opportunities to take on tasks from people in your community, that they hate, and that you love. Conversely, ask people in your community to take on tasks that you hate and they love.
- Create Dream Teams. Start playing the Matchmaker between your connections who have similar passions and complementary gifts. Many connectors do this naturally, but anyone can dabble.
- Engage in *Who First* Problem Solving. Take a page out of the playbook of both *Good to Great* and *The Power of Who,* when looking at a problem to solve. Create the habit of asking "Who can help me?" come before asking "What should I do?"
- Gain Wise Mentors. Exponentially accelerate your growth by identifying and joining forces with wise mentors who can identify shortcuts in your future, and guide you around roadblocks before you encounter them.
- Initiate Transparent Accountability. You need to have a completely open, accountable relationship with at least one person. If you have a spouse, this person should be outside of your spouse, because this person can help you get perspective on your marriage.

We will now explore each of these habits related to Joining Forces in depth.

My source material for these concepts includes extensive personal experience connecting and empowering teams at work, in ministry, creative endeavors, and in personal life. It also includes wisdom gained from the following books, which have given me the words to frame my experience. You'll see more references to these books in the pages to come. If you want to cultivate the passion and skill of Joining Forces, I highly recommend the following books:

Good to Great, **by Jim Collins.** I've already introduced this book and described it above.

The Power of Who, **by Bob Beaudine.** This book is a passionate exploration of why and how we need to leverage our community for radical progress. The tagline of the book is, "You already know everyone you need to know," and it gives practical, fatherly advice about how important it is to intentionally cultivate your relationships with existing connections instead of endlessly seeking to capture more relationships. I love this book.

Rocket Fuel, **by Gino Wickman and Mark C. Winters.** This is a business leadership book that describes the necessity for every company to have a *Visionary* and an *Integrator* at the helm of the ship. The combination of a high level, far-seeing entity with abstract goals and big picture insight (Visionary) with an organizational, tactical entity with the ability to convert vision into concrete steps and hold organizations accountable (Integrator), is like "Rocket Fuel" for any business seeking explosive growth and progress. This book is all about the need to Join Forces at the highest levels of endeavor. This book is powerful, especially in the context of business and leadership. It sets leaders free from thinking they need to be all things. For me, it was a deeply refreshing and encouraging book at a time when I needed to learn this principle in order to be healthy in my leadership.

3.2
Ideal Alliances

The following section and tables will help you identify your ideal candidates for Joining Forces and accomplishing great things. These simple tables will help you create a written description of the kinds of people who can provide you with the most benefit, and who can most receive benefit from you. The Ideal Alliances process includes the following resources:

Pre-Profile:
- Required Partnership Values
- Non-Starters for Partnership

Profiles:
- Counterpart Alliance Profile
- Comrade Alliance Profile
- Custom Alliance Profile #1
- Custom Alliance Profile #2

For all of the following tables, you can add our responses to your Hero Profile at **superpowerquest.com/myprofile**

The Superpower Quest

Superpower Quest Hero Profile

Pre-Profile: Character Considerations

The following is a place to meditate on the kinds of people you can and cannot partner with, on a fundamental level, based on the character traits that are most essential to you. Partnership requires trust. If you are going to trust someone, you are placing yourself in a place of vulnerability. Trust is a risk! You can't eliminate that risk, but one way to mitigate it is to isolate the values that most predict success and failure in a partnership, with an honest understanding of your deeply held core values.

Required Partnership Values

Required Partnership Values are the characteristics that you hold most dearly in a partner. These words are your best predictors of a successful partnership. You don't need your partner to be perfect in these things, or even as good at these things as you are. But you do need to have a sense that they have a basic adherence to the characteristics that you have elevated in your life. If you and a partner are not synced, on a basic level, on your RPVs, then your partnership could become difficult, or even toxic. Knowing these things up front means you can observe, ask around, and check for these things with any potential partnership candidate.

REQUIRED PARTNERSHIP VALUES (RPVs)	
These are two non-negotiable values that I look for in a partner. They are the characteristics I most value in a relationship. (For example: Humility, Gentleness, Follow Through, Willingness to Risk, Honesty, Patience, Communication.)	
Required Partner Value #1	
Required Partner Value #2	

146

Non-Starters for Partnership

We all have tender spots, and areas where others can easily trigger us. No one likes to be lied to, but this action is traumatizing to some people. Tardiness is a problem, but for some people, it's more than a problem—it can create massive relational tension. Non-Starters, like Required Partnership Values, are huge predictors of the success or failure of a potential partnership. Now, you can't always control who you work with. And this is a good thing, because sometimes we need to be sharpened and humbled and grown by working with people who we'd never choose to work with. However, insofar as you can, it's good not to choose to partner with people who seem to possess your Non-Starter characteristics.

NON-STARTERS FOR PARTNERSHIP (NSPs)	
Two non-negotiable flaws or vices that cannot be present in someone you partner with. These probably reflect the ways you've been most damaged by others. For example: dishonesty, selfishness, pridefulness, overbearingness, etc. (It's OK if these are just the opposites of the above, or not RPVs, or not.)	
Non-Starter #1	
Non-Starter #2	

Profile #1: Counterpart Alliance Profile

You know the saying, "opposites attract?" When you link up with your opposite, the potential energy is massive. So is the potential for things to blow up. You are most likely to misunderstand, and be misunderstood by, people who are wildly different from you. Your Counterpart is the type of person that is most different from you on the Superpower scale, and that has the most potential to bring things to the table that you lack. There is INCREDIBLE power in finding these people and linking arms with them, assuming you can find a way to establish trust by picking people with the minimum Required Partnership Values that you selected above.

The Superpower Quest

I have experienced the power of leveraging my Counterparts at work, in my marriage, and church leadership. It has become a passion for me to both find and leverage Counterparts in my life, and to help others find their Counterparts. I don't know where I'd be without Organizers, Achievers, and Leaders in my life. It's easy for me to gravitate towards Dreamers, Connectors, and Nurturers. These are the people who process like me, who often value Harmony, and act accordingly. But as much as I need people who will encourage me, I also need people who will challenge me—people who will advocate for Order in my life and hold me accountable.

My friend and mentor, Alan Briggs, once said something that stuck with me. "Seek to spend time with people who are unimpressed with you." Dreamers, Connectors, and Nurturers tend to be impressed with me. I've got to work a lot harder to impress Organizers, Leaders, and Achievers. It's humbling. It takes my ego down a peg. And this is a very good thing.

In "Lincoln the Unknown," Dale Carnegie, an influential writer and lecturer, gave insight into the life and character of the American president that stirred my heart. Lincoln's election was a MASSIVE fluke. He beat out the top candidates, not because he had the most votes, but because infighting within the parties caused frontrunners to be weakened. This meant that all of the politicians that were available to be a part of Lincoln's cabinet had great reason to resent and despise him. Everyone thought they had greater merit to be in office than Lincoln did, and were often vocal on this point. Lincoln proceeded to take this "team of rivals," and to place them in positions of power in his cabinet, each appropriate to his gifts, exercising incredible humility and strategy. I remember being brought to tears by the utter humility that Lincoln was able to show in the face of contempt. One of Lincoln's greatest critics, William H. Seward, ultimately became Lincoln's close friend as they served together and prevailed in one of the most volatile moments in the nation's history. Lincoln intuitively knew how to leverage his Counterparts. He understood the need he had for the unique strengths of the people around him, and used humility as a powerful tool to sidestep the contempt that, taken personally, could

SECTION 3 | Join Forces

have ruined his administration. It staggers me to think of the strength of heart it must require to lead a team of people who despise you in a time of unprecedented pressure. Lincoln is probably my favorite historical figure because of this.

Joining Forces with a Counterpart can be difficult. But if you can find a place of trust and mutual respect; if you can understand how much you need each other's gifts, and how far you can go together, then you might just find yourselves traveling at a velocity you never anticipated to incredible destinations that you never dreamed.

COUNTERPART ALLIANCE PROFILE (CHALLENGE)	
This covers the people who are most opposite to me, with the potential to provide the most value and progress to my life.	
Ideal Core Drive *This is my Hindering Core Drive, which is also my Counterpart's Ideal Effective Core Drive. (Order, Progress, Harmony).*	
Ideal Hero Types *These are my Hindering Hero Types. These are my Counterpart's two Ideal Hero Types.*	
Challenges *When I partner with someone described above, here are some problems that can happen*	
Positive Outcome *When I partner with people like this, in a healthy way, then "x" happens.*	

Profile #2: Comrade Alliance Profile

Look at your life. Think about the people who are closest to you. These are the people who feel safest to you. People you can confide in. People who know you and accept you as you are. I realize this might actually bring up some grief for you. Many of us are lonely and starving for more of these kinds of relationships. We need Counterparts, but we need Comrades just as much. Use this section to get an accounting of the Comrades who already exist in your life, and to build a profile for others, so you can be on the lookout for more potential candidates.

COMRADE ALLIANCE PROFILE (SAFETY)	
These are the kinds of people who make me feel safe and understood.	
Ideal Core Drive *I am most comfortable with people who have the following as their Effective Core Drive. (Order, Progress, Harmony)*	
Ideal Hero Type *I am most comfortable with people who are strong in the following two Hero Types.*	
Challenges *When I partner with someone described above, here are some problems that can happen.*	
Positive Outcome *When I partner with people like this, in a healthy way, then "x" happens.*	

Profile #3: Custom Alliance Profile (1)

Think about your life, and think about other partnerships that have worked well for you, and enter them here. Think of circumstances when you were able to work with someone, and you were able to accomplish something great together. Try to pinpoint that person's makeup, so you can look for that combo in the future.

CUSTOM ALLIANCE PROFILE (SAFETY)	
These are the kinds of people I've worked well with, or think I would work well with.	
Ideal Core Drive *(Order, Progress, Harmony)*	
Ideal Hero Types (2) *(Leader, Organizer, Dreamer, Achiever, Connector, Nurturer.)*	

SECTION 3 | Join Forces

Challenges *When I partner with someone described above, here are some problems that can happen.*	
Positive Outcome *When I partner with people like this, in a healthy way, then "x" happens.*	

Profile #4: Custom Alliance Profile (2)

Same as above.

CUSTOM ALLIANCE PROFILE (SAFETY)	
These are the kinds of people I've worked well with, or think I would work well with.	
Ideal Core Drive *(Order, Progress, Harmony)*	
Ideal Hero Types (2) *(Leader, Organizer, Dreamer, Achiever, Connector, Nurturer.)*	
Challenges *When I partner with someone described above, here are some problems that can happen.*	
Positive Outcome *When I partner with people like this, in a healthy way, then "x" happens.*	

Of Course! Context Matters

It's great to isolate and describe, in specifics, the kind of people who you can generally lock arms with to move each other forward. But I don't want to forget to mention that context matters. It also depends on what you are trying to accomplish.

There's a Biblical proverb that states, "Where there is no ox, the stall is clean. But much increase comes from the strength of the ox." Some people don't want an ox, because they don't want to clean up all of its stinky poop. But the strength of the ox is worth the inconvenience.

All humans have their own baggage, and some of this is just the negative side of their incredibly positive Superpowers.

If you want to make progress, lock arms with an Achiever. Achievers can be brash and impatient. That's the "stall cleaning" side of the Achiever. Are you willing to endure some impetuousness? Are you willing to endure some push and pull? If so, then you will see that *much increase* comes from harnessing the power of an Achiever. Sorry Achievers—I'm not saying you are oxen. The same can be applied to any Hero Type. You want a creative vision for the future? Go find a Dreamer. But we Dreamers make a mess, and this mess can play out around being scattered and inconsistent.

These Ideal Alliances are only the starting point. From here, the rest of this section will talk about specific tactics for leveraging the power of Joining Forces more effectively in your life.

3.3
Know Thyself

> "There are three things extremely hard:
> steel, a diamond, and to know one's self."
> —Benjamin Franklin, "Poor Richard's Almanac"

The rally cry of the first two sections of this book, Discover your Superpower and Understand your Weak Spot, is to *Know Thyself*. Truly knowing yourself is the basis for knowing others well, and the heart of Joining Forces is knowing yourself and others so well that vibrant collaboration is possible.

Joining Forces and Negotiation
This book, considered carefully, has given you the foundation for effective collaboration, which is true self-understanding. Now, you may ask, why is self-understanding necessary for effective collaboration? You can loosely think of Joining Forces as a form of negotiation. In the book *Never Split the Difference: Negotiating As If Your Life Depended On It* by Chris Voss and Tahl Raz, negotiation is defined as "communication with results." [3]

We have things we want in life. We have goals and aspirations. That is simply a perpetual reality of human existence. Negotiation is how we communicate with others to achieve our mutual goals.

The Superpower Quest

Although negotiation can carry a connotation of "us versus them" or competition, negotiation is not inherently bad, and doesn't have to be exploitative. It's the foundation for cooperation just as it is for competition. Voss and Raz's book gives this gem of wisdom: "He who has learned to disagree without being disagreeable has discovered the most valuable secret of negotiation." [4]

When you are negotiating, you need to know three basic things: what you have, what you lack, and what you want. What do you bring to the table for the other person's desired outcome? What do you lack that makes you dependent on others? What do you ultimately want?

In the context of joining forces, the answers to these questions come from the Superpower Quest framework. What do I bring to the table? It's my Superpower. What do I lack? That's my Weak Spot. What do I want? That's the larger mission that I'm leveraging my Superpowers, and the Superpowers of others, to accomplish. This is the effective self-knowledge that is needed for you to enter into meaningful negotiation with the Superheroes around you.

- What do I have? (Superpower)
- What do I lack? (Weak Spot)
- What do I want? (Mission)

To give you a sense for the categories where we can fall short, there are three levels of activity in life: Vision, Direction, and Execution.

The Visionary level is big picture, abstract, conceptual. It is the realm of big ideas and creativity. Visionary people answer the *what* and *why* questions, as well as the big picture where, which is the destination. The Direction level has to do with planning in preparation. This is where the maps are, and the supply lists, and the overall strategy. Direction people answer the *how* and *who* questions. The Execution level has to do with actual motion, in accordance with the direction, that ties back to the vision. This is where the plans are executed. This is where the steps are taken. This is where all the actual movement happens to get from point A to point B.

SECTION 3 | Join Forces

- Dreamers and Connectors tend to live in the Visionary sphere.
- Leaders in Organizers tend to live in the Directional sphere.
- Achievers and Nurturers tend to live in the Execution sphere.

Being a Connector/Dreamer, my areas of genius only exist in the top layer. Many people that I know have Superpowers, or at least competencies, across two of the three areas. But I am incredibly lopsided towards the abstract creative side, to the total detriment of my abilities in either the planning or execution sides. This just means it feels like I've had a steaming double helping of weakness in my life, which has given me an incredible amount of opportunity to reckon with my weakness over decades.

> In fact, the weakest of us might be the most prone to Join Forces with others, which makes the weakest of us, potentially, the very strongest.

Now, I will readily admit, maybe your weakness feels as much of an overwhelming mountain as mine does. Our weakness has a tendency to loom like that, and sometimes blot out the sun. I'm hoping to communicate with this book, with my life, with this section, that there's hope for the weakest of us, the poorest of us, the least experienced of us. A mountain of weakness might mean that you are difficult, but it does not mean that you are impossible.

In fact, the weakest of us might be the most prone to Join Forces with others, which makes the weakest of us, potentially, the very strongest. If I know that I'm ignorant, I can Join Forces with others to gain wisdom. If I know I'm inconsistent, I can Join Forces with others to gain structure and accountability. If I know I'm reckless, I can Join Forces with others to gain checks and balances. If I struggle with expressing myself and connecting with people, I can Join Forces with people who will ask me questions and draw out my authentic self.

If I know myself, if I know my strength, if I know my weakness, then every strength can become something to share with others, and every weakness can become an opportunity to lean on others. In this way, I have the greatest opportunity to fulfill my mission and the missions of others. Remember, the purpose of this book isn't to show you your Superpower so that you can become an impregnable island of self-determination and self-reliance. I included this chapter to build your conviction that you were made to run with a pack! You were made to feed the dreams of others, and to gain sustenance from others for your dreams, and even to dream in community!

The greatest things I have accomplished in my life are creating a healthy marriage, creating a loving environment for my children, helping to build a vibrant Church community, helping to rebuild and revitalize a dead company, and writing this book; all of these things would have been impossible without Joining Forces with insanely gifted people who were willing to put the hand to the plow with me, and I with them.

Nothing has made me more open to partaking in the excellence of others than the depth of self-knowledge that has been granted to me. And this, only as an extension of God's incredible kindness towards me; God, who I see as the ultimate helper and equipper to Join Forces with—my first love, my first father, and my first friend.

I've given you a tool, this book, for radical self-knowledge, but not as an end unto itself. I've given it to you as a means to the end of understanding where you fit inside of partnerships and communities, and to enable you to fit well, and contribute masterfully, and receive graciously.

Know Thyself…and Join Forces like a boss!

3.4
Pay Attention

"Know this, my beloved brothers: let every person be quick to hear, slow to speak, slow to anger."
—James 1:19, The Holy Bible (ESV)

Many people want to speak more than they want to listen. This is certainly my tendency, and I've had to work on it quite a bit. Listening well—paying attention—is a key element in Joining Forces.

This chapter specifically leverages my experiences as a pastor, a CEO, and a father, in the sense that these were all roles in which I was entrusted to lovingly understand the strengths and weaknesses of the people in my care, in order to help them unlock their potential and function as an effective unit.

Knowing thyself, as you do, and having gone through the SPQ process; let us now talk about strategies for recognizing the strengths and weaknesses of others. This means you will have to pay attention and be keyed in to the ways that the people around you carry themselves, and the ways that they see themselves. This will be easier for Nurturers and Connectors than it will be for people who are weaker in these Hero Types.

Being that I am a Connector, I realize that this book might be weighted towards a Connector's perspective. In fact, I recognize that it can't help but be so. I've tried to gain outside perspective from many people with different Hero Types, in order to avoid weighting it so much in that direction that it places unnecessary burdens on those who do not have the Connector as a strength. However, I was serious early on when I said that everyone must function, to some degree, within every Hero Type in order to be functional in the world of humans.

This is a section that will sound like it has more application to the Connector then to other hero types. And it is certainly true that Connectors will tend to execute the principles of this chapter more often than the average person. However, from the most extraverted person in the world to the most introverted, we will all need to Join Forces with others, and this means we will all need to be able to understand and recognize others. And the only way to understand and recognize others is to pay attention.

The following are techniques for getting the depth of understanding about the people around you that you will need to effectively Join Forces.

Know Your Personality Classification System. Your classification system is the personality framework that makes the most sense to you. It's the one you're going to study and double down on until it becomes intuitive. Your system of choice may end up being the SPQ Hero Types, or some other classification system; like Enneagram, Myers-Briggs, DiSC, Big 5, Clifton Strengths, or others. You don't have to make everybody else buy into the classification system that you choose. But it will give you the advantage of perceiving your world through the lens of a framework. This will give you a huge leg up on being able to identify where the people around you fit within that classification.

- **Spend Time.** I will cover this more in depth in the upcoming *Tend Your Garden* chapter. Suffice it to say, you need to spend time with the people in your circle in order to have the depth of knowledge you will need to be able to Join Forces appropriately.
- **Share Yourself.** It won't work to invite others to share about

themselves, if you're not willing to share about yourself. If you want to Join Forces effectively, there's a level of vulnerability that is required. I will talk more about techniques for being more vulnerable in the *Utility Belt* section.
- **Ask Questions.** In my experience, ninety-nine percent of people desperately want to be known. The primary mechanism for knowing people is asking the right questions and demonstrating that you are actively listening to the answers, which is the next point. People don't ask good questions because: a)They don't know the questions to ask, and b)They are nervous to take the risk. I can help you with both.

The goal of asking these questions is to gain deep insight into the design of the person. In order to share themselves with you in this way, the other person will need to feel safe, respected, and valued.

A posture of curiosity is the best way to create this environment. Asking questions that touch on the person's passions, stories, and dreams will often cause that person to "light up" and give you treasures from the deep storehouse of their longing.

Here are five questions that will help you get right down to the essence of people: their passions, their priorities, and their dreams.

- What are you passionate about?
- What was a defining moment in your life?
- What is your Big Dream? How can I help?
- What is a movement you'd like to be a part of?
- Can you tell me about a book or mentor that influenced you?

I know, to some of you these questions are going to sound really scary. Maybe you aren't used to asking questions like this, so you think they may sound fake coming from you. Maybe you're afraid they will make things awkward. Maybe you're afraid the person will say something controversial that you don't agree with. To all of these concerns, and all the other ones that I haven't listed, I say…fair. These are all possibilities.

But they are merely bumps on the road towards intimacy. You cannot have intimacy without risk. You cannot Join Forces more effectively without having closer connections with people. I'm not telling you to do this all the time, or even a lot. Start with one time. Then twice. See what it feels like to get someone lit up and telling his or her unique and beautiful story.

I suspect you won't want to stop.

Listen Actively
Now, you can't just ask a question like the ones I listed above and sit back, like pushing play on a movie. It's not that easy. The question is only the beginning of a powerful, authentic interaction. Even though you're the listener, you'll be doing most of the work. The work is concentrating, asking follow-up questions like, "Tell me more about that," being authentically curious, finding points of connection in your own story without derailing the conversation and train-wrecking it back into yourself by making it all about you.

Part of effective listening is creating safe spaces. Release yourself from the burden of having to judge or correct what the other person says. There are conversations where correction needs to happen, but they are rare, and these conversations happen in the context of established trust. Getting to know someone, even someone you've known for years but don't really "know," is the time to listen, drink the person in, and understand who they really are, even if you don't agree with what they think or believe. If you can only have intimate, respectful conversations with people who think like you, then you will be left with only having relationships with people who think like you. That's like living in a hall of mirrors. You'll have trouble making an impact in the world outside of your closed community, and you'll have trouble finding blessed correction in the blind spots where you need it most. That is the path of stagnation, not growth.

Notice Weaknesses with Charity
Can you become aware of, and privately acknowledge, another person's weakness, without feeling superiority or disdain?

It's a beautiful, sacred thing to be entrusted with the knowledge of another person's weakness. It's also terribly easy to abuse, if it triggers judgment or condemnation. A sense of judgment or condemnation upon another person's weakness is a sign that you haven't accurately appreciated the depth of your own weakness. Speaking to myself, first, on this one, because I sometimes struggle with this.

If you become aware of another person's weakness or limitations, this has not been granted to you for the purpose of contempt, or even fixing it. How much do you enjoy it when people try to fix you? It is possible that you may be of service to the person someday, but you won't make a positive impact outside the bonds of trust and good timing and humility.

There are ways to handle the revelation of weakness that bring only benefit. When I talk with people about their weaknesses, or allow others to talk with me about mine, it's only by mutual permission in the bonds of mutual trust. Permission is super important in the sensitive areas of a person's Weak Spot.

However, I might know that a person struggles with the details, and not ask things of that person that I know are setting them up for failure. I might even offer help, gently and humbly, if I see the person struggling in an area of weakness. Observing and understanding a person's weakness can empower you towards more effective service and blessing in that person's life; but again, only if you can steward your understanding of their weakness with mercy and grace, not judgment and disdain.

Call Out the Gifts

Stewarding the weakness of another person is a private thing. Acknowledging a person's gifts is an opportunity for private and public affirmation. This can also help people recognize and articulate their own gifts, and gain confidence.

Here are some things you can say, publicly and privately, to call out the gifts of others.   "I noticed you're really good at …"

"It really helped me when you …"

"The way you [X] is really good for this community."

Make Connections

We will dive more into this concept in the *Create Dream Teams* chapter, but suffice it to say that, when you are paying attention to the gifts of the people around you, you will begin to see opportunities that work in your people's favor. You will have the power to foster connections between people that you know, and other people that you know, who can benefit each other. You will have the power to make them aware of opportunities that fit within their Superpower.

I hope these strategies for paying attention are beneficial to your life. There's no such thing as a boring human. The greatest treasures in your life are the people around you, waiting to be seen as treasure, waiting to be unlocked, waiting to be gasped over and delighted in. Pay attention and grow rich in insight and your ability to positively impact the people in your life.

3.5
Tend Your Garden

To inform this chapter, I'm leaning on my extensive networking and community building experiences. I will also be pulling some principles from Bob Beaudine's excellent book, *The Power of Who: You Already Know Everyone You Need To Know.*[5]

As I was writing this book, I deployed a survey to my entire network as part of my research. This was a miniature, introductory version of the first part of the Superpower Quest process, *Discover Your Superpower*. I asked people to self-identify their Core Drive, their Effective Hero Types, and then tell me their Big Dreams and Key Interests.

As I was going over my entire rolodex of contacts collected over the last several decades, I was both excited and floored that I knew so many people. I wouldn't be surprised if I asked 500 people to take the survey, and all of these people were people who really know me in some capacity.

I also asked my people to share the survey with their networks, and some of them did. The result was 200 responses at the time that I'm writing this section. Two hundred people were willing to share deep, personal information with me.

About twenty percent of the surveys came from people that I didn't already know in some capacity, but the majority came from people who know my name, and who know what I'm about. People I've served in ministry, people who have pastored me. People who knew me in high school, people who knew me in college. Family members. People who I consider mentors, people that work for me, people that have done business with me, people that have been with me in my moments of greatest agony, and greatest joy. People in my current small group Bible study who have been meeting for nearly a decade.

I learned some really cool things. The fairly even distribution of selected Core Drives and Hero Types across people from a variety of backgrounds helped me confirm and feel confident about the accuracy of my categories.

But the real gold for me was the answers I received to the questions about Big Dreams and Key Interests. I was inspired and overjoyed to hear my connections dreaming big. I found myself sometimes becoming breathless, looking over a new survey submission, and thinking, "I can help this person achieve that dream!" I began to feel like something special was happening. I was looking at a beautiful painting of 200 people's dreams in one place and beginning to draw the lines between people with similar passions and complementary gifts, people who could help each other. Then I began to make the introductions. Dozens, since the time of that revelation. One day it will be hundreds, and then, maybe thousands.

I learned that one of the men in my small group, a good friend named Jon, was interested in leadership training. It just so happened that I was attending an amazing leadership cohort that my company had paid for, and I had a free pass to invite others. I invited Jon, and he was stoked to attend the last session with me. This created an awesome point of connection for the two of us, as we began to share our experiences in business and leadership more often. But here's the thing; I had been meeting weekly with Jon and his family for many years, and it took a survey for me to uncover this common interest.

It made me wonder; what important things do I not know about the people closest to me? Are there ways we could be helping each other achieve our dreams if we only knew the points of overlap?

SECTION 3 | Join Forces

There's an opportunity right under our noses, and it might be the most powerful accelerator of progress that we have access to.

In *The Power of Who: You Already Know Everyone You Need To Know*, Bob Beaudine presents a thesis that you "already know everyone you need to know." The common approach to networking is adding connections left and right. It's a game of chasing a quantity of connections. You focus on growing your network instead of tending to your network.

Beaudine challenges this conception by advocating that you stop neglecting your greatest resource: the people in your life who already know you, care about you, and are more than willing to help you. This is your *Who*.

> There's an opportunity right under our noses, and it might be the most powerful accelerator of progress that we have access to.

Think about the inner circle of people in your life that would do anything for you. Now consider the number of people just outside that circle who would do a lot for you. Now consider that each of those friends has a close circle of friends who would show you favor, simply if your friend asked them to, on your behalf. Adding all these people together, it's possible that you have hundreds, even thousands of people in this world, with strong motivation to use their means and connections to help you.

And consider that the traditional networking idea takes emphasis from investing in, and benefitting from, these people, and tasks you with pursuing strangers.

Yes, there is a time and place to focus on extending your network. But that should never take priority over tending to—and leveraging—your existing network of closer relations.

The irony is that when we have critical needs, such as a new job, or a better job, or a side-hustle breakthrough, or an entrepreneurial opportunity, or a need for certain goods or services, it's easier for most of us to ask strangers, because of the shame of appearing needy to people we know, love, and respect. Or maybe we've fallen out of touch with key people, and asking them for help seems tacky.

So, instead of putting the word out to our people, we reach out to strangers for help. We put our resume or application in the pile. We fill out a "contact us" form. We make a cold call or send a cold email. When all along, maybe the key to our problem was in the hands of someone who knows us, loves us, and remains completely unaware that we need anything they could provide.

The cure for this is being more intentional to invest in your people and trusting that they want to invest in you. Our culture has become increasingly individualistic, and there are benefits to that. But we are losing out on the satisfaction and effectiveness of locking arms with our people to rise together.

And so, with Bob Beaudine, I encourage you to tend your garden and make it healthy before you go do more planting.

Here are some *Connector* tips for tending your garden:

- Write out a list of your key connections. Set up a schedule to make sure you are touching base with each of them on a regular basis. You can leverage your Life System from your Utility Belt to make this happen. (We will talk about this in the next section.)
- Send out a monthly or quarterly email newsletter to your people. Substack is a great mechanism for this. Also, good to add to your Life System.
- Use social media to keep tabs, and give meaningful comments via the platform where you and your people are active. But don't end there. Convert from social media to something more personal, like a phone call or a face-to-face meeting. The influential LinkedIn/personal brand coach, Katelyn Richards, once posted, "Your people are HERE. But you need to talk to them off of HERE. Great content is fabulous, but face-to-face convos are even better. Use the first to do more of the second."
- When someone comes to mind, build the habit of reaching out immediately with a text message, asking how they are doing.

- Ask the big questions. There's nothing wrong with small talk, but make sure you are not missing opportunities to go deeper. Ask your people about their Big Dreams and passions. Don't assume you know, just because you've known them for a long time.

I don't expect everyone to be the Connector. If the Connector is a Hindering Type for you, this list is going to seem overwhelming. I don't expect you to do all of these things; I just wanted to give you a variety of things to choose from. Choose one, try it out, assess the results, and add it to your Life System if it works.

Keep your eye on the end goal. In order to Join Forces with others, you need to understand them. Start with getting a better understanding of the people in your nearest circles.

3.6
Make Swapsies

Once you've identified Superpowers and Weak Spots in the people around you, a powerful way to leverage this information is something I call *Making Swapsies*.

I got this terminology from my brother and sister-in-law, Drew and Rachelle Bartels. They are always making up silly words—I'm convinced this is part of Drew's Superpower. We call it *Swapsies* when my wife and I take their kids so they can have time together, and then they take our kids so Sarah and I can have time.

In the context of this chapter, *Making Swapsies* is the simple act of giving your Superpower in an area of another's Weak Spot, and receiving their Superpower in an area of your Weak Spot.

Swapsies is probably the simplest and most intuitive form of Joining Forces.

The Bartels, who I mentioned above, have an awesome method for doing this as a family with their two boys under twelve. The Bartels are bought-in to the Scrum task management framework, derived from Jeff and J.J. Sutherland's book, *Scrum: The Art of Doing Twice the Work in Half the Time*.[6] Scrum is a system of allocating tasks based on both capacity and disposition. The goal of Scrum is to understand the true capacity of everyone on a team, and to have everyone in the team working within their capacity, and working on the tasks that are most within their wheelhouse of ability and passion.

The Bartels have adapted the Scrum concept for family chore day. They write the weekend chores on a series of sticky notes. Then they have each family member give a numerical value on a scale of one to eight, of how difficult the task feels to them. One is easy, eight is hard. Then they divvy up the tasks, and add up the points, making sure that the point totals are similar across people. This process is a great example of *Making Swapsies* because it shows the negotiation aspect of allocating tasks.

For me, taking the kids out on an afternoon outing is a one or a three. For my wife, it can be more like an eight. For me, yard maintenance is an eight. For my nephew, Ezra, it's a one.

If someone in my community needs high-level advice on marriages, business, team building, conflict resolution, or professional development, I am happy to jump on the phone for as long as it takes to talk through the problem. The hours melt away. This is less than a one for me. This is joy.

I have a good friend who is at a growth stage in his career. I've spent time informally coaching him through some rough spots. He's a jack of all trades, so whenever I have a question about home repair, I have him on speed dial, and he always comes through for me. I value what he's done for me more highly than what I've done for him. I wonder if he puts a higher value on what I've done for him. It's possible! That is magic of Swapsies.

This doesn't have to be a formal arrangement, although it can be. Swapsies situations naturally arise as we become confident about the things we have to offer, and as we become more willing to receive, and even ask for, the offerings of others.

3.7
Create Dream Teams

Swapsies is about you exchanging your Superpower for someone else's.

Creating Dream Teams is going a step further and matching up people you know with each other. It's the art of strategic connection.

In the course of life, people in your circle will make you aware of needs and struggles. As you live out the Superpower Quest framework, you will become more and more sensitive to the Weak Spots and Superpowers of the people around you. Then, when one of your people makes you aware of needs or struggles, someone in your mental rolodex may come to mind— someone who can help. Someone with the right Superpower!

Then you will have the opportunity to make the connection! Here's how it works:

- Tell your person you have someone in mind who can help. Ask if he or she is OK with you making a connection.
- Check with the other person to see if they are open to the connection.
- If yes to both, then make a quick introduction. I usually do this via group text message or email, but I sometimes use social media if both parties are active on a platform that I am also active on.

- The introduction can be something like this: "I was talking with [PERSON 1] the other day, and [PERSON 1] expressed problem X. [PERSON 2], you instantly came to mind, since [REASON]. I'll let you two take it from here, if you want to connect."
- Then, you can see your way out. No need to hover or make it happen. Let it be if it's going to be. This is important. You're not going to want to keep doing this if you end up creating awkwardness or tension. And you don't want to create an unnecessary occasion for your people to feel pressure, or feel like they failed you in some way if the timing just isn't right for them.
- You can get a lot more detailed with these introductions, and I'm trying to make this into an art form. But it's more important that you give the opportunity than that you polish the method. Anyone coming to mind that you can help in this way?

These are the basic steps, but you can go crazy with it. I write huge email introductions, where I take my time affirming the unique greatness of the people I am introducing. In this way, I get to spread the love to people in my community, while giving them important insight into each other's gifts and qualities.

Bonus Content: You can visit **superpowerquest.com/resources** to view a sample introductory email that I sent, bringing to powerhouses together in my community.

If you want to get ridiculous boss-mode/mic-drop with it, you can take a page out of the playbook of my friend Alan Briggs, mentioned in other places in this book, who is a Super-Connector in his own right. He will actually do all the steps I listed for a formal introduction between two of his relations. But then he will sometimes go a further step to buy them a gift card for dinner together to sweeten the pot. Have you ever had someone say, "Hey, I want you to meet X person, who I think you can deeply benefit, and who can deeply benefit you. Oh, and by the way, here's a $100 gift card for you two to get dinner together." Amazing!

There's a lot more I can say about this. Really, building Dream Teams for mutual, interlocking benefit has become a joyful passion for me. This proceeds from my unique Superpower of "Authentic Connection for Mutual Progress." The whole Superpower Quest project, with the book, the online community, and the content I'm pushing out on multiple platforms, is really pointing towards refined, cultivated collaboration. I am creating a space where people can find their Dream Teams and flourish inside them. The Superpower Community at superpowerquest.com/community is really, at its core, just a Dream Team factory.

This is my passion; this is my playground: Turning the process of strategic connection into an art form. I'm writing about this with a fire in my chest. Why is that? Because this is my Superpower. Most of you wouldn't feel this way about this particular endeavor. There's something else that makes you feel this way. I want you to find that.

I'm going to sidetrack us a bit here, so bear with me. This entire book, and whatever movement comes with it, has its origin in a simple decision that I made at the outset. I decided somewhere in 2021 I was going to follow my Superpower, and then I set up a system of accountability to measurably increase the amount of time I spent operating in that Superpower. In the process, I discovered something. All my life, I've struggled with consistency. Consistency is more in the realm of Leaders, Achievers, and Organizers, which are all my weakest Hero Types. It's hard for me to finish things that I start. Sometimes it feels impossible.

Regardless of if you struggle with consistency or not, the simple reality of life is that you're not going to make real progress without sustained consistency in a single direction. You can't make extraordinary progress without extraordinary consistency. And most people I know struggle with sustained consistency.

Some of us can access a gear and just make sustained consistency happen. I stand in awe of people like this. They set their minds to something, and they do it. They say, "I'm going to work out every day for the next year," and then they do it. My friend Josh Jones, a Leader/Achiever, is like this. But what about the rest of us?

The Superpower Quest

Operating in your Superpower, in alignment with your passion, makes consistency happen. The key to sustained consistency, for people who lack extraordinary willpower (i.e. most of us), is operating in your Superpower. This is why I was able to write this book. This is what has carried me through seasons of disappointment, or lethargy, or times when it seemed like this wasn't going to amount to anything. When you are doing what you love, what you are meant to do, then you can endure much longer seasons of execution without payoff. Why? Because the execution is a reward unto itself. You have to find the areas in which the reward is the act of doing the thing. Then you're on to something. Then you'll keep doing it. Then you'll find the sustained consistency that will carry you towards an exponential result. People don't see exponential results because, somewhere along the way, they run out of willpower. A strong antidote for this is doubling down and focusing attention on the thing that brings you joy and excellence: Your Superpower.

> The key to sustained consistency, for people who lack extraordinary willpower (i.e. most of us), is operating in your Superpower.

So, back to the topic of this chapter, once I became aware that I was probably "one in ten-thousand" at fostering strategic connections, I started to invest my time and energy into doing more of that. Perfecting the art and science, so to speak.

The gift I have to give the person who is "one in ten-thousand" the opposite direction, and doesn't have a *Connector* bone in their body, is the approach outlined in this chapter.

#1. Listen carefully to your people. Be on the lookout.
#2. Follow the steps above, to make an introduction when appropriate.

But here's a cheat code for you, because I know that this habit might go against the grain for many people. #3. Leverage the Connectors in your life. If you have friends, or people on your radar, that need help, and you don't know anyone who can help, borrow someone else's rolodex. Reach out to a Connector. Introduce your person to a Connector. Connectors get energy out of strategic matchmaking. Get over your worry that you're going to be bothering a Connector by reaching out, and make the ask on behalf of your friend.

To extend the cheat code even further, you can #4. Introduce your friends to this book, and the Superpower Quest framework overall, and the online Superpower Community in specific, all of which are geared towards helping them find their *Dream Team*. When it comes to helping your pack, do the most. I learned this from my favorite book of 2022, *The Go-Giver,* by Bob Burg and John David Mann, and another great pick, *The Power of Who: You Already Know Everyone You Need to Know,* by Bob Beaudine. Both books are referenced elsewhere in this book. Let's get stupid-radical about opening doors and creating opportunities for the people in our respective spheres. Creating Dream Teams is a way to do this.

3.8
Who First Problem Solving

This chapter pulls from my experiences as a company leader and as a connector in my community. I am also pulling principles out of *Good to Great* by Jim Collins, and *The Power of Who: You Already Know Everyone You Need To Know*, by Bob Beaudine.

We face a lot of problems on a day-to-day basis. Have you ever had a day without a problem? Me neither. Solving problems is part of the responsibility of being human. Some problems are big, some are small. Some are in the area of your Superpower, some are in the area of your Weak Spot. Some align with your Mission, some don't. In this chapter, I am advocating a mental pivot in our default way of approaching problems.

In *Good to Great,* chapter three is called "Who First…Then What." [7] I quoted from this chapter earlier, to introduce the *Join Forces* section of the book. The *Who First* mentality indicates that the best strategy for success is to secure the right people before solving problems. In fact, this chapter indicates that pre-existing problems often dissolve when the right people are in place.

So much of the message of *The Power of Who …* by Bob Beaudine is that many of our problems are "Who" problems that require the right "Who" to help us solve them. Investing in our networks is the key to having consistent access to the people we need to help us overcome challenges.

Both of these books advocate a *Who First* approach to solving problems. This simply means that we can develop the discipline of always being ready to ask, "Who can help me with this problem?" instead of only asking, "What must I do to solve this problem?"

This will put you in a ready mindset to Join Forces more often, with other heroes who can help you. My family was struggling to find a good dentist. We have some severe dental fear in our family, and our many attempts to find a new dentist by trial and error were unsuccessful. But we did have a stellar oral surgeon—she just wasn't able to practice general dentistry. The oral surgeon had the right approach to calming dental fear and we valued her. Suddenly, I got the idea, why not just call the oral surgeon we loved, and ask her about a dentist? Typically referrals work the other way around (dentists refer you to an oral surgeon), which made this approach counterintuitive. That explains why I didn't think of it earlier. Anyway, I called the oral surgeon and she pointed us to a one-in-a-million dentist who was the perfect fit for our family.

This mindset makes you spend more time finding the right person, and potentially way less time solving the problem. Indeed, some problems are impossible to solve well without the right person involved.

In my role as a CEO of a company, I've assembled a team based on the *Who First* principle, and our plans for growing the team are firmly rooted in the principal as well. We've worked extremely hard to get the right people on the bus, and to maneuver everyone to the right seat on the bus. I am going to raise the hood so you can look at the engine behind our highly effective company, and how our unique gifts interlock to create the whole organism.

I am a Connector/Dreamer in the CEO position, which is right where I should be, casting high level vision and maintaining high level connections with our largest clients and partners.

Dan, our CFO, is an Organizer/Connector. He has the practical mindset to help keep our finances in order, with a heavy dose of

SECTION 3 | Join Forces

entrepreneurial spirit and business savvy, and a relational ability that you don't normally find with people in his position. He doesn't see his job as managing numbers—it's taking care of his people.

Caleb, our Operations Director, is an Organizer/Dreamer, with the ability to connect with me on high-level vision, and then do the thing that I've proven I can't do well—turn that vision into practical strategy and plans. He spends most of his time on the *Direction* layer, ensuring that the company has the structures, processes, and plans in place to make tangible progress. He makes sure that our ideas don't stay ideas or wishes. He is invaluable to me, and to the business. In Gino Wickman and Mark C. Winters terminology, found in their book, *Rocket Fuel: The One Essential Combination That Will Get You More of What You Want from Your Business*,[8] I am the "Visionary" of the company, and Caleb is the "Integrator."

Lydia, our Project Manager, is an Organizer/Achiever. She interfaces with Caleb to bring another concrete layer of organization and execution. She wants little to do with the vision. She has a passion for making sure that all tasks are properly documented, that everyone's workload is balanced, and that all tasks are being done right and on time. She manages our complex labor and delivery schedule, and builds out all of our schedules in our project management software.

Michelle and Alaine are experienced Researchers who execute their duties within the schedule. Michelle is an Achiever/Organizer who loves seeing her tasks for the day, putting her head down, and getting them checked off of her list. Alaine is a Dreamer/Organizer who is also high in the Achiever. She is able to put her head down and knock out her tasks in an organized way, but she also has the desire and ability to look at things from a new perspective and try new things.

Jordan is a Nurturer/Connector who also has the Achiever as a Supporting Type. She is our most public-facing entity besides myself, because she conducts telephone research, where her ability to make people feel welcomed and cared for is a powerful asset.

We know that our next entity is probably an additional Researcher who is an Achiever/Organizer. When I am ready to bring on a salesperson to take over sales from me, it will be a Connector/Achiever.

With this team around me, I've never felt so empowered in my entire career. We have a clear vision, we like and respect each other, and we've been through intense difficulty together. The right interlocking of gifts means that, most of the time, people are working on their areas of real gifting, sometimes in areas of competency, and rarely in areas of Weak Spot. My team feels like a living mural of the principal of *Who First* Problem Solving.

The truth is that people want to contribute their Superpowers to causes they believe in. People want to be helpful in the areas where they're gifted. People are dying to Join Forces. Even the cantankerous ones.

Who First Problem Solving is a way of seeing the world and being open to the potential of the humans in your world. Next time you have a need, or you're thinking about solving a problem, add this question to your due diligence: "Who do I know that might take joy and satisfaction from helping me with this problem?"

3.9
Gain Wise Mentors

"Where there is no counsel, the people fall;
But in the multitude of counselors there is safety."
—Proverbs 11:14, The Holy Bible (NKJV)

My friend Matt was visiting from Phoenix. We've known each other for over a decade. We were pastors together, once upon a time. Now we are both professionals, working our jobs and raising our families. Our lives have taken a parallel course, in some ways, and our conversations have become rich and reflective. He was telling me about a meme that's going around that's something like, "Many people may invest in your success, but a true father wants you to surpass him."

Matt is getting pretty gray in the beard. So am I. We both still feel a powerful sense of purpose in our lives, but more and more, we are finding ourselves in the background, instead of in the spotlight. Matt is pouring into several younger men who are full of questions about life and ministry, empowering them by giving them the real talk about the cost of leadership. He is giving away the true gold of his life, with no expectation of return. He's taking a personal and prolonged interest in several key individuals.

I asked him how often in his life people had done that same thing for him. He said it was very rare. I said it was rare for me, too, looking back over nearly five decades of living.

I've grieved that, in the past. I talk a lot about the longing for others, those who are ahead of me in life, to pull me aside and say, "Hey, I've been where you are trying to go. Let me help you get there faster than I did."

Most of us can identify with this longing. Remember a time when you were in a new and unfamiliar environment, feeling like a sore thumb, like the first day of high school? What would it have meant to you for one of the cool seniors to take an authentic interest in you? Not because their mom or some teacher told them to, but because they saw you and cared, and determined to be your advocate. Maybe this happened for you at a key moment; maybe not. At many formative moments, this did not happen for me. My conclusion? "I'm on my own. I have to figure this out myself, and be careful not to need anyone." It's taken decades to change that mindset.

At the same time, I can't complain. I've tasted this kind of investment and I wanted more. In the last five years, I stopped waiting for someone to pull me aside, and I started going after people who know things I want to know like a rabid dog going after a bone. I began to covet mentorship, and snatch it wherever I could. And I began trying to be this person for others.

I first noticed this concept of what I call *snatching mentorship* in the book, *The Ruthless Elimination of Hurry* by John Mark Comer. The following passage was an aside in the book, not reflecting Comer's main point about the importance of slowing down in the midst of our frenetic culture of hurry. But it branded itself on my brain, nonetheless.

Comer writes, "Last week, I had lunch with my mentor, John. Okay, confession, he's not actually my mentor. He's way out of my league, but we regularly have lunch, and I ask a barrage of questions about life, notepad open. John is the kind of person you meet and immediately think, 'I want to be like that when I grow up.'"[9]

"Yes," said my heart, when I read that. Comer was describing the very thing I knew I needed to do. He helped me solidify the conclusion that I don't need a formal mentoring relationship with someone to benefit from what that person knows and who that person is. This mindset has emboldened me to ask for time with people who are "out of my league," and then show up with my notepad in hand. Shout out to Richard Bliss, Guy Tasaka, Troy and Kim Smith, Robin Cook, Alan Briggs, Drew Bartels, Jayde Duncan, Katelyn Richards, and AnnMarie Wills; a few of the many generous hearted people who have invested their precious time dropping mad wisdom while I scribbled notes.

The world needs more fathers and mothers. I don't mean physical, although we need more of those too. I mean spiritual and emotional mothers and fathers. I mean the "older cool kids" who are now wise and gray, who have tasted deeply of the pain and joy of this life, who have fought for wisdom, and who have a story to tell. People have a burning desire to share what they've learned for the benefit of others. These are the people who know what only experience can teach.

The world also needs younger people who have tasted enough of failure and weakness to become humble, and teachable, and to become hungry for the wisdom of their elders. And to that hunger, I hope to add an unapologetic boldness to ask the wise people that you come across to share their treasures with you.

One of the marks of a wise person is generosity. I have found that most of the wise people I've attempted to meet, have been willing to share their wisdom without any expectation of return. If you are willing to humble yourself, and treat their time as if it were more valuable than yours, take on the burden of scheduling, and be tenacious to nail them down, and if you are willing to accept thirty minutes instead of an hour and come with a list of questions so they don't have the burden of keeping the conversation moving, you will find a wealth beyond imagining.

Joining Forces is a truly powerful way of living, because it leverages a key fact about our design. We were designed in such a way, with strengths and weaknesses, that we need others in order to reach our potential. These others are not optional. We need them. And of the many ways that we Join Forces, mentorship relationships are perhaps the most potent form of Joining Forces.

Talking with someone who is ahead of you in life, further down the path that you are on, may be the closest thing you can do to seeing the future. Joining Forces in a mentorship relationship gives you access to your potential future self.

Paid Consulting

Even when I began to see the value of mentorship, I still felt perplexed when hearing about people spending a hundred dollars or more per hour for consulting services. "You're gonna pay people that much money...to talk to you?" That's what I thought.

Now I've been on the receiving side of such services, and I can attest that those fees are some of the happiest checks my business writes. So I am certainly an advocate for paying the cost for what targeted mentorship is worth, especially as a business cost.

> You know things, now, that are solid gold for another person. Pursue excellence of wisdom and understanding in your niche. Then, give your wisdom generously to others.

This is because the payoff happens in units that dwarf the value of money. The payoff happens in units of time and energy and avoided chaos. How much would you pay for a year of your life? How much would you pay NOT to make your next catastrophic mistake? A consultant can accelerate your journey towards a goal and help you navigate roadblocks you can't even see. Let's say you are heading towards a goal that will take you seven years, as an inexperienced person. But someone who has been down that road can tell you how to get there in three years. What's the value of those four years?

I come from a poverty mindset, in which it would be inconceivable, even if it were possible, to pay hundreds or thousands of dollars for someone to tell me what they know. This is why I was resistant to the idea of paid consulting for so many years. I also understand that many of us can't afford, or don't have a company willing to invest in such services. The only reason I include this section is to plant a seed for anyone who grew up with a poverty mindset like me. Be open to the possibility that the best investment you can make, at a certain time of life, might be paying a wise person to be your guide. That's a mentorship mic-drop right there.

Be A Mentor

You know things, now, that are solid gold for another person. Pursue excellence of wisdom and understanding in your niche. Then, give your wisdom generously to others. I said earlier that a mark of true wisdom is generosity. Be generous with what you know. Give your wisdom to others with no expectation of return. Be the amazing upperclassman cool kid for someone else who needs to be seen and encouraged.

Take Action

In his book *The 4-Hour Workweek, Expanded and Updated: Escape 9-5, Live Anywhere, and Join the New Rich,* Tim Ferris coaches his readers to be careful about how much information they consume that is not converted into the right kind of action.

"Ignorance may be bliss, but it's also practical. It is imperative that you learn to ignore or redirect all information and interruptions that are irrelevant, unimportant, or unactionable. Most are all three…lifestyle design [intentional living] is based on massive action-output. Increased output necessitates decreased input."[10]

This principle is brilliant, and it has great applications to all areas of life. It is relevant to your journey to learn through mentorship, and I'm going to add a relational consideration.

In his book, Ferris is cultivating in the reader a *predisposition towards action* instead of passivity. That's probably the most important thing I took from his book. It's better to be a great doer than a great thinker. I want to be the kind of person that makes things happen in the world, even though, as a Dreamer, I have a predilection to over-analyze, fancy, and let big Ideas live and die in my mind without ever becoming action.

So, if you are going to sit at the feet of a sage, and receive the gold nuggets of wisdom that the sage will bestow upon you, there's one thing you need to remember. Those gold nuggets are only worth anything if you cash them in. You cash them in through application.

You cash them in by picking out something that you can apply in your life, and doing it. It's not good to ask for advice from anyone without a *disposition to act.*

As someone who has sat comfortably in both the position of the learner and the sage, I'm going to tell you a secret. The key to any teacher's heart is students who apply what they've been taught. Why does a teacher teach? Why does a mentor…*ment*? It's because we honestly and truly get joy out of seeing people make progress. We get joy from changing lives. We get joy from making an impact. The best way you can say thank you to mentors is to let them in on a success story of how you applied what you learned from them.

So much of the point of this book reaches its zenith in this section. For much of this book, I have advocated for you to embrace your design, with its strengths and its weaknesses. But I will reiterate that it doesn't end there. I don't want you to explore and unlock your Superpower so you can just be super for yourself. Let Spiderman's Uncle Ben's last words echo in your soul: "With great power comes great responsibility." That responsibility is to the communities in which you participate.

The giving and receiving of mentorship is one of the most powerful ways that you can impact your community. Mentorship, and even brief mentorship moments, will accelerate your growth in ways you can't even imagine. And then you will be able to pass on the fruits of this growth to those who are coming up behind you.

3.10
Initiate Transparent Accountability

Unlike Wise Mentorship, Transparent Accountability generally happens at the peer level. When I'm sitting under a mentor, most of the energy and wisdom is flowing one direction, from the sage to the student. In my Transparent Accountability relationships, the energy and wisdom is flowing both directions.

The foundation of a Transparent Accountability relationship is trust and authenticity. It's difficult, if not impossible, to be vulnerable with someone you don't trust, and a Transparent Accountability relationship requires vulnerability. This is the person you hold nothing back from.

If you have a spouse, it is ideal that your spouse is number one in your life, in terms of vulnerability and authenticity and trust, but your marriage or committed romantic relationship is not a Transparent Accountability relationship.

The goal of marriage is partnership, and transcends accountability. It can be damaging to a marriage if you make it a primary goal of the relationship to hold each other accountable. This can lead to conflicting interests and a sense that you need to control or fix each other. Since a spouse's issues and weaknesses have such an immediate impact on the other spousal partner, it's very difficult to be objective in a marriage, and accountability needs a level of objectivity in order to be effective.

Everyone needs at least one mutual confidante in his or her life, outside of romantic or spousal partnerships. You need someone who knows the transparent depths of who you are, what you dream to accomplish, your strengths, and your weaknesses. You need someone who can settle you in truth, help you find your way when you've forgotten it, and help you remember who you are. This works best when you are mutually transparent, meaning each knows the other's strengths and weaknesses, hopes and fears, victories and failures.

The greatest impetus for a sustainable trust relationship is mutual vulnerability and transparency. If I share my darkest secrets with you, and you don't share yours with me, there will always be a sense of unreciprocated risk, which doesn't feel like safety in peer relationships.

Mutual vulnerability is the hallmark of a healthy Transparent Accountability relationship. I actually have a few of these relationships, which is rare. One is my brother in law, Drew, and the other is my friend Dan. I meet with each of them weekly. These men know all of my dirt. They know all of my failures and all of my struggles. They've both seen me at my worst, they've seen me in tears, they've seen me out of my mind with pain and grief. I've walked with them both in similar places.

I cannot tell you what a burden has been lifted from me, to know that there are people on this Earth who know, and continue to know, the depth of my imperfection, and still love me. These brothers would do just about anything for me, and I would for them. They hold me accountable in my marriage, and I do the same for them. They tell me the things I don't necessarily want to hear, and I do the same for them.

I can safely say I would not be the man I am today without these brothers pouring into my life. I'm telling you, I would not be as healthy. I would not be as mature. I would not be as strong. There are many more humans that I could point to as massive contributors in my life, but these are my anchors.

I realize that this chapter may be hard for some people. Most of us are longing for this kind of vulnerability, connection, and even accountability. Many of us have tried very, very hard, and failed very, very hard. The idea of being this vulnerable to another human being could even be triggering to some of you reading this.

Practically speaking, let me just acknowledge that this is a heavy lift, and all the heavier for the fact that not all of it is in your control. You only have control over yourself. You only have the ability to invite others into this kind of relationship and prepare yourself to be in this kind of relationship. Relationship is a heavy concrete block with four corners and two sides. You can only lift your side. The rest is up to someone else, and that's the dilemma. That's why there's such a draw towards individualism. Why not just spend your time lifting things that you can lift by yourself? Because there is a range of things that can be built using just your tiny blocks, and there's a whole world of things that can only be built with the blocks that take more than one person to lift. And it's really lonely carrying bricks back and forth across the yard by yourself. And you are not made to be alone even if you find yourself alone. Swimming in water doesn't mean I was made to live in water. We sometimes find ourselves in places we didn't want to be, and that we weren't designed to be, long term.

> Relationship is a heavy concrete block with four corners and two sides. You can only lift your side. The rest is up to someone else, and that's the dilemma.

I've been utterly, grievously alone in my life. And I'm a Connector, so that was really painful. Gut wrenching, really. Nothing can distort your heart to despair or hate like living in a state completely opposite to your design.

I've had seasons where there were too many people in my life, and I began to break under the weight of all the felt expectations.

And in all these moments I had choices. Not necessarily to fix things outright. Not the power to wave a magic wand and change my circumstance. But the power to keep trying to angle myself towards something better, or to give up. And sometimes we give up. And even that is a choice that can be undone.

I don't have a better answer, and I don't think anyone else has a better answer, then to aim a little higher, instead of aiming a little lower; 180° turns are rare. They happen, but they don't happen often, for good or for bad, for glory or for destruction. And it's arguable that many of the 180s we see are just a tipping point in a war of degrees. I've read a lot of books looking for a lot of answers, and the wise ones say, "Baby steps."

I want you to find your Transparent Accountability relationship. Maybe you have it. Maybe you have something close. Maybe you have a prospect. Maybe you're looking all around you, hand over your eyes, and all you see is the vast desert 360° around you. The only answer I have for any of us is take a baby step. And then another. And then another after that. Sprint if you can for a bit. Then back to baby stepping.

Some of these baby steps might include:

- Know thyself. Keep investing beyond this book. When you know yourself, then you can share yourself.
- Isolate your candidates for Transparent Accountability.
- Share something tender and true that you wouldn't normally share.
- Sign up to create shared experiences with a friend.
- Tell a hard truth in a loving way to someone you think is mature enough to handle it.
- Get a weekly or monthly time on the calendar with someone you trust. See if they're willing to accept an invitation from you to urge each other on.
- In your meetings with friends, take notes. Check in with their Big Dreams. Ask about their struggles.
- Do what you can do. Some people have the energy to try this kind of connection every day, some people have the energy to try once a week, or once a month. Do what you can do.

You might ask, "What if it doesn't work?"

My question for you is, "What if it does?"

And you might say, "What if I walk and walk, and never get anywhere, and it ends up that I wasted my time?" "What if the next step is the one that gets you to a new place?"

They're both hypotheticals with equal weight. Which one keeps you stepping, and which one doesn't? I don't mean to be flip. But in a war of hypotheticals, both sides carry equal weight.

One thousand successes doesn't guarantee you won't have a catastrophic failure. One thousand failures doesn't guarantee you won't have an amazing success. Yes, the math works the same with a million. In order to leave the realm of hypotheticals, you have to decide something without all the data, because you never have all the data. It's a leap.

I'm writing a fiction novel called "Solomen" about a wandering storyteller with a magical afro. In a certain chapter, he finds himself in the middle of a desert.

> "And when I opened my eyes,
> I beheld in front of me
> A great desert, called
> The Barren Desert,
>
> Which no man can cross
> Or ever has or ever will.
>
> Across the great desert,
> In the heat-deformed distance
> I saw the Radiant City,
>
> Spires beckoning like ironic fingers.
>
> And it was so beautiful,
> It broke my heart like
> Fresh, steaming bread.
>
> I wept and wept,
> And the sun kissed
> My tears into vapor.

The Superpower Quest

> And I was parched
> Enough to cough.
>
> I looked behind me,
> Intending to turn back,
> But there was only
> Desert.
>
> And at that moment,
> I purposed in my heart,
> That I would rather die
> Forward than back."

Pick the direction you'd rather die in. I don't think there's another way, beloved. Fight your war of degrees, and know that the war is not over even if you take many clicks backward.

In the words of my favorite poet and rapper, Propaganda, "You don't gotta be fast, just don't run out of gas…"

3.11
Legos

This *Join Forces* section may be really encouraging for some people, but it may be hard for some people. That makes total sense to me. I've been living in this world for a while. I've lived through a pandemic, and watched what that did to us. I've lived in an age where there's more access to distraction and entertainment than ever before. I live in a world where we are constantly connected to one another through social media, and yet people are saying they are desperately lonely and something is wrong. Talking about community in our age of loneliness can feel like reading the Chick-fil-A menu to a starving man.

As I take a moment to think about how people might react to this chapter, or questions they might have, the question echoing in my mind is "How?" I don't know if that's everyone's question, but I can imagine it is the question for some.

Let me empathize for a moment if you're an Organizer, a Leader, or an Achiever on this journey with me. What I have to say is important, but it's coming from a Dreamer, and a Connector, and I know it probably feels like I'm speaking a foreign language sometimes. My wife is a Leader/Organizer, and sometimes she just stares at me like a riddle and a joke book had a baby. With her very presence in my life, she has helped me to bridge the gap to you, but I'm still me, and some of this stuff can't be put into an equation.

The Superpower Quest

Anyway, back to the question: "How, guy?"

"Can everyone do this *Join Forces* thing? What if I'm antisocial? What if I'm painfully introverted? What if I'm in a place where the people around me don't accept me? What if *Tending My Garden* and *Making Swapsies* and *Creating Dream Teams* seem frivolous and out of reach, based on my situation? Are these *Joining Forces* tips something that only the people with strong relational Hero Types like the Nurturer and Connector can do? And if anyone can do it, then how do I start? And what if this seems totally overwhelming to me? What if I have a major weakness in this area? What if I have trauma associated with being vulnerable?"

> I have decided to stand here, because to decide to stand, or to decide not to stand, both carry enormous risk. Neither is safe. One or the other must be done.

Some of these are practical questions, and some of these are heart questions. I've learned that you can't answer heart questions with data. Some of them can't be answered at all. I'll do my best to give an answer by reframing the questions a bit, and revisiting some core assumptions.

The entire premise of this book is founded on a series of core assumptions. I listed those assumptions earlier in the book. Those assumptions are either true, or they're not true. If they're not true, then this book is not true. Everyone has to choose the core assumptions that they will accept or not accept, and many of these core assumptions are impossible to prove or disprove in the framework of observable, quantifiable phenomena.

I'm saying that we have a design, and that this design is intentional. Many people of many faiths and philosophies believe this to be self-evident, just as I do. On the other hand, many people with many faiths and philosophies are either unconvinced or opposed to this view. I am not here to defend or to prove this view. I didn't come here to dig up the ground, I came here to build a house. This house only works if the foundation can hold it up. In my observation and experience, it does hold.

SECTION 3 | Join Forces

I admit to you that my starting place may be flawed, just as my understanding is flawed. But I have decided to stand here, because to decide to stand, or to decide not to stand, both carry enormous risk. Neither is safe. One or the other must be done.

So, I have to answer these questions first from the foundation of this work, since they are questions that strike down to that foundation.

I'm not only saying that we have a design, and the design is intentional. I am also saying that part of the intentionality of that design is that it requires communities to be fully expressed. Your design needs community like plants need water. No water, no plant.

Your potential requires community in order to be realized. This can look a lot of ways, and I'm not here to say what this has to look like, but the maxim is true, because it's rooted in the fundamental principle of design. You need others.

Do we have seasons of aloneness? Do we have seasons of isolation? Sure. Is this a perpetual condition that we were designed for? Not a bit.

I am saying we are designed to depend upon and to serve our communities. I do not mean this only in the sacrificial sense. I do not mean this to say that we were created to serve our communities and not ourselves. I mean to say that we were designed to serve our communities and ourselves, and that the greatest service we can do for ourselves is, in fact, the robust service of others. This robust service is a priority above service to ourselves, but not to the exclusion of it. I'm eating delicious Qdoba chips and queso as I write you this book, and it is well.

Self-sacrifice has a beautiful role in life, but that's not the picture I'm painting here. I'm painting a picture of a Lego table, where unique Legos of all colors, shapes, and sizes, are fitted together to create things of beauty and utility. Where every Lego, from the largest to the smallest, from the dullest to the brightest, has a place where it fits. Legos serve by the very essence of being what they are.

A Lego by itself is a tragedy to any creative child with big dreams of beautiful things. That is because there is no such thing as Lego, only Legos. "Lego" makes no sense without "Legos."

"Me" makes no sense without "us." An acceptance that you are not here for only you, but that you are actually here for others, is a kind of sacrifice, isn't it? And at the same time, it's an invitation into a joy that can't be purchased any other way.

My daughter, Eliya, has an incredible knack for baking. At the age of twelve, she's a magical baker. She loves baking; but it's not just the baking. She loves to give gifts that make people happy. This makes her happy. I'll be sitting in my office, working, and she will come up behind me silently, plate in hand, with some delightful thing or another. Most recently, it was a key lime tart. Then she'll lay the plate on my desk and give me a hug. Then, she waits for me to take a bite, eyes riveted, attentive. What is she waiting for? She wants to see the reaction, close up. She wants to see how her treats bring joy to her people. "How was it, Daddy?"

This is service. But is it sacrifice? I say "yes," in the most beautiful sense, and also, "no!" Yes, in the sense that she must go, and measure, and make her mistakes, and clean up her messes, and not all of this is joy. But it is all worth it for the joy of bringing other people joy. We are Legos. We interlock, and fit our designs together to create even bigger, more beautiful designs. This is one of the places where she "fits" in our family community. She's brought a thousand genuine smiles to the faces of her family and friends through her baking, and she'll bring ten thousand more.

So, can everyone Join Forces? Yes! It is not only possible, it is essential for you to see who you really are.

What about trauma? Trauma is real. Your design is also real. Your essential need for community is also real. How do we reconcile those three realities into anything that approximates a strategy? That's beyond my vision for you—I can't see your life, your trajectory, your healing, or any of the ways you will grow and change in the future.

I can only say that I know you have a design that is no accident, and your need for community is no accident, and your journey through life is no accident. And I know these things, only because I know them. And if I have expectation for you to know your design, and your Superpowers and Weak Spots, and learn to Join Forces wisely within your various communities, and to gain wise tools for your Utility Belt, it is only because you were designed for this.

I hope that this chapter provides you with the beginnings of a map to navigate from embracing your design to embracing your community via your design. Your communities need what you have as much as you need your communities. Your job community (or at least, the right job community) needs you. Your family and friend communities are not the same without you. Your groups and gatherings are not the same without you.

In *The Power of Who*, Bob Beaudine says, "Go where you're celebrated, not just tolerated."[11] This is true. Go forth and interlock with others to create beautiful things. Together.

SECTION 4
Build Your Utility Belt

4.1
Utility Belt

Many superheroes have a Utility Belt, which is kind of like their portable toolbox containing their most effective tools and weapons for winning the day. I imagine it's good for car keys and cell phones, too. Every hero needs a great Utility Belt, and I'm here to help you build yours.

Scream "Turtle Power!" if you hear me. Bonus points if you do it out loud. Extra bonus points if you decline to explain to the people around you why you did it.

I've been on a life journey for forty-eight years at the time of writing this book. I've seen good days and bad days. I've seen grief and joy. So much of life is struggle. When I was young, it just felt like survival. I found myself in a hostile world that seemed dead set on my demise. I didn't see myself as someone with a future. And if you don't see yourself as someone with a future, you tend to emphasize entertainment and escape over an investment in your own growth and development. When you are surviving, you don't see yourself as someone who is building something. Survival is good, but it's not living. This concept hearkens back to Maslow's Hierarchy of Needs.

Maslow's Hierarchy

Abraham Maslow was a well-known psychologist in the field of human motivation and psychology. His "Hierarchy of Needs" suggests that individuals have innate needs, and these needs must be fulfilled in a hierarchical order to achieve optimal personal growth.

In the hierarchy, there are five main levels of needs. In illustrations, these are usually depicted in the shape of a pyramid. From the bottom to the pinnacle, these needs are:

#1. Physiological Needs

These are the basic things you need to survive. These include food and water, shelter, sleep, and other physical necessities.

#2. Safety Needs

Only after physiological needs are met can you focus on safety needs, such as safety and security. Safety needs include personal security, financial sufficiency, health, and protection from physical danger.

#3. Love and Belongingness Needs

Once safety needs have been fulfilled, you can seek social interaction, love, loyalty, and a sense of belonging. You need meaningful relationships. You need family and friendships. You need to experience being part of a community.

#4. Esteem Needs

Once love and belongingness needs are met, you can seek self-esteem and recognition. You can now satisfy your drive to receive respect from others, achieving a sense of success, and cultivating self-confidence.

#5. Self-Actualization:

Self-actualization refers to the desire to fulfill your potential. This is the highest need in the hierarchy and reflects becoming the best version of yourself. This stage involves personal growth and self-fulfillment. In Self-actualization, you pursue individual goals, and realize your true capabilities.

Maslow believed that people proceed through these stages in a sequential manner, from the bottom of the pyramid to the top. He posited that lower-level needs had to be fulfilled before higher-level needs can even become feasible as motivators. Maslow also left room for nuance and exceptions; human motives don't always follow a logical or structured course. People's unique experiences and situations can always influence the prioritization of their motivations.

Maslow's hierarchy of needs has been influential in many fields, and has found widespread acceptance in psychological frameworks. I find it useful in understanding human motivations and the paths of personal development. It also sheds some light on my own story and experiences.

You can learn more about the Hierarchy of Needs in Maslow's book, *A Theory of Human Motivation*,[1] which I have researched around, but have not read myself.

Surviving to Thriving

People generally don't seem to be able to devote time and energy to their higher-level needs of purpose and fulfillment, until they have taken care of their more basic and primal needs.

The first twenty years of my life felt like striving to get above water so that I could breathe. Fear and anxiety were so prevalent in my life, they became like the repetitive sound you forget is there. I wonder how many people feel like that, living a life where anxiety is the constant background track?

Part of my healing process was watching my wife's reactions to my life stories. She would sometimes wince, sometimes tear up, sometimes get angry. She gave me an outside perspective that helped me begin to understand that my childhood wasn't "normal." Or maybe it was normal, in the sense that many people have traumatic childhoods. But it was not healthy. It wasn't fine.

We probably all have childhood trauma to work through. But we're generally not going to work through it unless we intentionally give ourselves permission. And we're not going to give ourselves permission unless we can accept the ramifications of admitting that everything wasn't fine, and facing up to the things that weren't fine. It's much easier to leave the past in the past, than to dredge it up; especially if you're a functioning person. It can seem pointless to rock the boat.

But so much of life is alignment with truth, and challenging the narrative that we've embraced, if it conflicts with the truth, is painful. Author John Delony talks about this in-depth in his book *Own Your Past Change Your Future: A Not-So-Complicated Approach to Relationships, Mental Health & Wellness*.

"This book is about stories. The stories you are born into, the stories you are told, the stories that happened, and the stories you tell yourself...These stories carry physical weight and impact our bodies and minds and become our mental and physical health, faith, and future."[2]

My wife's compassion in helping me challenge my stories has enhanced my mental health, and helped me to mature in my thinking.

We are truly effective and healthy in life to the extent that our fundamental assumptions about life are based on truth. And this is just plain difficult. We are complex beings with complex perception. It is a lifelong process to try and orient ourselves towards the actual truth at every turn. This is the ever-expanding process called wisdom.

My parents loved me. But they also damaged me. To say that they were imperfect, or even destructive, was not to say that they are not good people worthy of love. I now have loving relationships with both of my parents. In honor of them, I will not go into detail about the specifics, nor do I blame them for being imperfect. Now, as a father of four, I have great appreciation and understanding for the complexities of being a flawed and imperfect human raising other humans.

I can acknowledge that things were wrong in my upbringing, and that the consequences were real without a.) using this as a blanket excuse for all my faults, b.) rendering my parents as villains, or c.) comparing my traumas with the traumas of others to determine if mine are valid. They are valid.

I can just say, "Dang…some of that was really messed up, and I'm not crazy to grieve. The scars I wear are not fabricated. I have been harmed and I do need healing."

Swimming up from the depths of my childhood has been like the process of ascending Maslow's hierarchy.

#1. Physiological Needs

My needs for food, water, shelter, clothing, etc. were always taken care of by my parents. My dad worked long hours, and my mom was a stay-at-home mom for much of my childhood. I'm grateful to say that I was not worried about my physiological needs.

#2. Safety Needs

In my old neighborhood, the best scenario was not to be noticed. Leaving the neighborhood of my upbringing and going to college provided a measure of physical safety that I had never experienced before. Prior to that I was in fear of bullies and gang members.

#3. Love and Belongingness Needs and #4. Esteem Needs

Healthy relationships in college began to provide some emotional safety and a sense of self-worth. I found out that I was good at connecting and inspiring people around me. I had a crew around me for the first time, bound together over creative endeavors such as art and poetry. We threw multiple successful open mics on campus. I felt that I had the respect and love of people that I respected and loved. That was glorious!

#5. Self-Actualization

First, let me say that I don't like this term "self-actualization." When I hear it, it tends to carry a connotation of untethered personal freedom to "be whoever we want to be." It seems mostly used in the promotion of narcissism. I don't know whether or not this is how Maslow meant it, but the way I mean it includes the reality of design, purpose, and virtue. Self-actualization is the wrestling down to a deep clarity of purpose that enables a person to live an effective life in line with deep and virtuous conviction. It involves knowing oneself and being one's best. You could say this entire book takes place inside the pinnacle of Maslow's hierarchy.

If you subscribe to the fact that you have to gain victory in all four lower tiers in order to approach the fifth tier of Self Actualization, then it's ironic to think that the most foundational fifth tier is by far the easiest to take for granted. It is the easiest to miss. It is the easiest to ignore. It is the easiest to save for later. One of the great tragedies of life is that it is certainly possible to live all your life without a higher purpose. Even as I write this, the veracity of this statement is chilling to me.

Simply put, your Utility Belt is your unique toolbox full of tools for living. I mean *living* in Maslow's Tier 5 sense of living effectively and living with purpose, as opposed to the Tier 1 sense of basic physical survival.

You may be locked into one of the four lower tiers at the time you're reading this book. I know what it's like to be in that place. I know that swimming up from those depths can be agonizingly slow. I also know that knowing a good destination exists can help to inspire the hope and determination required to reach that destination. Is this book anything less than a trumpet in the streets, calling you higher? I'm indeed calling you higher. I'm calling myself higher. This is so much of the purpose that I have found inside that fifth tier of Maslow's pyramid.

This section of the book will document my journey. This is an effort to share my Utility Belt with you. My Utility Belt represents decades of living and striving. Decades of tears and laughter. You will not use all the tools in my tool belt. You may not use any of them. Your tool belt is uniquely yours and contains your own hard-fought life's wisdom.

Finding Your Tools

My dad is a mechanic. So often when I would see him, his hands were black with engine grease. He used to call engine grime, "clean dirt." That metallic, musky smell comforts me to this day.

Bonus Content: For more about my dad, and what he means to me, check out my poem "Father's Touch" at **superpowerquest.com/resources**

My dad has hundreds of tools. When he sent me off into adulthood, he gave me a toolbox and filled it with the handful of tools that he deemed most essential. It was not intended to be my complete, lifelong toolbox. It was a seed. It was a starter; and it was incredibly useful for me to launch out with tools of my own that I could test and utilize. I hope to do that for you. I hope to give you a toolbox and a few starter tools to begin, but not to complete, your journey towards ultimate effectiveness and joy.

> I hope to give you a toolbox and a few starter tools to begin, but not to complete, your journey towards ultimate effectiveness and joy.

If you are a mechanic, you are constantly growing your tool set. You run into new situations and edge cases as you tinker with cars over the decades, and you purchase new specialty tools to deal with those edge cases. Your Utility Belt is like that. I don't think it ever stops growing, because you never stop growing and gaining experience.

There are many uses for the word "tool". On a basic level, tools fix problems and create efficiencies. For the purposes of the Utility Belt, the word "tool" can refer to any useful piece of knowledge that helps you live a more effective life. It can refer to a system, a maxim, a process, or a framework.

I'm sure you already have many tools that you have adopted. You may just not have named them yet. As I share with you the words that I've given for my tool set, I hope that it will help you awaken the names of yours.

There are two categories of ways to manage, and even harness, your Weak Spot. *Joining Forces*, discussed in the previous chapter, was the first. *Building Your Utility Belt* is the second. This section delivers hacks and systems that can help you compensate and overcome your Weak Spot.

I am a big fan of the "easy button." Greg McKeown's bestselling book, *Effortless: Make It Easier to Do What Matters Most*, has had a huge influence on me. The book taught me to be constantly open to finding ways to make your essential tasks easier. McKeown notes that

The Superpower Quest

many of us tend to idolize hard work as an end unto itself, rather than choosing efficiency and ease where possible. This happens when we get locked into routines and don't zoom out to look for better ways to do things. Work ethic is great. But you can have a great work ethic, and spend ten hours on something that could have been accomplished in two hours. Poor judgment cancels out the benefits of a good work ethic, and we end up wasting energy that could have been spent on something important.

"What if, rather than fighting our preprogrammed instinct to seek the easiest path, we could embrace it, even use it to our advantage? What if, instead of asking, 'How can I tackle this really hard but essential project?,' we simply inverted the question and asked, 'What if this essential project could be made easy?'"[3]

To this principle, I will add another dimension, factoring in your unique design: You are operating in your most effortless state when you are working within your Superpower. You are generally wasting time and energy if you are grinding things out in your Weak Spot areas. This must, sometimes, be done, but it should be done sparingly. And if there are tools that can help you limit, or eliminate the grind, why not use them to your advantage?

The Utility Belt is usually worn by superheroes who don't have official, supernatural powers, or who need a boost in battle. These belts contain gadgets that help their owners gain the upper hand on their opponents. The Utility Belt might contain explosives, or weapons, or tracking devices, or grappling hooks. There's no end to the possibilities. The concept of the Utility Belt originated with Batman, from DC comics.

Applied to comics, I am using the phrase, Utility Belt, to refer to a broader category of technological or mystical enablement. This can include super-suits, such as those worn by Iron Man and Ant-Man. It also refers to implements, such as Thor's hammer, or Dr. Strange's flying cape, or Green Lantern's ring.

Some heroes have powers that live inside of them, and can be accessed at will. Some heroes have power as a benefit and byproduct of something outside of themselves. All of the latter fit into the category of Utility Belt.

I want to help you build your own personal arsenal of tips and tricks and techniques that will help you mitigate your Weak Spot areas, and even potentially turn those areas into areas of strength. Your Utility Belt will be unique to you. There is no one-size-fits-all solution. Our weaknesses are diverse, and so must be our methods to address them.

I have collected dozens, if not hundreds, of tools over the years. Some have come from mentors. Some have come from books. Some have worked well for me, and some I have discarded. Some worked for a season, only to be replaced by better tools. Building your Utility Belt is a journey that never ends. Just as heroes are constantly improving and upgrading their gadgets, you should be looking for new and better ways to accentuate your strengths and mitigate your weaknesses. For now, there is important work to be done—important, because having taken the time to identify your Weak Spot, you now have an opportunity to achieve truly amazing things. You must first learn to steward it well.

In the Merriam-Webster dictionary, Stewardship is defined as "the conducting, supervising, or managing of something."[4] Stewardship is a responsibility—something that can be done well or poorly. I am a steward of my money, my family, and my job duties. I want to take these responsibilities seriously. I want to execute these responsibilities with excellence. Part of honoring your design is learning to steward your Weak Spot. Supervise your Weak Spot. Conduct your Weak Spot, like a symphony. What a different mindset about weakness than the one we are generally taught! This perspective will guide you into a growth and productivity mindset instead of a punishment mindset, or a shame mindset. You have been given both strengths and weaknesses to manage. How will you manage them both well? Joining Forces, covered in the previous chapter, is one way. Utility Belt is another.

This is the question to be asking yourself as you delve into potential tools and elements for your Utility Belt. How can I manage my Weak Spot well? What systems can I implement, and what tools can I use, to thrive in my areas of weakness?

The Superpower Quest

Helen Keller

At the time of writing this section, I'm reading the autobiography of Helen Keller, *The Story of My Life*.[5] This book offers a beautiful illustration of the principle I'm trying to convey in this chapter. The right compilation of tools, systems, and hacks (aka your Utility Belt) can enable us to navigate our limitations, and to some degree, even transcend them.

Helen Keller faced incredible limitations. She was both deaf and blind. However, she was able to live a life of notable achievement. She was famous and influential in her time. She was able to thrive because of the love and investment of a teacher, Anne Sullivan, who took the time to give her—by touch alone—a full and robust education. I would dare to call this a customized Utility Belt that enabled her to flourish.

Sullivan inherited and developed a complete educational system that bypassed Helen's sensory limitations, utilizing touch as the mode of communication. Through time, the teacher was able to convey complex ideas through the writing of English letters upon Keller's open palm. They spent immeasurable hours in nature, with the teacher giving Helen objects to touch, and spelling the names into her palm.

This was one of many systems and habits utilized to foster the radical growth and development of her pupil.

With creativity, resilience, and time, Keller learned a way of living that enabled her to accomplish amazing, seemingly impossible feats of imagination and intellect. She was an author of many books, and a lecturer on behalf of the American Foundation of the Blind.

She never had an "ordinary" life. She was never cured of blindness, or given the ability to hear. But in her autobiography, she describes a rich life, full of wonder and meaning. She achieved, within her limitations, the thing that we all long for— she achieved a life of impact.

This would not have been possible if Sullivan had not been willing and able to invest the massive time and energy to give her the tools and systems she needed to be able to interpret and navigate a complex and dangerous world, in spite of her limitations. Sullivan, and other mentors along the way helped Keller fill her Utility Belt with the tools of success. Joining Forces is a prerequisite for how we build our Utility Belts over time.

Keller's Utility Belt comprised many tools, including memorization of her environment, navigation through touch, palm spelling, lip reading by touch, and eventually braille. Keller learned how to communicate via an interpreter. She learned how to type. She harnessed her matchless determination and intellect to find a path towards effectiveness and impact. And I would guess that there were many more tools, methods, and systems that enabled her to navigate her physical environment as well as the mental and imaginative environment of self-expression.

The story of Helen Keller is an extreme case that offers hope to many. Some reading this book may very well deal with physical, mental, or emotional disabilities. Some may deal with particular talent deficits and capability issues, which is this book's primary area of concern. I do not seek to make these limitations (disability and talent deficit) equivalent in nature; nor do I claim to know what it's like to live with physical or mental disabilities. I use Helen Keller as an example only in the sense that she, having encountered serious limitations beyond her control, was able to face, embrace, and ultimately overcome those limitations in a way that, I hope, inspires each of us to positively confront and overcome our own limitations, whatever they may be.

At this point, you have identified the areas of weakness and limitation that must be addressed in order for you to truly thrive and to be effective in the world. What are the tools, systems, and habits that can help you achieve greater impact?

What follows is a list of methods and frameworks for enhancing your Superpower and stewarding your Weak Spot. This list is not comprehensive—there must be millions of tools and systems out there, and no one person's collection of tools will be 100% transferable to any other person. We are far too unique and nuanced for that. Just like I can't look at someone with vision problems and just give them my prescription for eyeglasses, I can't give anyone else my Utility Belt and expect it to work for them. I have chosen a variety of tools below to address many different types of Weak Spots, but consider this the beginning of a lifelong journey to collect the right tools that work for you.

Utility Belt Map

The following table is a place to collect notes from your journey through this section of the book. Once completed, you will be able to see in one place all the five tools that you most want to implement (or keep implementing) in your life. These may be tools you encounter in this section, or other tools that you already use in your life, and want to double down on.

As noted above, you can also input your answers into your online hero profile at superpowerquest.com/myprofile

Superpower Quest Hero Profile

SECTION 4 | Build Your Utility Belt

Tool Name	How It Works	How Will You Use It In Your Life?

4.2
Pursue Truth

I'll never forget the sound of my father's weeping. It was right after the divorce. I was thirteen. My brothers and I were on visitation with my dad. We only got to see him on Sundays now. He was driving us to his tiny apartment. He began to make a strangled coughing sound, and I realized with a jolt that he was crying. My big, black, muscle-bound dad was crying like a child in front of us. My whole life, I had never seen him cry. And here he was, completely undone before me. It was almost feral, like watching an animal bleed out. My stomach tightened and I felt the wailing sound brand itself onto my soul.

This is a vignette from my father's defining moment. This was his second divorce. His second bout with some of the greatest misery a human can endure. I get the distinct sense, now, that my dad was looking for a reason to live.

In this season of desperation, he began studying the world religions. Spent time with books like the Quran and the Book of Mormon. He told me later he didn't care which one was right. He didn't have a dog in the fight. He just wanted to know the truth. His life depended on it. He eventually found his way to the Bible, and that was where his search ended.

My dad has an intensity about him. Age has mellowed him out, so you can easily miss it. But get him talking about the right topic and you will see his eyes sharpen, and his back straighten.

The Superpower Quest

If there's one thing that I've learned from my dad, it's that intensity in regards to mental exercise. My dad grew up in a very poor household in Chicago with eight siblings. He was the pensive one; the thinker. To this day he handwrites massive treatises on theology that perhaps no one has ever read, or ever will read. He's not afraid to think. Thinking is a worthy endeavor; an end unto itself. I think he would say the primary reason for existence is to discover the truth through strenuous mental exercise.

This is the fundamental lesson that I learned from my father: the serious pursuit of truth. The willingness to engage in deep mental exercise. In a sense, it's the tool that makes all my other tools possible.

We can know truth. The pursuit of truth is the foundational usage of the human mind. This may sound self-evident. However, we can tout this as self-evident without living as if it were true.

We live in a time in which it's easy to embrace the view that there are many truths. This is the idea of relativism. However, if there can be many contradicting truths, then there is no truth. In a world where the truth is relative, a serious and dedicated pursuit of truth makes no sense.

There's a huge difference between searching for a treasure that might exist versus a treasure that does exist. You cannot rally the same fortitude to pursue a possibility that you can rally for a certainty.

I remember I was trying to repair the kids' trampoline, and I dropped a screw into the grass. It was a screw that I needed. I didn't have any others like it. I began searching through the grass, peeling through the layers with my fingers. After many minutes of searching, I couldn't find it. I was about to give up in relative despair. But then a thought echoed through my head: "The screw exists. It HAS to be here somewhere." For some reason, the affirmation of that reality eliminated my despair, and I made a pact to myself that I wasn't going to give up until I found it. The reality that I knew, beyond the shadow of a doubt, that there was something there to be found, was the reality that galvanized my ability to search and keep searching. Eventually, I did find it.

I believe that truth exists, and that truth can be leveraged to improve my circumstances. So I give thanks to my dad; the eccentric, solitary mechanic, war veteran, Jesus follower, who was still driving forklifts for the U.S. post office 'till he was like seventy-eight.

I'll never forget the way he looked at me when I graduated high school. My Chicago ghetto dad, who has known racism, and poverty, and traumas untold. I had received my diploma, and I had come back from the platform to sit with my dad and my brothers. After the ceremony was over, I had to decide if I was going to party with my friends or come back home with my family. I remember I was standing up, and my dad was just staring at me. He had a faraway look in his eyes, and he was tearing up. I'd been accepted to Colorado State University. Neither my dad, nor anybody in his family, had ever gone to college. I can still feel the weight of those eyes; deep and brown with longing and pride. He said, "I'm proud of you, son." I didn't go and party with my friends. I went home with my dad.

> You can't let feelings drive your life. Feelings have an incredibly important role, but it's not unquestioned leadership.

You did not do everything well, Daddy. You were a working single father of teens, trying to figure it all out. But you loved me, and you earnestly longed for my success, in the way of a true father. You longed for me to go further than you, instead of holding me back. You gave me a platform to launch from. You taught me to strive, pursue, suffer, and long for the truth, for the truth is worthy.

Feelings are the Caboose

Another tool that attaches to the first tool, *Pursuit of Truth*, is the idea that "Feelings are the Caboose." This helps me to place my feelings in the right position, relative to truth.

I once had a mentor tell me, "Feelings are the caboose, not the engine." Shout out to Robin! In other words, you can't let feelings drive your life. Feelings have an incredibly important role, but it's not unquestioned leadership.

A feeling is true in the sense that it is an experience that I'm having. If I feel sad, then it's true that I feel sad. Sadness can be an emotional reality. This reality is important, and valid, and not to be stuffed down, or denied, or ashamed of.

But just because it can be true that I feel sad, this doesn't mean that what my sadness is telling me is true. For example, I might tell one of my daughters that she cannot have ice cream. This might make her sad. Her sadness might become a conviction that I'm being unfair. Whether or not I'm being unfair is a completely separate matter from how she feels.

In a life dedicated to truth, it's important to understand the role and function of feelings, and to give them their proper weight as an indicator of reality outside of themselves. Just because I feel something about the world, doesn't mean the thing I'm feeling about the world is true. I may feel the world is unfair, or out to get me. I may feel that I will never be successful. I may feel that I'm never wrong, and that I'm justified in all of my actions. All of these feelings are claims about reality that need to be evaluated, and can be found to be true or untrue.

It is important to be able to detach and observe your feelings. Be curious, not condemning. Notice your feelings. Notice the claims they might be making about reality. Then evaluate those claims based on more evidence than how you feel.

Let me emphasize here that I don't believe feelings are to be discarded. Your feelings are incredibly useful when it comes to self-discovery. They are an indication that introspection is needed. Feelings can also be accurate intuition about things that are happening around you. *Know Thyself* is the cry of the Superpower Quest. How can you know yourself if you ignore and abandon your feelings? Your feelings are a part of who you are.

Think of feelings as the starting point of a journey of discovery. Let's say I have a bad feeling about a person. For some reason I feel that I cannot trust them. This is a signal for me to tug on the rope of the feeling and see what lies on the other end. It could be a variety of things. It could be that I have unresolved conflict with that person. Maybe they hurt my feelings. It could be a misunderstanding that I need to clear up with that person. It could be that this person is legitimately toxic. Or I might find at the end of the rope that it's tied to nothing; it's just a raw intuition. Should this intuition be discarded? Probably not. But it probably shouldn't be treated as gospel truth either.

Most of the time, when I have an unexplainable feeling, and I start tugging on the rope, I find my own insecurity at the other end of the rope. It's incredibly useful and liberating be able to see that and say, "Oh that's my insecurity!" Since I readily acknowledge that insecurity is my Weak Spot, and I don't want to live a life that is ruled by insecurity, I end up with the ability to make a choice rather than being carried along by my subconscious predilections.

The Journaling Method
One of the ways I take the time to sort through my feelings and identify truth is by writing. People journal for all kinds of reasons. At the core, journaling helps us achieve a reflective state and get our thoughts and feelings out into the open. Tim Ferris, a successful author, entrepreneur, and thought leader, talks about how he uses journaling to clarify his mind on his web site, *The Blog of Tim Ferris*. This is a bit meta, because I'm quoting Tim Ferris who is quoting Julia Cameron in his quote.

"I don't journal to 'be productive.' I don't do it to find great ideas, or to put down prose I can later publish. The pages aren't intended for anyone but me. Morning pages are, as author Julia Cameron puts it, 'spiritual windshield wipers.' It's the most cost-effective therapy I've ever found. To quote her further, from page viii: 'Once we get those muddy, maddening, confusing thoughts [nebulous worries, jitters, and preoccupations] on the page, we face our day with clearer eyes.'
[Back to Tim speaking] Please reread the above quote. It may be the most important aspect of trapping thought on paper (i.e. writing) you'll ever encounter. Even if you consider yourself a terrible writer, writing can be viewed as a tool that you can and should use. There are huge benefits to writing, even if no one—yourself included—ever reads what you write. In other words, the process matters more than the product."[6]

I love Ferris's description of writing as "trapping thought on paper," and the idea that "the process matters more than the product." Journaling is an incredibly powerful tool in the Utility Belt.

Journaling is so important to my life, that I will write in great detail about the "Right Side Up Journal" by Alan Briggs, which is a tool that I use daily to bring focus and structure to my days. This journal is a reflective tool, but it also functions for me as a complete life system. Of all the tools I discuss in this Utility Belt section, the "Right Side Up Journal" has had the most practical, measurable impact in my life. I will dive into that later.

Use the *Pursue Truth* principle to ground yourself in your journey. This will help you become humble and open to the truth, even if the truth is inconvenient. In fact, it is the inconvenient truths that often lead to the most growth. For those who wish to grow, the pursuit of truth is a necessary foundation.

4.3
Push the Easy Button

I was a teacher at a high school for at-risk kids in my early to mid-twenties. These were intense, sleepless times. During the days, I prepared and taught lessons for amazing, troubled, sometimes violent kids. Many nights I went out as the wingman for Tim, who was recognized and respected on the streets and within the two local gangs. We did street intervention together, rolling around in his beat-up car to the hotspots of the city, looking for trouble so we could defuse it.

Tim basically gave me a genius-level education on conflict resolution. Watching him was like watching a magician. There are a lot of amazing things I could say about Tim.

But this chapter is about something I learned in the classroom. More accurately, it is something I began to learn in the classroom and have continued to learn and refine throughout the intervening decades: The Easy Button.

The science teacher in the school was a man named Bruce Hallman. He was deeply respected by the students, and was an able mentor for younger teachers, like me. He was the kind of teacher who passionately loved his subject and was able to make science fun for the students.

I'll never forget that he once told me that the sun is so hot, that if you had a piece of the sun the size of a grain sand, and you put it at the top of the capitol building in Denver, about 100 miles away from us in Fort Collins, that it would kill us all by burning us alive, even at that distance.

That's a great picture of how Bruce used strange facts and illustrations to captivate the minds of his students. He took such glee in grossing them out and shocking them. What an incredible teacher.

I was wrapping up my grading one year. I had one of those red teacher notebooks where you input all the scores and add them up. This was tedious work that took hours. I hated it. Hated it. My guts were screaming. I just wanted to get done so that I could feel the summer sky on my skin and frolic through the grass.

Bruce came in. He was done with his grading for the year. He saw me struggling and told me he had a better way. Something called Microsoft Excel. I was resistant. I didn't really like learning new processes, and I was afraid of technology. Plus, I had already done most of my grading in the manual format. He pushed and prodded and persisted until I finally yielded. I remember thinking, "What's this guy's deal? Why is he pushing me so hard?"

He sat me down and taught me how to use Excel. And then I understood.

Before you knew it, I was set up with auto-calculating spreadsheets that I used every day the following year to track attendance and input grades. When it was time to finish up grades at the end of the year, it took a fraction of the time.

This was a moment when it dawned upon me that difficult things could be made easier. My default mindset had been a fatalistic resignation to the necessity of grinding out unpleasant tasks. This just seemed to be a fact of life. The idea that I could use systems or technology to radically reduce the time investment of unpleasant tasks was a revelation.

The book I've read that best sums up, and expands upon, the tool that I'm calling the *Easy Button* is the book *Effortless: Make It Easier to Do What Matters Most* by Greg McKeown, mentioned elsewhere in this book. In his book, McKeown advocates that we develop a perspective in which we are constantly asking, "How can this essential task be easier?"[7] This enables us to stay open to the possibility that there are better ways to execute our tasks that free up time to invest in our greatest passions and priorities.

This principle has changed my life and the lives of people around me. Every week I meet for two hours with one of my closest friends, my brother-in-law Drew Bartels. We share everything and hold each other accountable to our goals. I shared with him what I've been learning from the book *Effortless*. Drew is a born encourager. He is a Nurturer/Achiever with a Superpower of inviting people into community, and helping them move forward towards their goals. In typical form, Drew got excited about what I was learning, applied it to his own life, and we began encouraging each other to look for more opportunities to push the *Easy Button*. He even bought me a big red button with the words Easy Button on it, that shouts "That was easy," whenever you push it.

> This is the power of the Easy Button. You look for ways to achieve big wins by creating systems of efficiency and economies of scale. You look for ways to leverage your life and leverage your schedule.

One of my big goals for the year from my *Growth Game Plan*, (another tool that I'm going to talk about in depth later,) was to set up recurring weekly dates with each of my three children who are still at home. I was struggling to figure out a time to make this happen consistently. I shared my frustrations with Drew. He looked at my schedule and encouraged me to push the *Easy Button*.

I pick up my kids from school every Tuesday at 3:30 p.m. Why not go an hour early and take one kid per week out of school an hour early to have a daddy date while I was already in the neighborhood?

I did this, and was able to achieve a level of consistency that is very difficult to achieve for a person like me who lacks time awareness and conscientiousness. My kids love their hour, and they are jealous over it. They never forget when it's their turn.

This is the power of the Easy Button. You look for ways to achieve big wins by creating systems of efficiency and economies of scale. You look for ways to leverage your life and leverage your schedule. You take the time and apply the mental energy to find easy, obvious answers to complex questions.

To tie this back to the main subject, working more within your area of Superpower is the ultimate way to enter an effortless way of being. Work done inside your area of Superpower doesn't feel like work. In a sense, leveraging your Superpower is a powerful way to push the Easy Button in your life. And pushing the Easy Button in areas of your Weak Spot, will free up more time for you to operate in your Superpower. Life isn't easy, and it's never going to be easy. But it could be *easier*.

4.4
Be Vulnerable

My college freshman Creative Writing teacher, Mr. Vigil, was the single most impactful person on my writing journey to date. I have continued to write poetry for a quarter of a century because of that man's influence.

He also gave me another cherished tool in my Utility Belt—the tool of *Vulnerability*.

Where I grew up, anything to do with vulnerability or feelings (like poetry), was considered weakness. The cardinal sin in my neighborhood was showing weakness. You had to be tough and strong. I wasn't good at that, but I fronted like I was. I brought that baggage out of my childhood, through high school, and into the college classroom with me.

Vigil walked into the classroom with creased Dickies, a black t-shirt, and a rosary. I immediately associated him with the people from my neighborhood and walk of life. This gave him instant credibility. He was also a poet who wore his heart on his sleeve. It was a conundrum.

He would always read my writing, and say, "Show me, don't tell me." He wanted the truth of who I was to show through in my writing. I really struggled with that. I didn't know how to access that level of vulnerability. I didn't know how to access my authentic self.

The Superpower Quest

He guided and challenged me to write my first poem—"Mama's Cross," which was full of the pain and loss from my (at the time) tortured relationship with my mother. She and I are good now. Shout out to my Mama. Anyway.

I read this poem out loud in class—the most vulnerable thing I had ever done. I looked up, and Vigil was crying. My heart changed in that moment. I realized the power of words to move people. I became a poet that day, and never stopped.

"Show me, don't tell me." It's a mantra that I still hear when I write. "Show me, don't tell me." It helps me put my authentic heart into the things that I do.

My childhood environment taught me that vulnerability was reckless, and weakness was something to be ashamed of. Vigil taught me that vulnerability is beautiful. He taught me that vulnerability has the power to draw others to you—to move others in a way that is impossible for polish, or pretense, or toughness. He broke a powerful yoke off of me. It remains broken to this day.

If you were to follow me around in my day, you would see where the magic happens. The magic happens for me when I'm connecting with people. Vulnerability is the tool in my Utility Belt that most contributes to my ability to create immediate, deep connection with the people around me. The thing that was such a weakness for me in my childhood, such a foreign concept when I walked into Vigil's classroom, has become a Superpower.

The exercise of this tool will come harder for some than for others. Connectors and Nurturers will have an easier time. But this is a tool that anybody can use. If you know yourself, and if you love yourself, then you'll find that you have the power to share yourself, as you are, even though it's a risk. Some people will not receive you. Some people are not here for that kind of party. But it will draw you immeasurably closer to the people who matter.

Bonus Content: For a poem from that season of my life of "show me, don't tell me", a poem about vulnerability and connection, check out "Touch" at **superpowerquest.com/resources**

I hope this tool brings for you what it has brought for me: closer, more tightly knit relationships. Less small talk. Deeper and more passionate conversations. A growing sense in others that you are a safe place to share their hopes and secrets, and even their failures and weaknesses.

4.5
Know Thyself

This is a single tool in my Utility Belt within the Superpower Quest framework, but it is also the foundation for the entire Superpower Quest framework. I include this here, because it is a mindset shift that can help you embrace tools like this for greater impact in your life.

It just so happened that what I learned from decades of learning myself was that I had a passion for helping others to learn themselves. *Knowing Thyself* means investing time and energy into understanding yourself as you are. You are exercising this tool by reading this book.

There isn't a particular person who gave me this tool. But there was a particular moment when I discovered it for myself. Early in my marriage, my wife and I took a personality test called "Lion, Otter, Beaver, Golden Retriever." We were having some tension in our marriage at that time. We weren't prepared for how very different we were from each other. My test results declared that I was an Otter/Golden Retriever. My strongest category, the Otter, is playful, gregarious, and social. The Golden Retriever is loyal and protective. Sarah's test results showed that she was a Lion/Beaver. The Lion is an authoritative, results-oriented leader. The Beaver is detail- oriented and ritualistic. I was floored to find that we were basically opposites. It explained so much. For me, it put words to my lifelong struggle with my inherited ideas of what it means to be a man.

All men were supposed to be Lions, weren't they? This was the perspective that I had been chipping away at my whole life. Vigil had taught me the power of vulnerability. I had become more serious about my Christian faith, and the example of Jesus had done damage to my inherited ideas of "action-hero" masculinity. But this moment in my life was a moment of naming. I had always, unconsciously, held myself against the characteristics of the Lion and found myself lacking. In this moment, I held myself against the characteristics of the Lion and found myself…different. There are thousands of miles between the idea of "lacking," and the idea of "different." I was not a Lion, and that was okay. My wife was, in fact, a Lion, and that was also okay.

It didn't matter if she or I wanted me to be a Lion. You don't become what you are by wishing; you are gifted what you are by fiat. You have a design. Sarah and I recently looked back on those early years of our marriage, applying some of the wisdom and perspective that we've gained over nearly twenty years of marriage to diagnose our issues at that time.

We traced some of our early problems to an early misunderstanding, back when we were first getting to know each other, and the expectations we had going into marriage. Sarah's father is a Lion. He's a truly great man. Jerome is decisive, authoritative, and dignified. He has also learned a huge measure of gentleness, which is a thing that does not come easily for Lions. Sarah had great respect for her father, and was looking for someone with similar characteristics.

In my college friend group, which is the context in which Sarah first got to know me, I seemed like a leader. We had big ideas and big dreams, and I was at the center of those conversations. My group of friends Joined Forces and did some pretty amazing things. One example (referenced earlier) was a series of open mic poetry nights. I was often the MC at these events, and also a big contributor to vision. But behind the scenes, I was never delegating tasks or giving direction or instruction to people. I was always inspiring people, connecting people, and getting them excited. People were self-motivated to do their parts. That was all. I was a Connector and a Dreamer, and from certain angles, that made me look like a Leader.

Sarah got the impression that I was more like her dad than I really was; more of a Lion. Imagine her surprise when she found out, after she married me, that I basically didn't have a Lion bone in my body. She crawled into bed with a Lion and woke up with a playful Otter. I wasn't purposely trying to deceive her. I was still trying to figure out what I was, and often trying to be what I thought I was supposed to be. Have you ever seen an Otter in a Lion's den, living with a Lioness, trying to act like a Lion? It's ugly, trust me. The Lioness is not amused.

It's a good thing we loved each other. That was a jarring discovery to have, and it took us some time to work through it. Now she understands and embraces what I am, and what I'm not. I understand and embrace what she is, and what she's not. We challenge each other to grow in our areas of weakness, without denying the fact that a level of weakness must always exist. We have mutual respect and appreciation. The fact of our differences certainly creates tension from time to time, but we've learned to shorten the cycle of issue identification and reconciliation.

The "Lion, Otter, Beaver, Golden Retriever" personality test was a beginning for me. It showed me the power of naming personality characteristics to help people transition from a sense of "lacking" to a place of embracing the idea that they might just be "different."

From there, I gained a hunger to dive deeper into the art of self-assessment. I exposed myself to new personality frameworks like *DiSC, Enneagram, Myers-Briggs,* and *Big Five,* and other self-discovery tools like *Unique Ability* and *Ikigai*. I learned important lessons from each of these, and the consistent similarities confirmed my findings.

Every human has a unique design. People can learn to understand their design. And if they do, they can cooperate with that design to soar to greater heights of success and joyfulness.

Use this tool to set yourself up for success, to the best of your ability. If you hate enclosed spaces, don't take road trips. If you are an introvert, give yourself breaks in social situations. If you hate managing people, then maybe skip that promotion.

Live with yourself according to understanding. That is what it means to *Know Thyself.*

4.6
Establish an Anchor Habit

I have a theory that everyone has, or can have, an Anchor Habit. An Anchor Habit is the daily habit that brings the most sense of control and intentionality to your day.

We all have many habits, but an Anchor Habit is special because it has the power to make or break your day. It's a sign of something greater than itself. Anchor Habits communicate something to your brain. Confidence, a sense that everything is okay, a sense that you are not totally overwhelmed, a sense that you are in control of yourself.

There was a time in my life when I was drowning under the weight of my responsibilities. I was working a demanding job, raising young kids, and helping to pastor a church. I would wake up in the morning full of dread. I felt utterly incapable of executing my responsibilities. I was dropping balls and disappointing people, both of which are very triggering for me. I remember thinking that I could not continue this way. I needed time to think, time to pray, time to reflect. But I did not know where to get the time. I couldn't take it from my family.

So I did one of the hardest things that I've ever done. I established a morning routine in which I woke up hours before anyone else. It was rugged. I set several vibrating alarms. I would force my eyes open, begging God for strength to get out of bed. I would plop one leg out of bed and then the other. I would shamble out of my room, feeling like death on a stick. And then I would get my coat and walk around my neighborhood in the pitch blackness, because the morning wind on my face and the motion of my feet was the only thing that could keep me awake.

This habit came from total desperation, otherwise I never would have done it. It changed my life. Ultimately I realized that the bigger problem was that I had too much on my plate, and I went through a process to accept that and rectify it. But this habit was a treasure forged in that chaos. It has remained with me, in some form, to this day; so we're talking seven years or more.

Even when my life is at its most chaotic, or when I feel untold pressures, my daily quiet time gives me the ability to actually process my grief, confront my fears, or reflect on my joys. It gives me the time and space to be intentional about my life.

If I don't get my daily quiet time, it throws off the equilibrium for my whole day. I feel overwhelmed and it" a sign that something is seriously wrong. When I'm getting my quiet time, which is more than 95% of the time, then I feel like I am in the driver's seat of my life, no matter what's going on. A huge part of my Weak Spot is inconsistency. This is an example of the fact that sometimes it is truly unavoidable to reckon with your Weak Spot. You can't always avoid it. Sometimes you have to wrestle it down to the ground to the point of tears and beyond. So, being as inconsistent as I am naturally, I feel that if I can have an Anchor Habit, then anyone can.

Everyone's Anchor Habit is different. My wife's Anchor Habit is working out. When she's working out consistently, her life is consistently better across all metrics. When she's not, it's disproportionately worse.

My brother-in-law, Drew, needs to run in the morning. Preferably, outdoors. He needs to feel the wind on his face, and the ground beneath his feet. This is where he feels free, alive. This is where he feels God's good pleasure.

Our minds simply need external confirmation that we are doing okay. In order to be healthy, we need a sense that we are actors and initiators in our lives, not victims or bystanders. Otherwise we get inexplicably nervous and unsettled. An Anchor Habit is a signal to our subconscious that we are holding the reins and moving in a chosen direction.

Here's the recipe for an Anchor Habit:

- It needs to be daily.
- It needs to happen at roughly the same time or at least the same time-frame every day.
- It needs to be something you can do at least ninety percent of the time.
- It needs to leverage one of your true passions in some way.

I'm passionate about writing. My wife is passionate about weightlifting. Drew is passionate about running. The love of what we're doing is ultimately what sustains the Anchor Habit over periods of high stress or allows us to get back on the horse when we fall off.

I would encourage you to identify your Anchor Habit, and then fight like hell for it. Treat it as life or death. If there's a place in your life to put a flag in the ground, this is it. Do what it takes to make it happen, and don't give up. One of the keys to success is not fighting a war on ten different fronts. Pick a single front and double down. Throw all your firepower at it. Once you have established your Anchor Habit, you can build on it and move on to other things.

Habit Stacking
The idea of an Anchor Habit interlocks well with James Clear's concept of "habit stacking." James Clear is the author of *Atomic Habits: An Easy & Proven Way to Build Good Habits & Break Bad Ones,* an amazing book that has greatly benefited me.

Clear does an incredible job of illustrating the psychology behind effectively establishing new habits for a more consistent and effective life. According to Clear:

"When it comes to building new habits, you can use the connectedness of behavior to your advantage. One of the best ways to build a new habit is to identify a current habit you already do each day and then stack your new behavior on top. This is called habit stacking."[8]

Once you have established and named your Anchor Habit, you can use this as a post in the ground of your life to tie off new habits.

My morning quiet time eventually became the controlled and consistent moment in my day that enabled me to "stack" an additional high-leverage habit on top of it: The "Right Side Up Journal."

4.7
Choose a Life System

One of the greatest challenges of living a successful life is consistency in one direction over time. Even for the best of us, our minds and hearts are so distractible. The highs and lows of life, the trauma, the stress, the weight of our responsibilities, our natural forgetfulness, and the intensity of our passions and addictions, all conspire together to make it difficult to hold to any sort of consistent plan over the long haul.

Even people who are naturally organized need systems. The system helps take a load off of the fallibility of the human mind and memory by transferring the burden of memory to an established routine or structure. My twelve year old daughter has a way better memory, and far more conscientiousness, than I have. Let's say I'm a four out of ten, and she's a nine. Still, even with this incredible advantage, she only has so much mental capacity to work with. Systems extend our mental capacity.

Capacity Extension
A very simple example of this is the system of written language. People used to have to memorize things for those things to have any chance of being transferred to others. They used songs, anecdotes, and other techniques to transfer wisdom. Even still, the transference of thought

to others via speech as the only mechanism left a lot of room for fallibility in the transmission of ideas. The success of the transmission was limited by the ability of each invisible mind to give and receive and retain information through invisible, audible words that fade immediately after they're spoken. Also, with no source material to verify against, changes over time, either by accident or by connivance, would be untraceable with the passage of enough time.

Written language is a system that actually allows people to think their thoughts onto a visible, shared, editable platform, thus creating a visible, persistent memento out of invisible thought. In this way, a person's invisible thoughts can physically outlast the span of their lives. Writing is the simplest and most efficient form of thought made into substance.

Writing automatically extends the mental ability of anyone who knows how to write, providing a substantive way to store information outside of the brain, and share this information with other brains, such that either brain can go back and consult the source material to ensure the continuity and accuracy of the thought expressed. This is nothing less than freaking magic. It makes my heart beat faster just thinking about this!

Systems extend our mental capacity, so that we can conserve our limited mental capacity for more essential endeavors. Going back to the writing example, I don't have to spend hours and hours of my life memorizing ideas, since writing enables me to put them down on paper and come back to them.

All systems create this kind of mental bonus, enabling a reallocation and maximization of mental, and even physical resources.

Similar to the previous chapter, in which I theorize that everyone has an Anchor Habit, which is the king of habits among all other habits, I also believe everyone needs a Life System, which is the king of systems among all other systems. The right Life System will give you a massive boost of effectiveness and productivity in the areas where you most need it.

My Weak Spot of inconsistency has been a lifelong impediment to growth and success. Everyone who knows me well knows how much of a factor this is for me. I have failed in this area thousands, if not hundreds of thousands of times in my life. And every failure hurts, because these are the failures in which I have let people down, or made people's lives more inconvenient, by forgetting details, not following through on commitments, missing key deadlines, etc.

Now, I will reiterate from earlier chapters that this is a very typical weakness of the Dreamer. We care much more about big ideas and creativity than we do about effective execution. But all dreams and no execution means a life of incredible frustration for both the Dreamer and all the people that depend on that Dreamer to contribute more than just ideas to the general welfare.

The fact that this was an innate deficiency in my nature was not an excuse to leave off from addressing it. I wanted to stop letting people down. I knew that consistency was never going to be a strength for me, but I had hopes that the right systems would help me to reach a basic level of proficiency. It was the pain of failure that drove me to exploration. It was pure frustration and desperation.

I tried many different systems in my search. I built a system from scratch using a software called "Smartsheets" that worked for a while. The goal was to log all my tasks on a spreadsheet, complete with due dates, where the rows of each day's particular tasks would change color to alert me to what needed to be done that day. Creating and maintaining this glorified spreadsheet took incredible time and energy for me.

The system was amazing, and it yielded success for a while, but it was too burdensome to maintain. When I would fall off of the horse and miss a few days, it would often be weeks or even months before I could muster the mental energy to get back on. The system was not sustainable during seasons of greater than average stress.

I still love Smartsheet though. That technology is top five for me, when it comes to creating interactive spreadsheets with complex triggers from multiple users and events. Truly great.

Organize Tomorrow Today
I began to get real traction when someone introduced me to the book *Organize Tomorrow Today: 8 Ways to Retrain Your Mind to Optimize*

Performance at Work and in Life by Jason Selk, Tom Bartow, and Matthew Rudy. This book introduced me to the idea of radical prioritization.

"Prioritization may very well be the most underrated skill of the highly successful."[9]

"The most successful people don't get everything done; they get the most important things done."[10]

This book advocates for readers to adopt a series of systems and/or habits, guaranteed to help them organize their lives. The book cautions the reader to take the time to implement one habit at a time, until you've nailed it, before moving on to learning the next habit. The book describes the habit as nailed if you have performed it with a ninety percent or greater success rate over the course of three consecutive months.

The first system in the book has the same name as the book title, "Organize Tomorrow Today." It's the creation of a task list in which you daily list your three most important tasks, and earmark one of those three as your "one must-do" task. Here's a paraphrase of how it works:[11]

- At some point today before you go to sleep, write a list of the three most important things you must do tomorrow. (Three Most Important)
- Put an asterisk next to the most important one of the three. (One Must)
- Tomorrow, check in with the list early in the day. Prioritize these things over everything else that needs to be done, most especially your One Must.
- Cross them off of your list as you complete them.
- Rinse and repeat.

The utter simplicity of this mechanism may be a stumbling block for you. You're probably thinking, "I have a hundred things that need to be done in a day, and you want me to prioritize three?"

Yes. Here are a few reasons why this works. The authors accurately identified that the reason most people don't make satisfactory progress is that they don't keep their promises to themselves. You heard me right. The first and paramount problem is that we don't trust ourselves. We don't trust ourselves because we've consistently endeavored to do things that we have failed to do. This is probably because we were trying to do too much, but it doesn't matter. The underlying narrative this creates is that we can't really trust ourselves to do what we say we're going to do. This plummets morale and leads to apathy and a sense of futility. We need to start getting wins instead of losses if we're going to change that narrative.

We also need to learn to prioritize. Busyness isn't the same as productivity. You can complete twenty non-essential tasks that won't move you a fraction of the way forward that one essential task will. Imagine if you could identify and accomplish three important things every day, instead of two dozen things that may or may not be essential.

> You heard me right. The first and paramount problem is that we don't trust ourselves. We don't trust ourselves because we've consistently endeavored to do things that we have failed to do.

Finally, think of the psychological benefit of having an achievable standard, instead of a murky, ambiguous one. People with a murky and ambiguous destination never know if they have reached it. They live with a sense of that failure. People with a clear destination know if they've reached it or not. If they have reached it, they can rejoice. If they haven't reached it, they can recalibrate. Both are productive activities and mindsets as opposed to defeating ones.

Using the system, you will begin to gain confidence and so will the people around you. You'll have the confidence that if something makes it to the list, it will get done. You will begin to see yourself as a man who keeps promises to himself or as a woman who keeps her promises.

My wife began to preface her honey-do requests to me with, "Can you add this to your must do list this week?" After I had nailed this habit, she and I both knew that if it made it to the list, it would get done.

This mechanism has many advantages, but the greatest is its utter simplicity. The barrier of entry to this system is the lowest I've ever seen. You need a pen and pad, an established five minutes to think about the next day, an established time in the morning to check your list for the day, and a habit of checking off each task once you've completed it. This thing is crazy powerful. This works especially well for people like me, who have almost given up hope that any system could help them.

The "Right Side Up Journal"

And now, the moment you've been waiting for. Call me a nerd, call me a geek. Call me crazy. But one of my best friends in the world is my black leather binder. It makes me happy when I look at it. My wife sometimes refers to it as the competition, but she's just joking, man!

This binder is my version of the "Right Side Up Journal" by Alan Briggs and StayForth Designs.

Bonus Content: Check out **superpowerquest.com/resources** to find the link to get your own Right Side Up Journal.

Alan Briggs, as you can probably tell by previous mentions, was a huge influence on this book. He was the one who challenged me to set an initial deadline and push through, and provided accountability and support along the way. This book would not exist without his help.

Alan created the "Right Side Up Journal" as a resource for helping leaders create traction in their lives. He has a passion for helping leaders move from confusion to clarity, from clarity to courage, and from courage to consistency. He is a person who knows his calling, and I've witnessed him walk out this calling effectively in my life and the lives of others.

The RSU Journal is a mix between reflection, life management, and accountability. As I mentioned before, I stacked my RSU Journal habit on top of my established daily quiet time reflection, ensuring that I always start the day off with a powerful mix of reflection, prayer, goal setting, and trajectory confirmation.

Here's how the RSU Journal Daily Template works:

- Go to the current day in your journal.
- Do any short, reflective exercises. These are scattered throughout the journal to help you zoom out, track progress, and celebrate the wins.
- Write your daily filter. This is a short vision statement about the day, and serves to create a context for your daily priorities. It might be as simple as "invest in family" or "rest and rejuvenate." It might be "finish strong" or "give yourself grace." It should reflect the main focus of the day.
- Fill in the *Morning* section with the main things you need to accomplish in the morning.
- Fill in the *Afternoon* section with the main things you need to accomplish in the afternoon.
- Fill in the *Evening* section with the main things you need to accomplish in the evening.
- Fill in the *One Thing That Must Be Done* section to identify your highest priority task for the day.

The RSU Journal comes preloaded with all the things you need to maintain a macro and micro view of your progress, priorities, and tasks. Ninety-nine percent of people will be able to use the journal right out of the box for massive life traction.

I made adjustments because of the fact that I am a Dreamer, and very creative, and I get joy and energy out of using my creativity to customize tools for my specific make up. I also wanted to incorporate elements of my Superpower Quest into my life plan.

Based on Alan's personal feedback, I also developed an *at a glance* Weekly Vision page template that sits face to face with the Daily Template, and moves from day to day through the week (days change, but week stays the same for seven days), so I'm always planning my days with the larger goals of the week in mind. My weekly template also summarizes my personal Superpower Quest results, and lists my Power Punches so that I'm always holding myself accountable to schedule as many high-leverage Superpower actions as possible into my days and weeks.

Here's how the Weekly Vision template works:

- Each week has its own blank Weekly Vision template.
- This gets filled in on Monday mornings, first thing. Once filled in, it gets moved to each consecutive day, and gets reviewed daily.
- The first action is to enter the weekly filter. This is like the Daily Filter, but zoomed out to a general focus for the week.
- Next, I review of my answers to the following questions:
    - ▸ Who am I beneath all appearances?
    - ▸ Why do I exist above all?
    - ▸ What is my main Superpower?
    - ▸ What is my main Weak Spot?
    - ▸ Next is a review of my seven to ten Power Punches. These are my highest leverage activities, and should be scheduled as much as possible into each of my days.
    - ▸ Next is my Repeatable Steps table. This list the specific actions (slightly more specific than my Power Punches) that I will perform each week. This includes checkboxes for the number of times each of these activities should be repeated during the week. For example, I post five times to LinkedIn every week, so the row reads "LinkedIn Posts" and has five checkboxes.
    - ▸ Next is a table for inputting my weekly Dragons, Frogs, and Unicorns.
        - ▸ Dragons. These are the one to three things that I'm most scared to do, or most challenged by, that need to be done this week.
        - ▸ Frogs. These are the three to five most inconvenient things that need to be done this week. This comes from the popular concept and book, *Eat That Frog! 21 Great Ways to Stop Procrastinating and Get More Done in Less Time* by Brian Tracy.[12]

▸ Unicorns. Unicorns are the two to three metrics I'm using to judge success for the week. These are my ideal outcomes.

Bonus content: You can check out my "Weekly Vision" page at **superpowerquest.com/resources**

Ultimately, the "Right Side Up Journal" replaced "Organized Tomorrow Today" as my Life System. Once I mastered Organize Tomorrow Today, I was able to transition to a system that could accommodate more complexity, and had more built-in accountability towards specific, lofty goals. This is also the way. Sometimes you have to upgrade your tools within your Utility Belt.

Because I have low conscientiousness, I lean heavily on my "Right Side Up Journal" binder. Throughout any given day, I am reviewing my plans and checking off tasks ten to twenty times a day. I can imagine that people with higher conscientiousness would need a lower touch solution than that.

Here are the results of the integration of the "Right Side Up Journal" and my Weekly Vision doc into my life:

- I am far more productive than ever before.
- I am identifying and executing my priorities more than ever before.
- I am operating more in line with my Superpower more than ever before.
- I am able to proactively structure my days to account for days of low motivation or high stress. I can assess how I'm feeling, or unforeseen challenges, early in the day, and then adjust the Daily Filter and/or the number of daily tasks to accommodate.

This may or may not be the Life System for you. My system works to address my specific Hindering Hero Types of the Organizer and the Achiever. For me, it has turned an area of weakness into a strength. My system helps me remember things; deadlines, commitments, and details, that even conscientious people would forget. But here's the caveat…the detail has to make it into my system in order to be remembered. When I forget to write a deadline into my journal, or if my journal is unavailable, I'm just as prone to forget as I ever was. Even with its limitations, my system extends my capacity more than I, or my close family and friends, could ever have imagined.

Put in the work! Take the time! Find your Life System that most supplements your Weak Spot areas. Use trial and error. Fail fast. Learn as you try.

Here are some tips and steps to find the Life System of your dreams.

- Understand your Weak Spot, and begin dreaming about specific systems that might extend your capabilities in those areas.
- Look for others who have similar Weak Spot who seem to have learned to manage their Weak Spot. Ask them how they do it.
- Look for books that seem to address key areas where you need help. There are many self-help books covering thousands of topics. There's a good chance you will find things to incorporate into your Life System. Read these books like a treasure hunter looking for the mother lode. You might find it.

  "Atomic Habits" is a great place to start. It provides excellent psychological insight about habits to help set you up for success.
- Look for habits you can "stack" on top of Anchor Habits, in order to increase your chances of long term success.

4.8
Run If You Can!

I watched an interview with a man named Jocko Willink, a former Navy Seal who is now a famous author and podcast host. This guy is the epitome of toughness. You can tell by the thick neck and broad shoulders. Anyway, when asked what he would do in a situation when someone approached him to fight, he answered, "Run away."

Those were the most unexpected words I could have imagined coming out of his mouth, or the mouth of anyone that I perceived as a tough guy. When challenged to fight, he would run away. He proceeded to explain that when you enter a fight, there are many variables that you cannot foresee or control. What if your opponent has friends nearby that want to jump in? What if he has a weapon? Or what if you enter the fray and fight with the man, and hurt him badly, and get arrested as a result?

Sometimes you lose the fight by fighting the fight. Willink affirmed, over and over, that fighting is something you do when you have no other options. Fight to save your life and physical well-being. Fight to protect your loved ones. But exhaust all safer options first—including running away. The logic was compelling, and applicable to the premise of this chapter.

Choose your battles wisely. Do not willingly spend more time than you absolutely have to on activities within your Weak Spot.

The Superpower Quest

There are many things required of you on a daily basis. Some of these are in the area of your Hero Types and your Superpower. Some are in the realm of your Supporting Types. Invariably, there are some things that you take on, and even do every day, that are in the realm of your Weak Spot. Those are the things that cause you the most frustration and angst. Those are the areas where you feel the most drain. The goal of this chapter is to give you permission to re-evaluate the work you do in your Weak Spot areas, and abandon or adjust these activities where possible.

One simple illustration of this principle can be found in video games. In the game "The Legend of Zelda," you, the hero, Link, must defeat all manner of monsters to rescue Princess Zelda from the evil overlord Ganon.

You could spend the whole game fighting hordes of monsters. Defeating some monsters is essential for advancing your quest, opening doors, and getting the equipment you need. But there are many monsters that are just there, in all their orneriness, with the single goal of chipping away at your health. Sometimes you can run right past certain monsters and leave them behind, never having to engage.

For some, this might feel like cheating. But strategically, you have to zoom out and think about your goal. Am I here to rescue Zelda and beat the game? Or am I here to fight all the monsters? Either answer is acceptable, but the question needs to be asked so that you can create the experience you're looking for.

Little did you know that a video game like Zelda would have a nugget of such incomparable wisdom!

The first step of *Run if You Can* is to think about the areas where you experience the most fatigue and drain. What kinds of activities lead you to the most disproportionate amount of frustration and even rage? What are the things you dread doing?

Often, these are little things. They seem insignificant, and you wonder why they give you such a negative reaction. In the past you may have even chided yourself about your averseness to doing these things that seem so easy to everyone else. You may feel like you're lazy or lacking, or like you just need a muscle up and get it done. You may indeed need to muscle up and get it done, but that's not always the answer. In fact that should be the exception and not the rule.

I absolutely hate putting things like furniture together with instructions. Even Ikea stuff, that is made for the mechanically disinclined, gives me plenty of heartburn. For whatever reason, converting written instructions into actions is an operation that leaves me feeling frustrated and inadequate. I often do things wrong and misinterpret the instructions, and end up having to go back and redo elementary things.

I also have a tight relationship with the three kids I have at home, all under twelve at the time of writing this book. They love to do everything with me. Including building projects. They love to help. They fight over who gets to be the one to turn this screw or that screw. They ask me a million questions. It's all very cute.

Except it's not…to me. If I'm honest, it multiplies my stress by a factor of ten. I'm already on edge having to do a building project. Having my kids involved pushes me over the edge. I get very irritable and snappish, which is not like me. I feel the ugliest version of myself coming out.

Initially, I would always let my kids help, because it felt like the right thing to do, even though it would almost always end up in frustration for all of us. They would say, "Please let us help Daddy!" And I would crumble, initiating the cycle.

My internal picture of a "good dad" was someone assembling things with his kids, smiling, giving patient encouragement, and teaching life lessons along the way. And the truth is, there are awesome dads out there doing exactly that.

But I finally came to terms with the fact that I am not that dad. Building projects are squarely within my Weak Spot. Having an audience while I stumble along only enhances the misery. Having kids distract, question, and need to be managed raises the stakes to code red.

At this stage, I only take on projects like this when absolutely necessary. My wife knows that I will do them, because I love her, but I have my conditions:

- I can't be rushed. Time needs to be set aside, and ETA's need to be quadrupled.
- I have to be alone. No kids, no spouse, just me and the tools and the thing that needs to be put together, and maybe the "Hamilton" soundtrack to make it less miserable.

After five or six years of creating infrequent moments of unnecessary frustration and angst for myself and my kids by saying yes when I could have said no, it has felt good to give myself permission to make these adjustments. I pour into my kids at other times and in other ways. This minor adjustment enables me to have more energy for better things.

This is how you run away, and these are the kinds of scenarios to run away from. With this short chapter, I hope to give you permission to question your assumptions behind taking on tasks within your Weak Spot areas unnecessarily. Give yourself some room to maneuver. Give yourself some room to question. Give yourself permission to run away.

Value your time. Value your energy. Try to spend more of your life exercising your Superpower. Buy more time for this by identifying and pruning the activities that waste your time and energy.

4.9
Punch the Doohickey

There's a common trope in superhero and action movies: Picture the scene in which the team of heroes has rescued a *doohickey* from enemy forces. This gadget is the ultimate boon that can save the world. They push the button to activate it. Nothing happens. It's been damaged somehow in all the fighting, and they don't have the time or skill to take it apart and fix this alien technology. Suddenly, one of the heroes steps forward. He's not the smartest one in the group. He is the lumbering one with super strength. He squints at the device and… punches it. Suddenly it whirs to life with a hum of blinking lights. And the world is saved!

Sometimes your Effective Hero Types can be used to compensate for your Hindering Types. In the example above, the hero uses super strength to *hack* a situation where intelligence and technological skill are the more obvious answer.

I'm sure you've heard the saying: "If you're a hammer, every problem is a nail." This saying has a negative connotation, and rightly so, implying that people can become blind and narrow-minded in their approach to solving problems. But, with some situational discernment, treating "non-nail" problems like a nail can be very effective. There may be some opportunities to apply your special genius, in creative ways, to solve problems that might have otherwise been beyond your ability. If you're a hammer, be a hammer for as much of life as you possibly can.

On a scale of one to ten, you would rate an easy task as a one, a moderate task as a five, and a difficult task as a ten. Let's say that each person only has so many points to allocate in a given day. Side note—I am borrowing a bit from concepts in the book *Scrum: The Art of Doing Twice the Work in Half the Time* by Jeff and J.J. Sutherland.[13]

> They say the shortest distance between two points is a straight line. This is true. But what if that straight line is vertical?

If most of your workload is tasks that feel like a one, you're going to get exponentially more done in a day than if you stack your day with sevens or tens. Furthermore, you and I could look at the exact same task, and I might rate it as a one, and you might rate it as a ten.

Now let's apply the same logic to the idea of Punching the Doohickey. There might be a thirty-minute task that feels like a ten to you. What if there's a way to address this task that takes sixty minutes, but it's sixty minutes spent doing something that you are very good at, and that you enjoy? Which is the better gambit?

Well, when something feels like a ten, you tend to procrastinate and push it to the back of the line. In this way, it often doesn't get done at all, or gets done late. It also takes ten points of energy away from your total energy stash for that day. So it's not just time, it's energy output that is the issue.

Which are you better off doing? Something that takes thirty minutes, that leads to frustration and exhaustion, or something that takes longer, but fills you up and energizes you? When *punching the doohickey*, you're tapping into your areas of strength and allocating that strength to conquer a task creatively, even though you're not going the shortest distance between two points.

They say the shortest distance between two points is a straight line. This is true. But what if that straight line is vertical? What if you end up climbing the face of a mountain? That's why they create switchbacks. You go a longer distance with a smaller incline which makes it more manageable. That's Punching the Doohickey.

I'm a Connector. Connecting with people is not a drain for me. It's not neutral. When I'm connecting, it's a positive and joyful experience for me. I can and do spend hours and hours getting to know people, their strengths and weaknesses, their stories, their hopes and dreams. Honestly, this is where almost all of the magic happens in my life. It's the relational stuff that lights me up.

Home repair and maintenance fit squarely in the area of my Hindering Drives. I've already told you. Doing this kind of work takes a lot out of my mental and emotional bank account, and I'm not fast or efficient at it. So my lawn suffers, and my wife suffers, because order and tidiness are incredibly important to her. If I were by myself, I could easily be at peace being the smiley-chatty guy with the overgrown lawn. But for love, I have opted out of that life. So the lawn needs to be taken care of, and I don't want to take care of it. What's my *Punching the Doohickey* option? I leverage my *Connector* Superpower to solve the problem. Ears open, I find out that my landscaping genius nephew is in town and looking for work.

Better believe I hired him faster than you can say "Holy Guacamole, Batman!" Beautiful yard? Check. Happy wife? Check. Happy me? Double-check.

I leveraged the Connector to overcome an Organizer/Achiever problem. Does it always work out this way? No, but you better believe with successes like this under my belt, I am always looking to Punch the Doohickey when it comes to addressing problems that arise that are in my Weak Spot areas.

I know some people that are big in the Achiever gifting, but lacking when it comes to the Connector. How can you Punch the Doohickey? Can you leverage your Achiever abilities to somehow get Connector results?

On social media, I recently asked my people to share their Weak Spots. My friend Kenny, an entrepreneurial Dreamer/Achiever, responded to the call, describing a "Connector challenge" that he has when interfacing with large groups.

"Anyway, my [Weak Spot] is walking into a networking/social event and seeing a bunch of people and not feeling comfortable walking up to anybody and talking. To be fair I was always like that. I think it's just not my thing, especially the basic surface level convo stuff. Once there's substance I'm all in, but it's hard to get there. One of those things I've also just kind of surrendered to and then because of that it actually got a little easier so <u>acceptance but not giving up</u>…"

He described his strategy for dealing with this Weak Spot as "acceptance but not giving up." Dreamer/Achievers have no problem mustering the energy to power through and get things done. In other words, he keeps showing up to the difficult situation and "swinging the bat," even though it feels awkward and unnatural. This is classic Punching the Doohickey behavior. He's experiencing his Weak Spot in the Connector realm of action, but compensates by pulling from his Achiever toolbag. He gives himself permission not to be great at Connection; permission for it to be hard; and then leverages determination and tenacity to make it happen. Achievers don't really have a problem with hard things, as long as they can see the practical value of the task.

Kenny is an incredibly authentic, inspiring person, and he can relate with people on a deep level, once the surface ice is broken. His only trouble is getting there. He's learned to embrace a weakness and mitigate it with a strength. Punch that Doohickey!

There are many other applications of this principle. If you are an Organizer that is weak on the Nurturer, you might identify your key relationships, and then create a plan and schedule for investing in each one. This might sound off-putting or clinical, but if you are lacking in the Nurturer, it's going to be hard to instinctively feel your way towards the actions that create intimacy with others. In the absence of that, you'll need to leverage a strength, like consistency or diligence, to create a framework for success. In so doing, you might find yourself MORE consistent in your endeavors to care for others, than someone who is a full-blown Nurturer and lacks conscientiousness. You may find that your friends deeply appreciate your intentionality.

You might be a Leader with a Dreamer weakness. You might be a Dreamer with a Leader weakness. Regardless, you should be looking for ways that you can leverage a strength to creatively mitigate your weaknesses. Punch that Doohickey! Punch it all day!

4.10
Sequoias

The lessons, tools, and maxims that I have described in this section make up the bulk of the Utility Belt that I use for everyday living. I hope that some of them are useful and transferable to you. But keep in mind, your journey is your own. You can and you will assemble your own Utility Belt that works for you. Enhance your strengths and mitigate your weaknesses. You can do this!

My audience is people who want to grow. People who know they have potential but are encountering resistance in realizing that potential. People who long for that Benevolent Upperclassman to put an arm around them, invest in them, and help them unlock their potential. I can't picture that you would have gotten this far in this book if you aren't one of those people who earnestly wants to grow. This book is only one tool in your journey for growth. And there are many other books, written by people who are wiser and more experienced than I am. I have referenced some of them, and pointed you in their direction. The power of this book is that it is written by a fellow struggler, a fellow striver, a fellow longer.

When I was a kid, I erroneously thought I was nobody. But I couldn't shake the feeling that I wanted to be somebody. That longing felt like bees in my chest, or a screaming. I always felt like there was something huge inside me, throwing elbows to get out. If you know that feeling, this book is dedicated to you.

There are many things that I cannot speak about with confidence. But this, I can: Feeling like you are small— maybe smaller than anyone, and having a desire—no, a compulsion to grow. And see, I think maybe that's just what it means to be a human in progress. We are seeds. Maybe that's what seeds feel. The longing and the inevitability, way down there in the deep forgotten blackness, waiting for sun and water to tug them upwards. I want to feel that tug, and the older I get, the more I also want to be the one tugging. I want to bring rain and sun to the seeds around me, as others have brought the rain and sun to me.

I got to see the great Sequoia trees in California this year. Sequoia seeds are about the size of a pinhead, and are enclosed in a seed case from 1/4 to 3/8 inches long. Tiny. Insignificant. But they grow into monstrous trees 250 to 300 feet tall, and they can weigh over two and a half million pounds! Standing next to one feels like standing next to some massive, prehistoric beast. I'm 6'2", and I'm not often made to feel microscopic. Mind-bendingly massive things can come from tiny origins. Our smallness isn't a liability, it's an invitation.

My father craved something, and taught me to crave it. Knowledge. Wisdom. Growth. The older I've gotten, the more curious I've become. I hope this book has the effect of making people more curious, more hungry, to know themselves and to gain the wisdom of others. See the treasures of wisdom and excellence around you.

Do you have a tried-and-tested tool in your Utility Belt? Shoot me an email at **johnny@superpowerquest.com** and tell me about it. Your tool may be featured in our Superpower Community Newsletter.

Don't forget to log your top five Utility Belt Tools in your Hero Profile at superpowerquest.com/myprofile.

SECTION 5
Face Your Supervillain

5.1
Face Your Supervillain

And now it's time for the final section of the Superpower Quest. It is time to face your Supervillain; your greatest enemy. One consistent thing about superhero stories is that villains seek to destroy and exploit the community, and heroes serve and protect the community. The fundamental difference between heroes and villains is that villains are selfish and exploitative, and heroes seek the good of others.

Heroes, in the ideal, are driven by love. Villains are driven by power. The dichotomy between love and power will be very important for the remainder of the book. My mission in writing this book was to help you embrace your design and embrace your communities. In fact, I have advocated that you were designed for community, not for isolation. Your powers were not just granted to you for you, they were granted to you for others. Remember, with great power comes great responsibility. I hope I have helped you to see that you have great power, and that you were designed for great responsibility; to positively impact the communities in which you participate.

Now, who is your Supervillain? Who is the greatest threat to the communities in which you participate? Who is the greatest threat to your destiny as a glorious contributor to, and defender of your communities?

The Superpower Quest

Yes, there are external forces of evil and oppression in the world, but they are not your foremost villain. There are dictators and corrupt politicians and serial killers and unjust laws. There are natural disasters and pandemics and economic recessions. There's no end to the number of external forces that cause human suffering. But because these things are external, they are outside of your control. This is not to say that you cannot fight unjust laws, or bring aid to victims of natural disasters, or stay vigilant for criminals. But you truly cannot control when such things strike, or wave a magic wand and make them go away. You can only respond in a way that brings some measure of goodness to bear against the evil. And all of the good you can muster may not be enough to overturn the evil.

Jan Huss, the Czechoslovakian theologian, fought the same battle against church corruption that Martin Luther fought, but Yan Huss was burned at the stake. He was a link in the chain of reform, but he never got to see the results of his contribution. Martin Luther King spent his life fighting the oppression of racism, but he was assassinated before he could see his dream become a reality. Corrie Ten Boom, the Dutch clockmaker, author of "The Hiding Place," and leader of an underground resistance against the Nazis, was ultimately captured and placed in a concentration camp with her sister. She was unable to save her beloved sister, who died in the camp.

I can write a list a hundred miles long of all the great men and women who fought against external evil in the world, at great personal sacrifice, up to and including their own lives. People who gave all the good they had in opposition to the face of evil. Some got to see that evil toppled and put to flight. And some never got to see it. They were never in control of the outcome. They were only in control of themselves. What made them heroes was not the ultimate result of their labors, but the willingness to stand and battle wickedness with goodness.

But I will tell you that this battle was only possible because a greater battle had been fought and won. This was the battle to become the type of person who was able to love this lavishly, and risk this gloriously. This was the battle against cowardice, and selfishness, and the lust for power, and the lust for revenge, and pettiness, and rage, and

SECTION 5 | Face Your Supervillain

escapism, and despair. They successfully defeated their true enemy, which was the only reason they were free to set themselves against the external enemies of their respective communities.

The greatest harm that Martin Luther King could ever have done to his community was to not become the Martin Luther King that we know and respect and honor— the Martin Luther King who was willing to die for the healing of others. The battle could have been lost a thousand times, if at any point he had chosen to turn back and become a lesser man. He conquered his true enemy. He conquered himself. This doesn't imply perfection, it simply implies the level of mastery that enabled him to do what had to be done.

> The greatest harm that you and I can do to the communities in which we participate would be to not become the superheroes we are meant to be, and to give ourselves over to the selfish and exploitative ways of the Supervillain.

The greatest harm that Corrie Ten Boom could have done to her community would have been for her to not become the Corrie Ten Boom who was willing to stand up to the Nazis.

The greatest harm that you and I can do to the communities in which we participate would be to not become the superheroes we are meant to be, and to give ourselves over to the selfish and exploitative ways of the Supervillain.

In the song, "You Can't Stop Me," the rapper Andy Mineo says, "My biggest enemy is me…but even I can't stop me." I think he's right. The real battle, the battle that counts, the battle that comes before every other battle, is the battle that lives inside of us. You are the Superhero, and you are the Supervillain. Which of the two will emerge victorious? That's what this chapter is about.

- What is the Supervillain?
- What are your Triggers?
- How does the Supervillain emerge?
- What is your Shadow Drive?
- What are your Villain Names?

The Superpower Quest

- How can your Supervillain be stopped?
- What can be done if your Supervillain runs amok?

Supervillain Design Map

The following is a map for your journey through this section of the book. Once completed, you will be able to see the full map of your Supervillain design. Don't forget to input your conclusions into your Hero Profile at superpowerquest.com/myprofile.

TRIGGERS	
List your three to five Triggers below.	List the associated Weak Spot Word.

SHADOW DRIVES	
Domination, Chaos, Trespass, Discord, Obsession, Apathy	
#1.	#2.

SECTION 5 | Face Your Supervillain

VILLAIN WORDS	
Positive traits and tendencies…	
1.	2.
3.	4.
5.	6.

SUPERVILLAIN NAMES
Names given to your Supervillain Personas…
1.
2.
3.
4.

5.2
Your Supervillain is
NOT Your Weak Spot!

Remember: your Supervillain is not your Weak Spot. This is extremely important. We covered this in the Weak Spot section, but that was a long time ago, and I want to do some review and add a little bit of color.

Your Weak Spot is your weakness. It's a part of your design as surely as your Superpower. You can't erase it, you can't change it, but you can manage it, supplement it, and steward it. The two major ways I gave you to steward your Weak Spot were Joining Forces and Building Your Utility Belt.

To put it in practical terms, there are two forces in human experience, in the realm I'm addressing. One force is weakness. This encompasses your limitations, your inabilities, your disadvantages. These limitations can include anything that limits you from doing things other people can do, and it encompasses many things that have nothing to do with your choice. You didn't choose to be born 5'3", or to struggle with math, or to have a hard time connecting with people. You didn't choose a proclivity towards anger, fear, or insecurity. These were factory settings that usually have nothing to do with any choices you made.

The other force is malevolence. Malevolence lives in the will. Malevolence is an action whenever you choose to destroy yourself or others, either as a meditated act of destruction, or as a refusal to quench the fires of a destructive urge. My child is not morally responsible for being clumsy or distractible, and dropping a dish on the floor. She isn't even morally responsible for getting angry when her brother steals her toy. Anger is a feeling, not an action. We all have feelings, and often they aren't the feelings we even want to have, but they can stay feelings. They don't have to become actions.

My daughter is morally responsible for hauling off and hitting her brother, when the anger flares up in her chest and she lets it take control of her arms. An ordered and healthy society cannot exist where people cannot be held responsible for their destructive actions, even if their destructive actions feel automatic and uncontrollable.

A healthy family, a community, a society, is built upon an understanding that people are volitional beings that are responsible for their actions. One can sympathize with the environmental or internal disadvantages, like a tendency towards anger, or an abusive upbringing, that contribute to destructive action. But the destructive actions can only be ignored, permitted, or enabled at the peril of the greater good. To feel any semblance of safety, people need to have a common understanding that some behaviors cross the line, and must be condemned. in the extremes, these require external consequences.

If there is no justice, then there can only be a never-ending cycle of exploitation, destruction, and revenge. To treat people as if they're not responsible for their actions is the ultimate form of dehumanization. What are you as a human, if not a volitional, responsible, accountable being with the ability to make your own choices, whether for good or for bad? This is your dignity.

To see yourself as, or to be seen as, an entity that has no control, is the most damaging psychological perspective imaginable. That's why the greatest crimes with the greatest punishments are the crimes in which one person steals control away from another, through murder, through physical abuse, through theft, etc.

The Supervillain represents the crossing of the acceptable line into destructive behaviors, not limited to physical abuse, but any behaviors that caused harm to others.

SECTION 5 | Face Your Supervillain

The greatest thing separating the Supervillain from the Weak Spot is the element of choice. If you are prone to anger, you probably did not ever choose to be so. Being prone to anger may be your Weak Spot. And to be clear, you may have chosen to give way to this anger for many years, giving it more and more control of your life by not actively standing against it. Regardless of the back story, acting on your anger in ways that destroy others is almost always malevolence, although our laws justly make room for outlier circumstances of violence utilized in self-defense or the defense of others.

Your Supervillain is not your Weak Spot, your Weak Spot is not your Supervillain. Your Supervillain is the evil and destruction that you do to yourself and to your community. We all have a Supervillain. We all have the capacity for malevolence.

5.3
Who is Your Supervillain?

Have you ever become unrecognizable to yourself? Have you ever acted in ways that destroyed the people around you, and in the aftermath, wondered how you could have done such a thing? Your Supervillain represents the ways that you, personally and uniquely, tend to destroy yourself and the world around you. Every Supervillain is different. They can be sneaky. They like to hide out in their lairs. After the Supervillain wreaks havoc and sets the world on fire, he returns to his lair and leaves you to deal with the consequences.

My Supervillain is narcissistic and manipulative. He is incredibly sneaky. He masquerades as a grand, benevolent person who can do no wrong. How could he do wrong?

I'm a people pleaser—this is part of my Weak Spot. I try to do everything right. I try to never let anyone down. My Supervillain keeps score of all the good things I do. He believes we are owed prestige and a place of honor. If people criticize me, or disrespect me, or don't treat me the way he thinks I deserve to be treated, that smiling facade begins to crack—but not all the way. The Supervillain can't let people see that he is upset—that would be weakness. So the power of his anger and resentment burn inside my bosom, a growing ball of fire. I often don't even know I'm keeping track of offenses, adding to the blaze, until there is an explosion. When it comes out, it's not pretty.

I snarl and berate my kids. I belittle my wife with a "holier than thou" routine. I say I'm not mad, like the person saying I'm mad is an idiot. My family walks on pins and needles around me. But I'm not mad. What's wrong with everyone? I vent frustrations, I discipline my kids out of anger, I defend myself endlessly, unable to see what I am doing wrong, assuring everyone how "not mad' I am, while I go around being overly harsh.

> The Supervillain is bad, but he feels so good; so right.

Usually, I'll end up saying something totally insensitive, unkind, and hurtful. Because this is so out of line with my general disposition, it doesn't take much to do a world of damage. I don't have to scream or be physical to cut deeply. Because I'm a Connector, I have a lot of relational power. In the worst-case scenario, I wake up as if from a dream, and look around me, and I can see the trail of destruction that I've caused. These are the times I most wish I had the power to turn back time.

The great author and theologian CS Lewis has described hell, not primarily as a place, but as a condition. In "The Great Divorce," he describes the gates of hell as locked "from the inside." People can leave whenever they choose. But they don't leave. Having given themselves over to their vices, over a lifetime and beyond, they see nothing wrong with their pettiness and evil, their narcissism and tyranny. Their vices, rather than virtues, have become their identity. Hell is who they are.

Evil that we do, unresisted over time, has this deadening effect. If you let the Supervillain come out all the time, and do not seek to depose him or rectify his damage, then over time, you become the Supervillain. The attitudes and perspectives of the Supervillain become more predominant than those of the Hero. I could be such a powerful and glorious Supervillain. So charismatic. So justified in everything that I do. I could sit in my golden throne, surrounded with the bones of my loved ones— the broken relationships that inevitably follow the descent into self-absorption.

The Supervillain is bad, but he feels so good; so right. He is the sum total of all your power, poured out upon your own head like wine. He is the great parasite of your community, gorging himself on their blood, taking all that should be given, and giving nothing in return.

You can see some of Tolkien's wisdom on this very topic in his passage in "The Fellowship of the Ring" when Frodo tries to offer Sauron's ring of power to Galadriel, the elf queen, feeling unworthy and unable to carry the burden. The ring represents the evil potential in all people. Galadriel, though good, is tempted by this power. Seeing the ring triggers a preview of what she would become if she were to accept it. She transforms momentarily into a being of horrible light and awesome power. She responds to Frodo, "Instead of a Dark Lord, you would have a queen, not dark but beautiful and terrible as the dawn! Tempestuous as the sea, and stronger than the foundations of the earth! All shall love me and despair!"

And then, at the key moment, she turns aside and refuses the ring. Having confronted her own capacity for evil, she rejects power in favor of peace. She gives her final answer, "I have passed the test. I will diminish, and go into the West, and remain Galadriel." She has resisted and rejected her Supervillain. She's won her battle against her own darkness. And the spoils of her victory? She gets to remain who she is, a good and benevolent queen.

This is what we're fighting for. We're fighting for our very selves. This is why the battle against the Supervillain is such serious work. You're Supervillain isn't only the momentary manifestation of your own potential for evil. Your Supervillain is the person that you could ultimately become, given the right series of choices.

5.4
Triggers

One major factor that contributes to the release of your Supervillain is your set of Triggers. I learned the term Triggers in a therapy session, and it was a huge step in helping me understand my sudden, disproportionate, negative responses and actions.

It was amazing to be able to look back and deconstruct the origins of my most intense negative reactions.

Triggers are the events in your life that are most likely to drive you towards a disproportionate negative reaction. Trigger responses are incredibly difficult to control. We can feel confused and dismayed and self-critical when our Triggers are in play, because situations that might seem trivial, or at least moderate, yield an intense negative reaction. Our Triggers can make us feel like we are less than others. We chide ourselves, and berate ourselves, and maybe even feel contempt. We get upset, and then we are upset that we're upset, which only compounds the force and duration of our negative response.

In my experience and observation, Triggers usually play on your Weak Spot in some way. The combination of Triggers and Weak Spot can feel explosive. Trigger moments are the moments when we feel the most out of control, and are the moments when we are most likely to harm others in a variety of ways, either by shutting down, becoming aggressive, or acting out in some other way.

Some of my Triggers are the following:

- When someone is overly critical of me, or puts me down, or disrespects me.
- When someone has unreasonable expectations of me.
- When someone tries to control me or manipulate me.
- When I fail in a way that lets people down.

You may have noticed that all of these relate back to my primary Weak Spot Word: Insecurity. My Supervillain can manifest from this in many ways, and can be expressed as shut down, meanness, or escape.

If you know your Triggers, then you can begin to anticipate the situations that will most lead to destructive outcomes, and hopefully take a moment to face the pain that is driving you towards a destructive expression of your worst self.

What are your three to five Triggers? Think of the times when you've felt the strongest negative emotions. Think of the times when you've felt out of control. Think of the times when you've become a stranger to yourself, or when your responses felt most disproportionate to a stimulus. What was happening at that time?

For each Trigger, identify the *Weak Spot Word* that most relates with that Trigger. This will give you deeper insight into the "why" behind your Triggers. When phrasing your Triggers, they usually start with, "When someone…" or "When I…" or "When something…"

You can enter your Triggers into your Hero Profile at **superpowerquest.com/myprofile.**

Superpower Quest Hero Profile

Triggers Worksheet

TRIGGERS	
List your three to five Triggers below	List the associated Weak Spot Word

Managing Triggers

I am not a therapist, so I am going to try not to get out of my depth. Let me preface by saying that I am a fan of the value of therapy, and Joining Forces with the right therapist can be life-changing. I always thought that therapy was for damaged people. Like a medicine for a deep sickness. Sure, it can be that. But therapy is also for healthy people who want to improve their mental health. I know healthy people who go to therapy, which has helped them to become more healthy. Therapy doesn't have to be the prescription for a critical disease. It can be the health supplement you take to optimize performance. I'm preaching to myself here, because I grew up with negative connotations around therapy.

So, I will say that the first step of managing Triggers is being able to accept the fact that *sometimes you get Triggered*. And that's OKAY. You will be more effective at dealing with your Triggers if you can relieve yourself of the extra layer of being Triggered that you're Triggered; mad that you're mad; upset that you're upset.

I have found a key to gaining perspective on this inside of my faith. As a Christian, Jesus Christ is my ideal person. I believe he lived a perfect life. And even Jesus experienced intense, negative emotions. Before his crucifixion, in the garden of Gethsemane, he wrestled with a palpable, oppressive weight of fear. The Bible says that he began to be "deeply sorrowful and troubled" to the degree that he actually began to sweat blood. I take great comfort in the humanity of Jesus, picturing him curled up in a ball, guts hurting, crying out to God, face to the ground. If it's okay for perfect-Jesus to struggle with intense, overwhelming emotion, then it's okay for imperfect-me. It's not wrong to struggle. It's not wrong to be Triggered. It's not wrong for me to have to get by myself and take whatever time it takes to face my suffering, and the source of my suffering, and seek a way through it that doesn't destroy myself and the people around me.

The simple ability to recognize when you are Triggered, and to even say, "I'm Triggered right now," is a huge step in seeking an outcome that is different from your automatic outcome, which nearly always terminates in some form of the Supervillain.

5.5
The Path to the Dark Side

How does the Supervillain emerge? Although your Supervillain is not your Weak Spot, there is a correlation between your Weak Spot and your Supervillain. Your weaknesses don't determine your choices, but by nature, they influence your choices, and they constitute the areas where you're most likely to make bad choices.

Throw in Trigger events that exacerbate your Weak Spot, and you can become a volitional powder keg, ready to explode. This explosion can look a thousand different ways: Shut down, aggression, manipulation, despair, escape, denial, defensiveness. The Supervillain has many colors and shapes, but the common theme is destruction.

The path from your Weak Spot to the emergence of your Supervillain is the Path to the Dark Side. The Path to the Dark Side really comes down to the fundamental motive of your heart. Which is at the top of your pyramid? Power, or love? The pursuit of power as the ultimate goal of the Supervillain. The pursuit of love is the ultimate goal of the Superhero. You cannot serve both masters equally; one will rise to the top.

There's a really good representation of this process in the "Star Wars" lore. In Star Wars episodes one through three, we follow the life of Anakin Skywalker, a powerful Jedi with some serious anger

The Superpower Quest

management issues. Anakin's mentor, Obi Wan Kenobi, is constantly teaching Anakin how to master his anger and negative emotions through self-discipline. However, Anakin comes into contact with an evil Sith Lord in disguise, who begins using his influence to encourage Anakin to access his angry, violent emotions, and harness those emotions to generate more power. This is called using the Dark Side of the force, and little does Anakin know that this is the path to becoming an evil Sith instead of a heroic Jedi. The reason Anakin is deceived, is that his evil mentor is encouraging him to access this evil energy in the pursuit of ostensibly good goals, like thwarting other, more powerful evildoers. But ultimately, Anakin is snared by his desire for more power, and he ends up becoming Darth Vader, a powerful Sith who is instrumental in the downfall of the Jedi order, plunging the galaxy into slavery to the evil, Sith-controlled Imperial Empire.

> You will not develop resilience without exposure to the temptation of its opposite. You will not develop real love without winning your fight against the hatred within you.

Anakin's descent to the dark side started with a trait that was completely out of his control—his tendency towards anger. This was his Weak Spot, plain and simple. The evil mentor's goal was to get him to voluntarily access and indulge in his most destructive feelings and urges, and channel them into destructive, though at first justifiable, actions. The evil mentor exploited Anakin's weakness, which was a vulnerability to his own urges towards anger and violence, under the guise of empowering him towards good outcomes. The lie was that Anakin could access and indulge in evil thinking for good and productive outcomes. Anakin was offered Frodo's ring just as surely as Galadriel—only, Anakin took it.

You might say that some of our Weak Spot is dormant evil. It is the measure of evil, by design, that has been allowed to dwell within us, for its essential utility in the development of the highest qualities, such as love, discipline, resilience, and wisdom. You will not develop resilience without exposure to the temptation of its opposite.

You will not develop real love without winning your fight against the hatred within you. You will not gain wisdom unless you win your war against stubbornness and pride.

I don't think that all Weak Spots are dormant evil, because Weak Spot is a broad category of weakness, covering everything from forgetfulness, which has no moral ramifications, all the way to a tendency towards rage, pride, or any other vice, all of which have massive moral implications when exercised.

But the Path to the Dark Side is clear, and often follows this series of unfortunate events:

- You have a Weak Spot area. Let's use "insecurity and a tendency towards dishonesty" as an example.
- External events set off one or more of your Triggers. Maybe you fail to complete an important project on time, and your boss gets angry with you. Let's say "People getting angry with you" is your trigger.
- You now have an external event (boss's displeasure) playing off of your internal Weak Spot (insecurity, and a tendency towards dishonesty.)
- Now you are feeling an incredible pressure to lie, in order to escape your boss's blame and wrath.
- Your Supervillain emerges, and you spin a very convincing tale for your boss about why the lateness was not your fault, and why it was out of your control.
- The result? You have cooled your boss's ire, but you have traded away your honest self in the process, and you've given strength to the liar within you. You have also increased the stakes for your practical consequences, if your boss finds out that you are not only a procrastinator, but a liar too, then your consequences will potentially be far greater. You've traded the future for the present. You've traded the truth for a lie. You've traded virtue for vice. You've traded community for isolation. The Supervillain won this round, and now he's stronger for the next round.

5.6
Shadow Drives

What is your Shadow Drive? Let's do a quick review of the different kinds of *Drives* in the Superpower Quest. We started with your *Core Drive*, to get a sense for your cause or calling. You selected an Effective Core Drive of either Order, Progress, or Harmony.

In the Weak Spot section, we checked out your *Hindering Drive*. Your Hindering Drive is the one of the three Core Drives that represents your area of greatest weakness. This is the general category where you struggle.

Shadow Drives represent the abuses that arise from a misapplication of each of the Core Drives. Each Core Drive has two abuses—the *Extreme* and the *Antithesis*. Both of these represent the ways that people are tempted to destroy and abuse their communities, either by over-applying or under-applying a Core Drive. The strength of any Core Drive becomes a destructive force at either extreme of its usage.

Order Shadow Drives: Domination and Chaos
- Extreme: Domination
- Antithesis: Chaos

Harmony Shadow Drives: Trespass and Discord
- Extreme: Trespass
- Antithesis: Discord

Progress Shadow Drives: Obsession and Apathy
- Extreme: Obsession
- Antithesis: Apathy

This means there are six total Shadow Drives: Domination, Chaos, Trespass, Discord, Obsession, and Apathy.

Domination

Domination is an overapplication of order. Domination pursues Order for the sake of power over others. Domination destroys the community by restricting it and taking away its freedom. Domination craves, and abuses, power. Domination includes tyranny, oppression, bullying, harshness, rigidity, legalism, callousness, coercion, and the destruction of individuality, micro-managing.

Chaos

Chaos is the rejection of Order. Chaos rejects Order for the sake of power. Chaos destroys the community by rejecting beneficial Order in the pursuit of false freedom. Chaos uses power to destroy order. Chaos mislabels all order as oppressive. Chaos includes rebellion, anarchy, disobedience, insubordination, frenzy, violence, riot, haphazardness, sloppiness, tardiness, defiance.

Trespass

Trespass is the overapplication of Harmony. Trespass pursues Harmony for the sake of power over others. Trespass destroys the community by transgressing the rights and the boundaries of the individual, in an effort to so join itself to the individual, that the individual cannot exist apart from it. Trespass tries to get people to behave in its favor, using emotional and relational leverage. Trespass includes manipulation, guilt trips, clinginess, passive aggression, crossing of boundaries, disregard of personal space, overstepping, codependence, using others, contempt, invasion of privacy.

Discord

Discord is the rejection of Harmony. Discord rejects Harmony for the sake of power. Discord sabotages relationships. Lonely, discord seeks to breed isolation in others. Discord mislabels all Harmony as exclusive and destructive. Discord includes strife, gossip, "blowing things up" (metaphorically), slander, quarreling, instigating, cajoling, deceiving, isolating, refusing to hear.

Obsession

Obsession is the overapplication of Progress. Obsession pursues Progress for the sake of power. Obsession destroys the community by driving itself and the community beyond their capacity, and treats people like machines. Obsession includes impatience, haste, recklessness, stress, inability to slow down, overwhelm, inability to rest, overcommitment, hurry, pushing, striving, overblown expectations.

Apathy

Apathy is the rejection of Progress. Apathy rejects progress for the sake of Power. Like a stubborn mule, Apathy destroys the community by withholding both inspiration and action. It holds back the community by being stubborn and self-involved, forcing the community to adjust to its pace. It mislabels any expectations of Progress as unfair and invasive. This includes laziness, lethargy, lack of motivation, disengagement, passivity, resignation, inability to persevere, fragility, shortsightedness, obliviousness, stubbornness, futility. When you're at your worst, when you have caused the most harm to yourself and others, it is usually because you have been following one of your Shadow Drives. Shadow Drives are the motives that drive your Supervillain's actions.

Here are some clues that you may be following your Shadow Drives, and your Supervillain might be in play:

- Your negative emotions are multiplied, either in fear, anger, sadness, contempt, etc.

- Someone who knows you well tells you that you aren't acting like yourself.
- Your reactions feel forceful; you can barely contain them, if at all—you feel out of control.
- You start asking yourself, "Why did I do that?"
- You see others as the personification of a problem, rather than human beings with feelings.
- You have a strong urge to blame others for your actions.
- You feel justified in cruelty or harshness or vengeance. You want to make someone else pay.

If you can name your destructive tendencies, you can begin to confront them. If you're unaware of them, they can run like invisible "scripts" in the background, driving you towards negative outcomes without being seen.

It's hard to see our own errors. The things we do seem right to us, otherwise generally, we wouldn't do them. If you have tried to understand your own motivations, you know what I'm talking about. For many of us, our default position towards ourselves tends to be acquittal. It's hard for us to be wrong.

Being able to understand and confirm the destructive scripts that play out in your life helps you to resist being incredulous about your culpability when you harm the world. This makes it easier for you to acknowledge wrongdoing and embrace responsibility, which will make it much easier for others to live with you.

What are the one or two Shadow Drives that most resonate with you, when you are at your worst? Make a note of them. You can also go to superpowerquest.com/myprofile to add them to your Hero Profile.

Superpower Quest Hero Profile

SECTION 5 | Face Your Supervillain

SHADOW DRIVES	
Domination, Chaos, Trespass, Discord, Obsession, Apathy	
#1.	#2.

5.7
Villain Words

What are the three to six adjectives that most describe how you behave when your Supervillain emerges? Choose your adjectives from the lists below, or use your own words. It's a good practice to get a second opinion from people who are close to you, as suggested in previous chapters.

Below, see words that are commonly associated with each Shadow Drive. You can start by circling the ones that best describe the ways you destroy yourself and the people around you when you are at your worst. These lists are far from comprehensive. Consider them a resource to get a head start.

It may be difficult to apply these kinds of words to yourself. That's natural. But naming the mechanisms by which you damage yourself and others will immediately give you power over them. There is so much power in owning responsibility. There is so much power in confession. This knowledge will not necessarily solve your anger problem, or your lust problem, or your deception problem. But confronting and acknowledging these realities is the first step towards a greater maturity in the areas of your struggle.

Try to be honest. Look into the dark mirror, and resist the urge to shrink back and minimize, deny, or deflect what you see there. We all have our handful of words like these that apply to us. Face the ugly, and just know that nothing in this section makes you less of a person, less worthy of dignity, or less worthy of love. You are a beautifully crafted being, and every human must wrestle his or her darkness.

My Villain words are Obsessive, Misleading, Passive, Mean, and Cowardly. Whooo. I don't like to say them out loud, or write them down for you to see. But I can. Because these words don't define who I am. They define who I can become, if I am not willing to confront myself and humbly accept responsibility when I falter.

DOMINATION

Dominating, Aggressive, Overbearing, Insensitive, Tyrannical, Coercive, Blustering, Bossy, Rude, Harsh, Explosive, Volatile, Oppressive, Belligerent, Bullying, Perfectionistic, Scathing, Insulting, Sarcastic, Verbally Damaging, Nitpicking, Implacable, Belittling, Disdainful, Contemptuous, Mean.

CHAOS

Rebellious, Defiant, Insubordinate, Unruly, Disobedient, Wayward, Recalcitrant, Obstinate, Defiant, Recusant, Contumacious, Mutinous, Seditious, Intractable, Refractory, Willful, Headstrong, Obstreperous, Nonconformist, Recusant, Uncooperative, Resistant, Contrarian, Iconoclastic, Unconventional, Defiant, Dissident, Subversive, Irreverent, Renegade, Oppositional.

TRESPASS

Overbearing, Controlling, Vengeful, Spiteful, Manipulative, Underhanded, Boundaryless, Overstepping, Intrusive, Interfering, Invasive, Meddling, Presumptuous, Pushy, Coercive, Insidious, Overzealous, Overcontrolling, Exploitative, Deceptive, False, Disingenuous, Misleading, Flattering, Slimy, Opportunistic.

SECTION 5 | Face Your Supervillain

DISCORD

Combative, Contentious, Confrontational, Belligerent, Gossipy, Outraged, Backbiting, Dissonant, Unruly, Noisy, Turbulent, Clashing, Unsettled, Rowdy, Jarring, Anarchic, Disruptive, Unrestrained, Clamorous, Erratic, Argumentative, Provocative, Pugnacious, Controversial, Unyielding, Opposing, Uncompromising, Inflammatory.

OBSESSION

Obsessive, Fixated, Self-absorbed, Narcissistic, Egocentric, Self-centered, Preoccupied, Consumed, Infatuated, Fanatical, Possessive, Compulsive, Single-minded, Absorbed, Fanatic, Prepossessed, Monomaniacal, Intense, Absorbed, Intoxicated, Insatiable, Overindulgent, Greedy, Avaricious, Consuming, Overzealous, Attached, Unrelenting, Manic, Steamrolling, Workaholic, Bulldozing.

APATHY

Apathetic, Passive, Lethargic, Indifferent, Listless, Uninterested, Inert, Sluggish, Inactive, Disinterested, Complacent, Phlegmatic, Dull, Spiritless, Torpid, Nonchalant, Lukewarm, Unmotivated, Unresponsive, Lifeless, Stolid, Stagnant, Enervated, Unenthusiastic, Comatose, Lazy, Negligent, Slothful, Aversive, Entitled, Resentful, Petulant, Self-absorbed, Dismissive, Withdrawn, Self-important, Oblivious, Consumed, Inattentive, Cowardly.

As in prior sections, take the time to narrow down and eliminate words that are most similar to each other. Once you have narrowed down to your three to six Villain Words, enter them into the table below, or go to superpowerquest.com/myprofile to input your Power Words into your Hero Profile.

Superpower Quest Hero Profile

VILLAIN WORDS	
Words describing your destructive tendencies and patterns…	
1.	4.
2.	5.
3.	6.

These words give you incredible insight into your Path to the Dark Side, or the ways in which you destroy yourself and others when triggered. Of all the documented parts of the Superpower Quest, I've gotten some of the most mileage out of identifying my Villain Words and being on the lookout. No one is going to be able to just muscle down their negative urges and drives through pure, white-knuckled strength. That's not what I'm advocating here. I'm advocating that you become so familiar with these words, that you can develop a greater sense for when they come into play in your life. And in so doing, I want you to give yourself permission to slow down and check in with yourself when you see these things in play, and start asking curious questions about what's going on. I want you to take the time and space to wrestle through to a place of clarity and understanding. How were you Triggered? How are you acting out? What are you believing about yourself and others? Is it true?

5.8
Supervillain Names

Are you still with me? I don't know if it's harder to face your weakness (Weak Spot) or your malevolence (Supervillain.) They are both pretty hard, but necessary as you make your way through your Hero's Journey to rescue yourself from the dark caverns of self-ignorance. Congratulations for making it this far. We're almost done.

In this short section, you are going to name your Supervillains. You are going to create simple personas as shortcuts to be able to identify when you are not acting like yourself; when you are abandoning the sacrificial, benevolent way of the Hero in favor of the exploitative, punitive, petty, and harmful way of the Supervillain.

You can do this by looking over all the words you selected for your Supervillain journey thus far. Look at your Triggers, your Shadow Drives, and your Villain Words. Now, you will pick the words that most describe the person you become when you are in full-on Supervillain mode. Think about that person. Feel what that person feels. Consider the destructive heat that proceeds from that person. Now, give that person a name.

My Supervillains are Mean Johnny, Shut-Down Johnny, Escape Johnny, and Puffed Up Johnny.

Mean Johnny does the most damage in my household. He is defensive. He is harsh in both his body posture, his facial expression, and his tone. He feels utterly justified to do what he does. He is almost always a product of fear and insecurity. He is a response to threat; specifically when I perceive that someone is threatening my dignity. In the past, he would come out for hours. He's difficult to depose. This is because the person I am perceiving as a threat may indeed have done something wrong. But there are actually infinite ways that I could respond to being wronged. An angry, defensive, harsh posture is only one way. It's not the only way. It's not the way I want to respond. It's a response that has been hardcoded into me through disposition and trauma.

> Knowing your Supervillains will give you a simple language for laying hold of your condition on a given day.

Shut-Down Johnny is downcast, paralyzed, silent, and passive. He shrinks from his responsibilities. Like a marionette with the strings cut, I crumple inward and withhold myself from the people around me as a defense mechanism.

Escape Johnny runs away from hard circumstances and hard decisions. He runs away into movies, audio books, or creativity as a way to avoid pain and pressure. He neglects the people around him, leaving them to their own devices, withholding his contributions to their welfare.

Puffed Up Johnny is in love with his own ideas. He tries to maintain a mask of humility, but he doesn't have room for other people's ideas. He treats their ideas as second rate. Given opportunity, he will take a lofty position over other people, making them feel small in order to make himself feel big.

Nearly all of the time, when I have destroyed the people around me, when I have caused tears, or frustration, or harm, I need look no further than to these four Supervillains. I'd love to water this down, but this is how I exploit, manipulate, control, and leverage the people closest to me, when I am at my worst. When I am stressed with work. When I am in the midst of a costly interpersonal conflict. When I have no peace. When I forget myself, this is the person that comes out of me.

Who are your two to four Supervillain personas? Enter them into the table below, or go to superpowerquest.com/myprofile to input your Supervillains into your Hero Profile.

Superpower Quest Hero Profile

SUPERVILLAIN NAMES
Names given to your Supervillain Personas...
1.
2.
3.
4.

Knowing your Supervillains will give you a simple language for laying hold of your condition on a given day. I've gotten to the place where I can wake up and tell which Supervillain is most likely to make an appearance, based on the particular Triggers that are at play in my life on a given day. Having done this difficult and beautiful work, I hope that you find great benefit in being able to see and name the Villain within.

And I don't mean, so you can punch him in the face. Like Dorothy's confrontation with the Wizard of Oz, you need to be able to look behind the curtain and see what's feeding him. You will only defuse him if you can regain presence of mind, identify the causes, and begin to move in health instead of being swept down the raging river. What lies are you believing as true? What pain are you refusing to acknowledge? What are you covering up, and why? What responsibility are you refusing to take? What happened, and how did you get here? These are the kinds of questions that can begin to help you turn the tide.

5.9
Aftermath

You have that sickly feeling in your stomach, or that pang of conscience that lets you know you've released your Supervillain upon the world again. You regret your actions (or your lack of action), but you are facing the reality that there is no turning back time, there are no do-overs. The damage has already been done. In a world where your Supervillain can and will run amok at some point, dealing with the Aftermath is a necessary skill. First, a note on severity. Not all rampageway, to respond to even the most catastrophic and inexcusable things that you have done. In the words of the blues, gospel, and rock singer Jonny Lang in his song, "Turn Around."

"The choices we make, might be mistakes
But it's never too late, to turn around ... turn around."

At the root, releasing your Supervillain is simply a bad choice. Bad choices can easily breed a string of more bad choices. But for those seeking the way of the Hero, there's only one remedy for your last bad choice—a good choice, and the next good choice after that. Your next good choice does not erase your last bad choice. It's not a quick fix, and the payoffs for good choices may be distant. But if you are playing the long game, the long game is a game of trajectory. You may not be able to heal a broken relationship in a day, or a week, or even a month. In fact, you have no guarantees of ever healing it. Despite the great lie of the Supervillain, power over the choices of others is a fantasy. Healthy relationships are never built upon control, manipulation, or deception. Your only real shot for healing the destruction you have wrought is authentic responsibility, actual redirection, and unconditional invitation. And this is not a guarantee, or a recipe. The best results come when you do the right thing for the right reason, and the right reason is never ultimately selfish to the exclusion of the well-being of those you have harmed.

For example, I have released my narcissistic, manipulative Supervillain inside of many relationships, most notably with my wife and kids. I'll describe a scenario below that's happened many times. I raise my voice with one of my kids; a typical aggressive Supervillain behavior. This action breaks and bruises my relationship with the child. Prior to my blow up, the child was entitled or disrespectful to me (big triggers), which were the triggers that ultimately led me to my choice to release the Supervillain. Now we are in the Aftermath, not speaking to each other, feeling tension.

> There are different timeframes and commitments for rebuilding, depending on the extent of the damage. It takes more time and energy to rebuild a city than it takes to rebuild a house.

Coincidentally, releasing the Supervillain never feels like a choice—it feels like an unstoppable compulsion. But naming your resistance as "impossible," instead of "difficult" means that you are making the ultimate concession to your Supervillain. You are claiming helplessness against his power, and abdicating the control of your choices. This puts you at the mercy of your Supervillain; and they are not renowned for their mercy.

In the common story above, my child releases her Supervillain, and then I release my Supervillain to fight her Supervillain. Supervillain versus Supervillain never yields great results. Go figure.

Now, in the aftermath, I can do one of three things. I can continue to nurse my resentment. Her faults and wrongdoings play like a highlight reel in my mind, where my faults and wrongdoings are conspicuously absent. Or, I can apologize, with the expectation that she will apologize in return. This is an example of doing the right thing for the wrong reason, and it's likely to result in another bout of Supervillain action, in one form or another. Finally, I can own my wrongdoings, full stop. I can take the time to sincerely articulate where I went wrong and ask for forgiveness. I can model the way of the Hero, which is the most compelling invitation I can give into the way of the Hero. She may or may not be able to join me there. But true Heroes realize it's not their job to make others into their own image. Freedom of choice is what makes us human, and it is always the final target of the Supervillain.

Your Supervillain will come out. We are imperfect beings, and total defeat is not an option this side of heaven. Have you watched any ongoing Superhero sagas? Here's the format: All is well in the community. The Supervillain hatches a plan and begins to put the community at risk. Just when it seems that the damage will be permanent, the Superhero arrives to thwart those sinister plans. The Supervillain, defeated, hurls threats, like, "I'll get you next time!" and escapes. Peace is restored. Until next time.

If you're like me, there's a part of you that's always screaming, "Why'd you let him get away?" My soul wants finality. I want to see evil permanently defeated, even the evil inside myself. Besides the fact that it would be a bad marketing decision on the part of any show's producers, since final victory over evil would mean no more show, it's also an accurate reflection of the way things really are. Good versus evil is a daily reality in the heart of every human being, until the day we die. You'll experience exhilarating victories and crushing defeats. The Superhero's path is incremental. Let's say the Supervillain won ten times last month, and only nine times this month. And when I let him out, I owned it. The Supervillain's path is also incremental. The more he wins, and the less responsibility you take, the stronger he gets, and the more often he will make an appearance. This is the episodic nature of the drama we've been born into.

The Superpower Quest

You may be dealing with an Aftermath right now. If not, it's only a matter of time. Here are some tips for how to nurture a Hero's response to your own Villainy.

#1. Take Responsibility.

Take responsibility without excuses. Although it is difficult to stop your Supervillain from coming out, maybe harder than anything you've ever tried to do in your life, we must maintain that it is possible, otherwise the battle is moot—you are equally well off if you fight or give up. Some patterns may take a long time—even decades—for you to break. But they will never break if you cede the match before the game is over. Taking responsibility empowers you to take action for change. A victim mentality empowers you to stay the same.

#2. Create Barriers.

A barrier is a system or habit that makes it harder for your Supervillain to come out. For example, if you struggle with the narcissistic pull of pornography, there are apps you can install, technology choices you can make, and accountability practices that you can put into place. These fit nicely into your Utility Belt. No single barrier will win you the game, but every barrier contributes something towards a better outcome. Putting barriers in place also demonstrates to your community that you are not content to tolerate your destructive actions.

It's incredibly important for your loved ones to see you taking the battle against your Supervillain seriously. In the aftermath, when you've done harm, they need to see more than just your sorrow over wrongdoing, and your willingness to take responsibility. They need to see action. They need to see concrete steps in a new direction. My wife is my best friend, and the love of my life. No one can hurt me like she can. No one tempts me to release my Supervillain more than she does. We've had horrible, mean-spirited fights in our past. Now that we've been married for nearly twenty years, we've learned a few barriers. One is to put things on hold. If we are getting increasingly more angry, and the quality of communication is plummeting, it's time to stop and reset. In the ancient Biblical proverb, Jesus says, "Why do you see the speck that is in your brother's eye, but do not notice the log that is in your own eye? Or how can you say to your brother, 'Let me take the speck out of your eye,' when there is the log in your own eye? You hypocrite, first take the plank out of your own eye, and then you will see clearly to remove the speck from your brother's eye." (Matthew 7:3-5) If you take a break, ask yourself the question, "What am I doing to contribute to the chaos here?" Then you can re-enter the conversation with a different heart—the heart of the Hero and not the Villain. This has been a great barrier for us, it has helped us seriously decrease the number and intensity of our fights.

One of the most valuable traits in maintaining peace in any community in which you participate, is the willingness to be wrong. This is hardest for those of us who pride ourselves on being right. But most of the time, in my experience, you can win the argument, or the person, not both. Winning the person means you just might end up with a person who is now willing to hear your perspective, outside of the framework of an oppositional argument. People don't generally change their minds because they're argued into it. They sometimes change their minds when they are loved into it. But to love someone well, you need to sacrifice your Supervillainous desire to win at their expense. These are just a few of the many Barriers that you can add to your Utility Belt.

#3. Get Help.

The battle against the Supervillain is a very personal battle. It's the most personal battle. But as in all other areas, we are stronger together. Transparent Accountability is a huge blow to the Supervillain. Villains thrive in secrecy and shame. They skulk around in their lairs, evading detection until they come out and create their destruction. They despise the light. In order to wreak maximum havoc, they need you to hide them, make excuses for them, and refuse to confront them.

It's a common theme in Hero movies that sometimes it takes a team to defeat a powerful Villain. There's no shame in receiving help when the fate of the world is on the line. And your world is on the line. Join Forces and live the truth that it's not just you against the world, or you against your Dark Side. It's you and your people, arms locked, standing against the darkness together—yours and theirs. It's a powerful thing to realize that we are all fighting the same war, and the shame that protects us from being exposed is the greatest ally of our worst enemy.

When I reveal my deepest failures and wrongdoings and struggles to a trusted companion, the power of my shame begins to fade. The Supervillain doesn't want to be named, discussed, pointed out. His massive, mountainous form begins to shrivel in the light. I become bolder. In confession, I attack my ugliest fear; the scary little thought that lives deep down inside all of us: "If they knew me; if they really knew me, and all of my faults, failures, and evil, they would reject me."

What if you could deal a death blow to one of your greatest fears? What if you could prove it to be the asinine drivel that it is? This is how you destroy the very ground upon which your Supervillain stands. This is how you take the offensive, and put your Supervillain on the defensive. Walk in the light. Get help from someone, or someone's. This could be a friend, family member, mentor, or therapist. Give someone you trust the gift of being able to decapitate your worst fear, and in so doing, maybe decapitate their own. If you can be loved as you are, maybe they can, too.

5.10
The Sticky Wicket

An understanding of your Supervillain requires an understanding of the following elements described in this section:

- Triggers
- Shadow Drive
- Villain Words
- Supervillain Names
- Aftermath Approach

Now that you have spent time familiarizing yourself with the attributes of your own Supervillain, you have the ability to wage war. You have named your greatest enemy, and you know that this enemy lives in your own skin. This is a huge step in being able to resist and overcome your tendencies for destruction. And not only this, but to begin a cadence of self-understanding that actually enables you to pull his plug.

When I was young, I thought something was wrong with me. I thought I was different from everyone else. I knew I was selfish. There was a moment in my childhood when an adult who was very close to me branded me with these words: "In this world, there are givers, and there are takers. You are a taker." As children do, I internalized this as a foundational truth, and I spent many years trying to figure out how to reconcile with the fact that I was a subpar human being. I acted out in a lot of different ways, like a beetle wriggling when it is pinned to a board.

> That's the sticky wicket of being alive in a world of good and evil. But the hope is that, through repetition, your will can be strengthened in either direction. Good choices compound themselves, just as evil choices do.

However I have many names—many names fighting for supremacy in a lifelong war for ultimate identity. Yes, I am the Taker. And I'm also the Giver. I'm the Connector, and the Dreamer, and the Pastor, and the Resenter, and the Hider, and the Screamer, and the Saint. Now I understand. I have a Supervillain. And that Supervillain is indeed selfish and narcissistic. But that person who named me with his name, Taker, was wrong about me, in the way that we are always wrong when we reduce people to their darkness, and constrain them to it. If I had chosen the path to the Dark Side, I would certainly be living in a narcissistic, manipulative, self-worshiping life. I could be living the life of the Taker. But I chose another path.

I know my Supervillain well enough to know what kind of person I would be if I had chosen to let him reign. But by the grace of God alone, I did not. Because there was also a Hero inside of me, unnamed and unseen. I was made to love and serve my communities, and gifted with Superpowers to do so with joy. I just had to find my way, like we all do. I had to make my choices. And I still have to make my choices, every day. Because I am painfully aware of the reality that, given the right circumstances and choices, I'm just moments away from becoming hell and raining destruction on myself and my people.

That's the sticky wicket of being alive in a world of good and evil. But the hope is that, through repetition, your will can be strengthened in either direction. Good choices compound themselves, just as evil choices do.

This is true. "Choices compound." Make good choices. But it is only part of the truth. This is a great conclusion, but it falls short of a crucial set of considerations that I will broach here, for conscience's sake, and for honesty's sake.

I have tried to create a framework for helping you understand your design. This Supervillain section is the most controversial, because here, more than anywhere else, I am addressing the moral ramifications of your design as a volitional being, and the relational consequences of leveraging your design for malevolence, evil, destruction.

I have not given a nuanced definition of morality, or a definition of evil, beyond saying that it is the mechanism by which we destroy ourselves and others. I tried to tread relatively carefully here, because I wanted people of my Christian faith, and people of other faiths, and people who profess no faith, to be able to benefit from the principles of this book.

But I must also be careful here, more than anywhere else in the book, not to lie. I have used personal testimony as the backbone for the claims in this book. I have put forth my design, authentically, within this framework, for you to observe and measure. I have shared my secrets, my weakness, and my sins with you. I've tried to be honest with you. And in this section of the book, more than any other, I feel compelled to address the very gap revealed by this chapter, rather than passing it by.

Here is the elephant in the room. I have not defeated my Supervillain by using the principles of this book. I've certainly made progress, in keeping him from maximizing destruction. But my Supervillain is alive, and overcomes me sometimes. Sometimes he breaks me, and makes me cry, and makes me wonder if I will ever be rid of him. Sometimes he hurts the people I love.

But the victory beneath the battle is that I can refer to my evil in the third person. And this is a hard-fought victory that comes from more than strategy. Infinity lies beneath this statement: "My evil is not me." In a book of assertions and techniques, I must here avow that this statement is a statement of faith. "My evil is not me." I can say this because God made this statement true for me in a way that I could not have made this statement true for myself. We must wrestle through our own process to come to our own conclusions, and I can't come to this conclusion for you, neither can this book and its process bring you there. And yet this book starts there, and gives techniques based on this assumption, "your evil is not you." I hereby just want to acknowledge the problematic-ness of that. You may or may not be convinced that "your evil is not you." I don't think I can solve it here, but I can at least acknowledge it. Suffice it to say that, in the war against evil, the Superpower Quest process is only half the story—if that. It is the strategic half, and not the spiritual half, and both halves must be present for there to be a fully robust and harmonious solution. I would not have written this if I didn't believe that there was an opportunity for any person of any worldview to find some benefit in these tactics. But I also know how gritty, how painful, how impossible, how real the fight with my own Supervillain is every day. And I would hate to hand you a bagful of techniques and say, "you can beat him now!" because techniques alone are not how I beat him, when I do beat him. I use these techniques, but I never overcome him without help from above, and help from others who love me. Ask me what I know deeper than deep, and I'll tell you that this is what I know.

So with this, the final section of the Superpower quest, I bless you into the world, in all your multifaceted complexity. You are beautiful, with a capacity for great ugliness. I've given you words to name your beauty, and your power, and your weakness, and now, your destructiveness. All so that you may cooperate with your design, for joy in life, and for impact in your communities. I call forth the Hero in you to live, grow, and love.

SECTION 6
Final Words

6.1
Hugs and Homies

The last chapter. I'm sitting here thinking about what I want to leave you with, as I wait to pick up my kids from Taekwondo class. It's a rainy day, and the trees look startlingly green. I think I'll go back to the beginning. "Embrace your Design, Collaborate with your Community." When I wrote this book, I set out to do two things. Those things have become more and more clear to me, the further I've progressed in my writing. The first principle of this book is Embrace your Design.

Embrace Your Design

This book is a love letter to the hungry. It is a ballad for those who long for more. This book is an arm around the lonely kid at the bus stop, tasting the cold smoke of his own winter breath. I am writing the book version of that *Benevolent Upperclassman* who miraculously sees through your Freshman angst to the treasure inside of you, and calls you forth into that inheritance. Many of you reading this are ahead of me on the journey of life and purpose. If so, I humbly submit these poems and lessons in the hopes that they might enhance or confirm what you already know. For those of you who are behind me on the journey, especially those who are just beginning, I hope this is the book that ignites a greater hunger, and a greater certainty of your destination. We were not made for mediocrity. All of my experience points to this truth. We were implanted with excellence like a buried treasure within us, glittering its question in the hidden darkness: "Will you look for me?"

The Superpower Quest

In the poem "Park Hill Son" that I shared early on in the book, there's a part where I picture myself going back in time and consoling my broken, battered childhood self, and my childhood best friend, and telling them everything is going to be alright.

"And I want to go
Back in time and visit
Myself, that Park Hill boy
In all his gangly
Nappy-headed insecurity,

That screechy voice that
Makes me sick whenever
I hear it on video.

That skin that wasn't
Black enough to be black.
And definitely not white.

That kid who was
Always out of joint.
Out of the socket. Kind
Of hanging there, limp.

I want to scoop him
Up, and his best friend, too,
And tell them both.
Like a big brother
Who made it out, and comes
Back with a sweet ride,
And big, booming stories
Of the wide world,
And gifts, and secret
Handshakes and

SECTION 6 | Final Words

Big hands cradling
Your knotty head,

And a grin that stares
Into your eyes
And knows you.

And somehow
Loves you.
And really does.
For some insane,
Incomprehensible
Reason.

And I want to tell them:

You guys are not worthless.
Look at me. Look at me.
There's more.

Park Hill isn't the world.
There are places out there
That don't eat you alive.
I'm serious.

You are precious.
Park Hill doesn't know any better.
Pitbulls make for bad
Nursemaids.

It was a setup
From the start.

Pitbulls bite you, not
Because they hate you,

The Superpower Quest

Not because something's
Wrong with you. They bite
Because they are pitbulls.
And that's what pitbulls do.

Can you imagine
A pitbull baking you a cake?
Come on, son.

You don't have to hate
The Pitbull.

But you don't have to
Put your arm in its
Mouth, either.
Hear me?

And it's OK for you to
Hug your homies and tell them
You love them. I know,
I know. You're going to
Pretend I never said that
Punk-ass stuff, but it's true.
I love you. Say it with me.
You love each other
Like brothers. And that's
A gift. You can say things
Like that.

You have no idea
What's possible.

You can dream, homies.
The world is big, and
She bites sometimes.

She bites hard. But,
There's more.

You are loved.

I don't know what to say
To you, now that you're
Here in my arms. It's
OK to cry. You can be
Who you are. Breathe
Out.

There are different ways
To be strong. Not just
The hard-edged
Bloody-fisted toughness
That Park Hill smiles upon.

Kindness is stronger.
Compassion is stronger.
Love is stronger."

—Excerpt from "Park Hill Son." Johnny Levy, (2020)

    That's the heart behind this book. I hate that so many of us down-low hate ourselves, because I know what that poison feels like on the tongue.

    Misfit, I sing for you. And I'm talking to the misfit inside of the popular kid, too. Everyone bears scars, and no one truly knows another person's pain. The world is not setting us up for success. My school taught me writing, math, science, and how to dodge bullies. It taught me how to measure myself against other kids who were stronger, more clever-tongued, smarter, better looking, or cooler than me. School is not designed to teach us ourselves, even though knowing ourselves is more important than any curriculum.

You are designed, you are handcrafted, you are beautiful. And the ugliness doesn't invalidate the beauty. Both are real, both are true. That doesn't make you a freak, that makes you human. But beauty is the main idea, ugliness is the footnote. Beauty is the intent, ugliness is the side product. No artist creates a work of art so that it will be ruined and forgotten in darkness. Art is created to showcase beauty. Some pieces end up ruined, or locked away in filthy attics, but that doesn't mean that was the intention behind their making. I am convinced the intention behind your life is good, and productive, no matter where you find yourself today.

I wrote this book because I want you to come to terms with who and what you are, and then I want you to run with the grain of that, and see how much further you end up than you ever could have imagined.

Collaborate with Your Community

The second foundational principle behind this book is embracing your community. I wanted to help people like me—broken people, people who fail to meet their own standard, needy people—come to terms with the fact that they were never designed to live effective, fulfilling lives on their own. In fact, the myth of the self-made man or woman is dangerous beyond imagination. It's dangerous because it seeks to authoritatively rewrite our essence. It seeks to edit our code and remove something fundamentally human: our dependency upon other humans. This dependency is not only okay; this dependency is good and right and essential. When I talk about the need to *Join Forces* and *Defeat Your Supervillain*, I am calling you forth into productive community, where you belong; where we all belong. We need others to truly become ourselves as we were meant to be.

My wife and I were in a therapy session just going through some hard times. The therapist had us take a personality test. He said our scores were more different from each other's scores than any couple he had ever seen before; and this was a man who had been doing therapy with a fully booked schedule for over twenty-five years of practice. My wife and I are, indeed, so incredibly different from each other. Some people would say that's a liability. And yes, at certain points in our marriage, it has felt like a liability. But we've also found that there's incredible energy in the pairing of opposites. The tension and the friction create heat, and this kind of energy is only destructive insofar as it is unharnessed. She has gifts and abilities that I couldn't dream of having. I do things that she could never do. Together we are very strong, much stronger than even we understand. We have faced incredible odds together. We're still friends and lovers after twenty years of this combo Disneyland-Circus-Wrecking-Ball, called life. We've raised children together and given them a loving household full of laughter and fun and discipline. We've been through incredible hardship together. We know what it's like to be crushed to nothing together, and what it means to keep going together.

> I want to put a knife to the throat of that form of pride, rampant in the world around me, that says we should be self-sufficient; we should be able to conquer all things through self-reliance.

I lost my wedding ring many years ago, playing football in the Thanksgiving frost. Sarah bought me a new ring made of titanium. She engraved the words "still sailing" on the inside. These are words from a poem she wrote to me about how we have sailed together through such painful storms in our marriage, and yet we have endured by the power of God. I treasure this ring and the complex mixture of joy and pain that makes for a steadfast, proven marriage. I am not *me* without Sarah. In spite of our differences, and more likely because of them, we have built a life together—something greater than ourselves. As much as we still frustrate each other, and even when it seems like we're both speaking completely different languages, there's still an incredible respect for what we lack that exists in the other person. This is what community means. It's interlocking parts, man. It's Legos.

I want to put a knife to the throat of that form of pride, rampant in the world around me, that says we should be self-sufficient; we should be able to conquer all things through self-reliance. Correction, this idea is not just rampant in the world around me, it's also rampant inside of me. The more I've learned to trust and lean on trusted members of my community, the more convinced I become that we most hinder our velocity, trajectory, and altitude in life by rejecting, either actively or passively, the incredible bounty of wisdom and progress that is only available to us in the minds and hearts of others.

The ancient Biblical Proverb says, "A threefold cord is not easily broken." Another says that "Many hands make light work." I'm not saying anything new. I'm saying something ancient. It's something we are losing in the age of the internet, and artificial intelligence, and the world at our fingertips, and a thousand Facebook friends, when what the heart really craves is one true friend who sees you and knows you. I know that trust is a risk. I know that some of you have been burned. So have I. Burned so hard I didn't know if the skin was ever going to grow back. I have no answer for you except to never stop risking where it counts—and this is where it counts.

And here's my final admonition: *Give.*

You are a treasure. I hope I have helped you see this a little more clearly than you did before. You are a billion dollars to be spent for someone else; for your community. Sure, buy yourself that hamburger. Get yourself those concert tickets. But don't forget to give that smile—the one that everyone says lights up the world—to everyone in your path. Or that wise and discerning counsel that helps your friends and coworkers avoid grievous errors. Or that "can do" attitude that makes all your friends call you first when they need help moving. Or that piece of art that brings a moment of joy and reflection to someone in your circle. Find your passion, find your joy, find that sweet spot in your design, and work that lever 'till it falls off. Give yourself away and see what comes back to you. This kind of giving is the loudspeaker of invitation. I don't know a better way to call forth the good and the beauty of others than to give the good and the beauty that is inside of you to others. I don't know another way, beloved.

One of the most impactful books I've read is *The Go-Giver: A Little Story About a Powerful Business Idea* by John David Mann and Bob Burg. If you liked this book, read that one next. The book advocates an approach to life and business that is completely counterintuitive to the prevailing, inherited mindset of greed and self-interest. The book teaches something called "The Five Laws of Stratospheric Success," which are as follows:

- #1. The Law of Value: "Your true worth is determined by how much more you give others in value than you receive in payment."

- #2. The Law of Compensation: "Your income depends on how many people you serve and how well you serve them."

- #3. The Law of Influence: "Your influence (social capital) is determined by the extent to which you put others' interests first."

- #4. The Law of Authenticity: "The most important thing you can offer is yourself."

- #5. The Law of Receptivity: "For effective giving, be open to receiving."[1]

These Five Laws are in resonance with the teachings of this book. Each of these laws, in its own way, obliterates self-interest as the primary goal, and makes your success contingent upon your authentic contribution to the success of others. This points to a higher form of community than most of us have experienced. True community is a system of reciprocation without expectation. The community that we are longing for is a place where we can freely give who and what we are, while freely receiving the benefits of others being who and what they are. Self-interest would be irrelevant in a setting in which the people around you were more interested in your success than their own. Maybe that is heaven. I don't think we can reach this ideal on earth—but it's good to aspire to have this attitude in ourselves, and promote it in our communities.

You've spent enough time with my inner voice at this point to have a sense for what I'm about. Connection is life to me. My passion for authentic connection, and for progress, burns like a fire inside of me. So obviously, I don't want things to end here, with you closing the book, standing up, and going on with your life. I mean, that's fine; especially if you gained something from this book that will help you in your journey. But, see, I want more than that. I want to connect. I want to know your experience. I want to bring you into something. I want to lock arms with you and a flurry of other Heroes to accomplish great things together.

So, one last time, join the Superhero Community at superpowerquest.com/myprofile. Submit your information into your Hero Profile, and receive access to your results, SPQ content, round tables, and updates on the movement. Our goal is to practically help you take your Superpower Quest to the next level, and continue to grow in power and purpose.

Superpower Quest Hero Profile

I wish you nothing less than completeness of joy and excellence in all that you do.

About the Author

Johnny Levy is a small business CEO, "Chief Connection Officer," poet, author, and speaker who lives in Colorado Springs. He is a passionate husband of one and father of four. His Effective Core Drive is Harmony, and his Effective Hero Type is Connector/Dreamer. His Superpower is "Authentic Connection for Mutual Progress." He has a passion for guiding people and companies into their potential. He also has a fire for strategic connections and collaboration for big wins. The principle that drives him is the conviction that our greatest challenges are truly "Who" challenges, not "What" challenges. Finding the right human to lock arms with is like hitting the lottery; like finding buried treasure. You are the key that unlocks a golden door for someone else, and someone else is that same key for your golden door. Living this truth means living a life of both generosity and humility: *generosity to give radically, and humility to receive radically.*

Partnership

Interested in collaborating? Below are some ways we can connect for progress.

Corporate Consulting. I help unlock the potential of organizations through consultative partnerships. I wield the Superpower Quest framework to help you identify the Superpowers and Weak Spots of your team members, so that you can Join Forces more effectively as a team, for increased job satisfaction and engagement. superpowerquest.com/consulting	
Speaking Engagements. I am a dynamic and authentic speaker who inspires and challenges. I love captivating and encouraging groups with the positive and encouraging message of the Superpower Quest framework. superpowerquest.com/speaking	

One-On-Ones. Purchase a slot on my calendar to have a lively discussion! superpowerquest.com/appointment	
Join a Collaborative. I host a series of monthly or quarterly "Super Collaboratives" in which I assemble small, niche groups around a compelling topic. This is a great way to harness the Superpower Quest framework in a specific area of growth within a relevant community. (ex. job seekers, marketers, fractional entities, creatives, etc.) superpowerquest.com/collaboratives	
Subscribe to the Superpower Community Newsletter. The newsletter covers three areas: Individual Growth, Strategic Connection, and Personal Affirmation. Subscribe to the newsletter for ongoing Superpower Quest personal development content (Individual Growth), collaboration opportunities (Strategic Connection), and Hero Profiles describing community members and their Superpowers and Big Dreams (Personal Affirmation). **superpowerquest.com**	

Endnotes

SECTION 1
1. Lewis, C. S. *Weight of Glory*. HarperCollins, 2015.
2. Campbell, Joseph, *The Hero With A Thousand Faces*. New World Library, 2008.
3. Nomura, Catherine; Waller, Julia; Waller, Shannon; Sullivan, Dan; *Unique Ability*. The Strategic Coach, 2006
4. Clear, James, *Atomic Habits: An Easy & Proven Way to Build Good Habits & Break Bad Ones*. Penguin Publishing Group, 2018
5. McKeown, Greg, *Essentialism: The Disciplined Pursuit of Less*. Crown Publishing Group, 2020.
6. McKeown, Greg, *Essentialism: The Disciplined Pursuit of Less*. Crown Publishing Group, 2020.

SECTION 2
1. Sullivan, Dan; Hardy, Benjamin, *The Gap and The Gain: The High Achievers' Guide to Happiness, Confidence, and Success*. Hay House Inc., 2021, 21.
2. Campbell, Joseph, *The Hero With A Thousand Faces*. New World Library, 2008.

SECTION 3
1. McManus, Erwin, *Mind Shift: It Doesn't Take a Genius to Think Like One*. The Crown Publishing Group, 2023.
2. Collins, Jim, *Good to Great*. HarperCollins, 2001.
3. Voss, Chris; Raz, Tahl, *Never Split the Difference: Negotiating As If Your Life Depended On It*. HarperCollins, 2016.
4. Voss, Chris; Raz, Tahl, *Never Split the Difference: Negotiating As If Your Life Depended On It*. HarperCollins, 2016.
5. Beaudine, Bob, *The Power of Who: You Already Know Everyone You Need To Know*. Center Street, 2009.
6. Sutherland, Jeff; Sutherland, J.J., *Scrum: The Art of Doing Twice the Work in Half the Time*. Crown Publishing Group, 2014.
7. Collins, Jim, *Good to Great*. HarperCollins, 2001.
8. Wickman, Gino; Winters, Marc C., *Rocket Fuel: The One Essential Combination That Will Get You More of What You Want from Your Business*. BenBella Books Inc., 2016.
9. Comer, John Mark, *The Ruthless Elimination of Hurry*. The Crown Publishing Group, 2019.
10. Ferris, Tim, *The 4-Hour Workweek, Expanded and Updated: Escape 9-5, Live Anywhere, and Join the New Rich*. Harmony/Rodale, 2009.
11. Beaudine, Bob, *The Power of Who: You Already Know Everyone You Need To Know*. Center Street, 2009.

SECTION 4

1. Maslow, Abraham H., *A Theory of Human Motivation*. Blurb, 2024.
2. Delony, John, *Own Your Past Change Your Future: A Not-So-Complicated Approach to Relationships, Mental Health & Wellness*. Ramsey Press, 2022.
3. McKeown, Greg, *Effortless: Make It Easier to Do What Matters Most*. Crown Publishing Group, 2021.
4. Merriam-Webster Dictionary, Merriam-Webster.com, "Stewardship." 2024 (Web)
5. Keller, Helen, *The Story of My Life*. CreateSpace Publishing, 2017.
6. Ferris, Tim, The Blog of Tim Ferris, *What My Morning Journal Looks Like*. (Web)
7. McKeown, Greg, *Effortless: Make It Easier to Do What Matters Most*. Crown Publishing Group, 2021.
8. Clear, James, Jamesclear.com, *"How To Build New Habits by Taking Advantage of Old Ones."* (Web)
9. Selk, Jason; Bartow, Tom; Rudy, Matthew, *Organize Tomorrow Today: 8 Ways to Retrain Your Mind to Optimize Performance at Work and in Life*. Hatchette Books, 2015, 5.
10. Selk, Jason; Bartow, Tom; Rudy, Matthew, *Organize Tomorrow Today: 8 Ways to Retrain Your Mind to Optimize Performance at Work and in Life*. Hatchette Books, 2015, 17.
11. Selk, Jason; Bartow, Tom; Rudy, Matthew, *Organize Tomorrow Today: 8 Ways to Retrain Your Mind to Optimize Performance at Work and in Life*. Hatchette Books, 2015.
12. Tracy, Brian, *Eat That Frog! 21 Great Ways to Stop Procrastinating and Get More Done in Less Time*. Berrett-Koehler Publishers, 2015.
13. Sutherland, Jeff; Sutherland, J.J., *Scrum: The Art of Doing Twice the Work in Half the Time*. Crown Publishing Group, 2014.

SECTION 5

1. Burg, Bob; Mann, John David, The Go-Giver: *A Little Story About a Powerful Business Idea*. Penguin Publishing Group, 2015.

www.ingramcontent.com/pod-product-compliance
Lightning Source LLC
Chambersburg PA
CBHW021143160426
43194CB00007B/676